The Culture of Conservative Christian Litigation

HANS J. HACKER

ROWMAN & LITTLEFIELD PUBLISHERS, INC.
Lanham • Boulder • New York • Toronto • Oxford

ROWMAN & LITTLEFIELD PUBLISHERS, INC.

Published in the United States of America
by Rowman & Littlefield Publishers, Inc.
A wholly owned subsidary of The Rowman & Littlefield Publishing Group, Inc.
4501 Forbes Boulevard, Suite 200, Lanham, Maryland 20706
www.rowmanlittlefield.com

PO Box 317
Oxford
OX2 9RU, UK

British Library Cataloguing in Publication Information Available
Library of Congress Cataloging-in-Publication Data

Hacker, Hans J., 1965–
    The culture of conservative Christian litigation / Hans J. Hacker.
        p. cm.
    Includes bibliographical references and index.
    ISBN 0-7425-3445-6 (alk. paper)—ISBN 0-7425-3446-4 (pbk. : alk. paper)
    1. Christianity and law. 2. Law (Theology) 3. Practice of law—United States.
4. Actions and defenses—United States. 5. Christian lawyers—United States.
6. Law firms—United States. I. Title.
    BR115.L28H22 2005
    340'.088'2773—dc22   2005004353

Printed in the United States of America
♾™ The paper used in this publication meets the minimum requirements of American
National Standard for Information Sciences—Permanence of Paper for Printed Library
Materials, ANSI/NISO Z39.48-1992.

The Culture of Conservative Christian Litigation

To Lisa Hacker—the friend and wife whose steadfast sense of love is my deepest motivation, and whose companionship is my chief reward—I dedicate this volume

Contents

Tables

Preface

During the late 1980s and 1990s, conservative Christian litigators from the New Christian Right participated in a series of high profile federal court cases involving religion and public policy. Over this period, these litigators achieved a remarkable set of victories, convincing courts to support the expressive and participatory rights of the religious in many policy arenas from religious expression in schools and public places to abortion protest and sexual orientation. We can trace their success during this period back to the adoption of what has been alternately called the free expression or the equal access argument.

In the past, courts had decided conflicts over governmental policy toward religion based on concerns for government entanglement with religion and religious causes. Under this rationale, any policy that advanced or inhibited a religion was constitutionally invalid. However, during the 1990s conservative Christian attorneys began to present courts with the argument that government sometimes penalizes legitimate religious expression in attempting to avoid entanglement, and that religious speech should be given the same protection from governmental intrusion as any other form of protected speech. As a result, courts began to shift their attention away from entanglement and toward the expressive nature of religious faith. In effect, conservative Christian attorneys presented courts with a pragmatic legal rationale forcing them to balance the governmental interest in avoiding entanglement against the need for inclusive policies that do not punish religious expression because of its content.

Not surprisingly, critics accuse New Christian Right attorneys of arguing for what amounts to tyrannical governmental power and claim that the risk of entanglement posed by government recognition of religion is great. They assert that, in pursuing an expanded sphere of religious rights, the conservatives' argument unbalances the Constitution. Ultimately, they surmise that the free expression/equal access argument has a caustic influence on individual freedoms by imposing Christian values on the unwilling. Thus, the question of the impact of conservative Christian litigation on court-crafted policy has generated considerable attention from scholars. Studies explore the development of the argument itself,[1] the impact of the argument on specific policy areas,[2] and the general parameters of involvement in litigation.[3] They also address the specific concern of policy influence.[4]

However, the history of conservative Christian litigation presents us with another interesting problem evolving from an overlooked aspect of litigation in the 1990s—not all conservative Christian litigators adopted the liberal perspective on religion articulated by their compatriots arguing free expression and equal access. Many find troubling the idea that Christianity is one among many valid public perspectives. Furthermore, they view the adoption of predominantly liberal notions of inclusion, tolerance, and respect for a diversity of ideas as a dilution of Christian principles. These firms take a principle-based approach to litigation and reject the rationale behind the pragmatic arguments and strategies of other New Christian Right litigating firms.

Why did some conservative Christian lawyers adopted liberal views on free expression and equal access while other eschewed such arguments, even if that meant less chance for success in the courts? This is the question at the heart of this book and its analysis of conservative Christian public interest law firms of the New Christian Right. To address this question, I explore the internal characteristics of three leading conservative Christian firms in an effort to grasp what motivates their behavior in court—what makes them distinct from each other and from the New Christian Right political movement as a whole. I examine how and why these firms differ in the goals they set, the cases they litigate, the legal strategies they employ, and the arguments they present to courts. This approach emphasizes a careful exploration of internal group characteristics rather than external factors to which groups must respond. Clearly, there is an important relationship between the choices groups make and the political environment they face. But, in this analysis, the accent is most decidedly on the structure of internal decision making, goal setting, and behavioral choice, rather than the external limitations placed on groups by their environment.

Because of this emphasis on internal group characteristics, I employ a methodological strategy best suited for an initial exploration of the research question. The study develops deep narratives of the three firms using a diverse set of data drawn from the public record and from in-depth personal interviews conducted at the law offices of each firm. Also included are empirical data on the litigation agendas of each group and their participation at all levels of the state and federal judicial systems.

I find that characteristics of organizational life have a profound influence on behavior, even while the legal nature of the organizations shapes and limits these characteristics. In particular, this study focuses on religious ideology as an explanation for the diverse arguments, choices, and strategies of groups, even ones with very similar goals. The internal significance of religious principle determines at least in part what kinds of behavior a group finds appropriate for achieving its goals in court.

The results reveal a much more nuanced understanding of motivations and their influence than one might suspect. Since some firms did not adopt the more liberal legal argument of their compatriots, we might conclude that they must then endorse the goal of cultural domination so prevalent among New Christian Right organizations that engage in legislative lobbying and electioneering. However, the study reveals a more subtle explanation. Those New Christian Right law firms most dedicated to religious principle are distinct in important ways both from their compatriots who adopted the free expression argument and from the New Christian Right movement as a whole. However, these highly principled firms take a unique approach grounded in the practice of law and legal tradition as well as religious principle. Most surprising is their understanding of the role they play in litigation. They have little notion of bringing God into the courts or forcing society to conform to religious doctrine implemented in law. In fact, they were convinced from the beginning that there was little hope they would triumph at all.

I begin the book with a chapter setting out the relationships among New Christian Right law firms, and between those firms and the broader movement. I define the parameters of the study and supply background information on the development of New Christian Right litigation since the 1970s. In the core narrative chapters (chapters 2 through 4), I characterize groups on a broad set of variables including resource acquisition, internal structure, litigation emphases, development, goal setting and implementation, and other features of internal organizational life. These characterizations become the basis for a direct comparison of the three groups in chapter 5.

While preparing to write this book, I learned quite a bit about what motivates attorneys of the New Christian Right. I also learned a good deal about what motivates my interest in conservative Christian litigation. I have wondered for the better part of a decade now why I am so fond of attorneys like Brian Fahling and Steve Crampton of the American Family Association–Center for Law and Policy, or Mat Staver of the Liberty Counsel. I find them to be bright, informed, and certainly good company. They are generous to a fault and genuinely excited by the prospect of yet another scholar asking them for an interview. During the interview process, one even insisted that I stay at his home with him, his wife, and seven boys for several days. They gave me almost complete free rein in access to documents, personnel, and facilities. They are, of course, very much on the dogmatic side. As Brian Fahling said, they are very opinionated.

In part, this project was born out of the recognition that conservatism has radically altered the landscape of American politics. Since the late 1960s, conservatism has reshaped American political and social institutions by defining the terms of debate over policy. Scholars have studied these changes and the impact of conservatism on everything from taxation to welfare reform and affirmative action. In particular, many scholars have explored conservatives' use of the courts in this effort to reshape policy and institutions. Less attention has been paid to why conservatives want what they want and how what they want structures the choices they make. It is easy enough to demonize a group that is dogmatic in its adherence to a particular ideology and worldview. It is much more difficult to comprehend the reasons for action. Thus, I hope to shed more light on the motives of litigators.

I have also learned that my interest in conservative Christian litigation is tied closely to my interest in civil society and civic participation. I think most observers of politics would conclude that today Americans are certainly no more civil in our public discourse on policy than in the past, and we may in fact be less so despite so many economic, social, political, and legal advances. As we segment ourselves into rigidly defined classes and interests, emerging every so often to do political combat, we lose an important component of Americanism—

the ability to bridge divides by building the trust and understanding at the heart of good policy choices.

Today, dogmatically religious Americans are in every way average Americans—in dress, manners, customs, education, finances, and especially intensity of religious belief. But, despite the extraordinary political success and prevalent policy influence of conservatism, conservative Christians are the most likely to turn dissatisfaction with the culture into sustained political action. There seems to be plenty of dissatisfaction, and scholars have recognized this. David Guinn has noted that "while . . . believers may be mistaken about the issues they have chosen to fight over, their concerns are legitimate and their anger is real."[5] Stephen Carter notes the level of disaffection among the religious in America resulting from the perceived ignorance of critics. He notes that "nothing creates political energy so well as insults."[6] As a political reality, this is a devastating blow to the civic engagement and cooperation that should characterize our politics. Where do we turn to mollify the cultural disaffection exhibited by those supporting our most dominant ideologies? As the most educated class among their movement, the attorneys of the New Christian Right are the best hope for schooling the religious and building a bridge between a rich religious heritage and a vibrant civic life.

There are many people to thank for their help. My deepest respect and grateful thanks go to Dr. Lawrence Baum, who advised me throughout the project. He read every word and made extensive comments before publication. His scholarly support, encouragement, tolerance, intellect, and humor were absolutely crucial. Wayne McIntosh, Paul Chen, Steven Brown, and Ron Claunch also read drafts of chapters, offering valuable comments and useful suggestions. Mark Tushnet, Clyde Wilcox, and Ted Jelen read very early drafts. While all of these individuals helped shape this work and should claim some credit for any success, I alone am responsible for its deficiencies.

A project like this cannot go to press without considerable institutional support. I receive it in abundance at Stephen F. Austin State University. Dr. Ron Claunch, chair of the department of political science, geography, and public administration, worked tirelessly on my behalf, helping me find funding, reading chapters, and providing general (and immensely valuable) encouragement. Dean Bob Herbert and Dr. David Jeffrey, associate vice-president of research, worked together and with the department to channel resources my way at a crucial stage in the process. Dr. Rick Abel provided a 1200 dpi press-quality laser printer, as well as the type of scholarly interaction and encouragement that can only happen while relaxing over martinis. At Rowman and Littlefield, Jim Langford, editor for religious studies, recognized the importance of this approach to the study of religion and politics. I am extremely grateful that he took a chance on this project. Assistant editors Katie Lane, Kim Smith, and Audrey Babkirk provided much appreciated encouragement and guidance throughout the process.

My wife, Lisa Hacker, endured four moves across the country over five years as we searched for a permanent place in academia. She also acted as my copy editor. All my love and thanks for everything you have put up with over these years. To my daughters, Greta and Sophie, whose births provided every reason to bring this project to press, thanks for being patient with the old man. Both my parents and my in-laws have offered extraordinary support during the many cross-country moves that taxed us emotionally and economically. To all my family (including Dean and Joyce Meadows), thanks for believing in me.

I am grateful to Jay Sekulow, Mat Staver, Nicole Arfaras-Kerr, Steve Crampton, Brian Fahling, Michael DePrimo, and Bruce Green for their participation in this project. Initial data collection was supported by a Graduate Student Alumni Research Award (GSARA) grant from the Graduate School of the Ohio State University. Stephen F. Austin State University funded this project through a grant from the Office of Research and Sponsored Programs.

Abbreviations

ACLJ: American Center for Law and Justice
AFA: American Family Association
CLP: American Family Association—Center for Law and Policy
DOMA: Defense of Marriage Act
FACE: Freedom of Access to Clinic Entrances Act
NCR: New Christian Right
RICO: Racketeer Influenced and Corrupt Organizations Act
RLUIPA: Religious Land Use and Institutionalized Persons Act
SJC: Supreme Judicial Court of Massachusetts

Chapter One

The Culture of Conservative Christian Litigation

The Historical, Religious, and Legal Context of Litigating
for the Religious Right

On May 13, 2004, U.S. District Court Judge Joseph L. Tauro issued an opinion in *Largess v. Supreme Judicial Court for Massachusetts*.[1] *Largess* was brought by three public interest law firms of the New Christian Right in response to an earlier decision by Massachusetts' highest court declaring the state's ban on same-sex marriage unconstitutional.[2] The three law firms—the Liberty Counsel, the American Family Association's Center for Law and Policy, and the Thomas More Law Center—sued in federal court, requesting an injunction preventing the state from issuing marriage licenses to gay couples. In making a case for the injunction, these firms argued that the Massachusetts high court violated the U.S. Constitution's Guarantee Clause,[3] which ensures the states a republican form of government. According to the firms, the Massachusetts court violated the clause by assuming the power of the state legislature to define marriage through legislation, thus violating the separation of powers mandated by Massachusetts' own constitution.

In refusing to issue the injunction, Judge Tauro wrote, "[I]t is the exclusive function of the [Supreme Judicial Court for Massachusetts] to decide issues that arise under the Massachusetts Constitution."

> And, there can be no question that the meaning of the term marriage is an issue that arises under that Constitution. To rule that . . . Defendant SJC usurped the power of the Massachusetts Legislature and violated the federal Constitution would be to deprive that court of its authority and obligation to consider and re- solve, with finality, Massachusetts constitutional issues.[4]

The attorney arguing the case, Mathew D. Staver of the Liberty Counsel, re- sponded that he would "appeal this case as far as necessary to ensure that the separation of powers principle is upheld in Massachusetts. . . . The republican representative form of government must be restored so the People can have a chance to define marriage."[5]

Only a few months later, another important event occurred within the New Christian Right—the Rev. Jerry Falwell announced the opening of the Liberty University Law School. Claiming that "we plan to turn out conservative lawyers the same way Harvard turns out liberals," Falwell introduced his newest project with a series of media interviews connecting the law school to the longstanding

1

mission of the movement—cultural revival and transformation. "We are on a mission to return America to her religious heritage," he said.

> We're hoping we are training lawyers who can turn the legal profession back to the right. I think we have plenty of lawyers. But, I'm afraid we don't have enough who are trained in America's religious heritage and in the Christian, Western intellectual tradition.[6]

Intimately involved in the creation of the third law school in the nation affiliated with the movement[7] was none other than Mathew D. Staver. Staver serves on the Liberty University Board of Directors and handpicked Liberty Law School's dean—Bruce Green, former general counsel of the Center for Law and Policy. Both *Largess v. Supreme Judicial Court for Massachusetts* and the announcement of the new Liberty University Law School raise several important concerns about the role of New Christian Right litigators in court and within their own movement over the next decade.

Largess is only one in a series of recent high-profile cases in which some New Christian Right litigators have departed from an approach to litigation that served them well in the past. Litigation has been an important part of the New Christian Right's political aspirations since the Supreme Court's decision in *Roe v. Wade* awoke conservative Christians to political action in the 1970s. During this period conservative Christian attorneys worked in tandem with states and the federal government to pass and then defend abortion legislation.[8] However, during the late 1980s, conservative Christian public interest law firms began pursuing an increasingly wide array of cases in important policy areas including religion in the public square and school, gay rights, abortion protest, and family values. With the aid of movement leaders, these firms proliferated, becoming some of the most active and aggressive litigators in the nation. The primary motivation for litigation activity among these firms is policy influence. Many conservative Christian law firms hope to influence the creation and modification of court-crafted policy. In fact, they have been relatively successful in doing so.

The primary reason for their success rests on the fact that many conservative Christian litigators adopted a philosophy fusing tolerance for diverse ideas, sophisticated legal arguments, and respect for professional norms of the practice of law. The primary vehicle for carrying that philosophy into the courts was the free expression argument. New Christian Right attorneys had tremendous success in making a free speech defense in cases involving First Amendment establishment clause claims. They exploited a tension between the free exercise and religious establishment clauses and offered courts a rationale for resolving disputes arising under them. Arguing that the free exercise of religion often involves an expression of faith that deserves protection as free speech, New Christian Right attorneys have applied this logic in cases involving public expressions of faith, equal access to public property, and abortion protestation.[9]

But, nowhere were these developments more evident than in cases raising the issue of religious expressive freedom in public schools. In some instances, litigators for the New Christian Right advocated a decidedly more liberal position on free expression than their liberal foes. For example, in *Board of Westside Community Schools v. Mergens*[10] the conservatives took a particularly open stance to the expressive freedoms of public school students. While the case centered on access to school facilities, they managed to turn the issue away from the question of whether allowing a student-led religious club to meet on public school grounds violates the religious establishment clause. Instead, they successfully shifted the case toward expressive rights and protection of minority views, arguing that a policy restricting only student-led religious clubs was non-neutral in application and inequitably limited students' religious expressive rights. Religious speech, they argued, deserves safeguarding by the courts just as they would safeguard any other form of speech traditionally protected under the First Amendment.

However, in several recent high-profile cases New Christian Right attorneys have departed from this philosophy. The results tend to confirm the notion that they fare better before appellate courts when casting claims in minoritarian terms. Where conservative Christian litigators severely test the limits of the court's willingness to accommodate religion in the public square and school, they either fail in their bid to expand the role of religion in public life or undermine the legitimacy of their free expression argument. For example, in *Boy Scouts v. Dale*,[11] New Christian Right attorneys participated as *amicus curiae* in support of the Boys Scouts' position that it could use sexual orientation as a criterion for membership and leadership positions. Although the Boy Scouts were successful in the effort, participation by conservative Christian attorneys effectively undermined their position relative to other minority views. Likewise, in *Board of Regents v. Southworth*,[12] the effort to allow Christians (or those of other faiths) to opt out of financial support for minority student-led groups through university fees suggested a conflicted view within the movement over the relationship between government and minorities. Finally, in *Santa Fe v. Doe*[13] New Christian Right attorneys argued for a high school policy allowing prayer at football games that, although placing control over selection procedures in the hands of students, amounted to state supervision of a religious practice. In other recent cases, movement attorneys follow their longstanding policy of depicting religion as the expression of a minority seeking constitutional protection.[14] However, in each of the cases mentioned above, those making the movement's case in court appeared to abandon their previous template for litigation or to select cases with facts that did not support their claims.

While litigation was an essential component of the New Christian Right's overall political strategy during the 1990s, the central ideas of the free expression argument did not resonate with movement leaders of organizations mobilizing voters, lobbying legislatures, and supporting educational institutions. Most found anathema the ideas that Christianity is a minority religion requiring protection, and the Christian church is one voice among a chorus of diverse interests all legitimately influencing policy. Instead, they endorsed the standard view of the relationship between the Christian church and political participation that

echoes in Rev. Falwell's announcement of the Liberty University law school—
Christians are fighting a cultural war to win back their nation from liberals promoting secular humanism.

The current close association with Christian educational institutions creates
a tension for New Christian Right litigators. How do they balance the traditional
culture war position of other movement leaders with their commitment to the
values embodied in the free expression argument? New Christian Right litigators
have assisted in defining the mission of conservative law schools as an effort to
exert a Christian influence on the practice of law and on the judicial branch.
Does this signal a shift among them toward the more traditional stance? If so,
should students of the courts be concerned about the future of New Christian
Right influence on the judiciary? As Joe Conn of Americans United for the
Separation of Church and State noted just after Rev. Falwell's announcement,
"[H]e wants to . . . fill up the courts and courtrooms with people who think just
like him. And, that has serious implications for people who don't."[15]

Taken together, recent events suggest that the approach of conservative
Christian litigators to influencing court-crafted policy remains in flux. One
might infer that as a group they have abandoned their commitment to tolerance
and dedication to minority rights. However, it is also possible that various
strains of thought exist within the movement's litigating wing, and that these
strains have expression in a variety of approaches to policy influence and reflect
the variety of arguments they present in court. If so, it is important to explore
just how those strains of thought influence behavior. Furthermore, if New Christian Right litigators have lost touch with the ideals that set them apart from other
organizations, this might also suggest a sea change in approach to litigation. Do
New Christian Right litigators now espouse the wartime mentality so dominant
among the movement's legislative lobbyists and grassroots organizers? If so, we
must explore what impact this will have on the ability of the New Christian
Right to continue its influence within the judicial branch. These are the two central issues addressed in this study.

The cases and their results discussed above raise the issue of how New
Christian Right litigators pursue their goals in court and what factors influence
their behavior. Clearly, the movement's litigating wing is not hegemonic. It is
composed of organizations that differ from each other in important ways. These
organizations present courts with very different arguments, some of which are
better suited for achieving long-term policy influence. Significant variation exists in their goals and objectives, motivations for entering the courts, and litigation strategies employed for achieving their objectives. This book is largely devoted to exploring variation in the behavior of New Christian Right litigators
and factors explaining that variation. I develop an account of litigation behavior
that explains why conservative Christian litigators pursuing the goal of policy
influence employ divergent litigation strategies and provide courts with arguments that differ significantly.

In what follows, I undertake a systematic evaluation of the characteristics
and behavior of three leading firms of the New Christian Right. I explore what

they hope to accomplish in court and what factors influence the strategies they employ in pursuit of their goals. I argue that we can best understand the behavior of New Christian Right litigators by exploring the internal organizational culture of the firms litigating the movement's agenda. The various strains of thought present within these firms are a product of their ideological commitment to religious principle and their ability to reconcile religious principle with the institutional norms of courts. I explore these features of organizational culture and relate them to their physical manifestations—the actions these firms take to achieve their goals.

In the remainder of this chapter, I will first explore the relationship between New Christian Right litigators and the broader movement. I undertake this task by situating conservative Christian litigation within the historical, legal, and religious cultural context of the New Christian Right. I then assess the theoretical basis for examining culture as a determinant of behavior. I examine social science theory connecting culture to political behavior and explore a particular facet of interest group organizational culture of particular importance for understanding conservative Christian litigation—religious ideology. Finally, I set out the methods I will use to pursue a systematic evaluation of interest group culture and behavior, laying out the general parameters of each case study and the general comparison among the three groups taken up in a later chapter.

Conservative Christian Public Interest Law and the New Christian Right

> We are not going to carry the day on the culture with politics alone. Our job is to keep [the] avenues open, make sure the church can be the church. . . . We are there to make sure the church's voice can be heard. Somebody said once we're Jesus' lawyers. Jesus doesn't need a lawyer. But the church does. I believe the church needs organizations that will defend the integrity of Christians in the public square.
>
> —*Jay A. Sekulow, 1998*
> *General Counsel*
> *American Center for Law and Justice*

One of the often overlooked ironies of the United States' late twentieth-century political landscape involves a philosophical disconnect between the political leaders of the New Christian Right and the Protestant Evangelicals making up the core conservative Christian constituency. Alan Wolfe argues that there are changes afoot in the mind of the Protestant Evangelical.[16] Defining this development as "The Opening of the Evangelical Mind," he notes that these changes are taking hold largely at conservative Christian intellectual centers like Regent University, Fuller Theological Seminary, and Wheaton College. Among scholars at these institutions, there has been a trend toward open attitudes on a variety of religious, social, and political issues.

Moreover, recent scholarship has been characterized by vigorous debate, tolerance for a diversity of ideas, and complexity in the understanding of the churches' place in society. Harvey Cox, a Harvard professor and liberal Protestant theologian, describes these developments across the landscape of Protestant Evangelical academic institutions where academic exchange that bridges theological divides seems to be more highly prized these days. Cox relates his own experience as a guest lecturer at Regent University where his remarks were given careful consideration. Both professors and students alike spoke with "enthusiasm about the value of this kind of dialogue between liberal and conservative Christians."[17]

Perhaps even more significantly, these changes are taking hold in the minds of average Evangelicals. Having been educated in the modern tradition of tolerance (often imparted from the unassailable educational sources listed above), they demonstrate liberal attitudes toward minorities and define pluralism in society as a virtue.[18] Clyde Wilcox notes that the more moderate stance of core New Christian Right constituencies on abortion, prayer in schools, and women's rights has prompted movement leaders to "take positions that are more accommodating in these areas."[19] In particular, Easton notes that Ralph Reed of the Christian Coalition crafted that organization around a message of "moderation, inclusion and, most of all, respectability" in an effort to appeal to educated and moneyed upper-middle-class Protestant Evangelical constituents.[20] Studies of conservative Christian activists often trumpet their significantly lower support for such democratic values as political compromise and tolerance of opposition. However, given the inflammatory and often outrageous rhetoric with which they are bombarded,[21] it is extraordinary that upwards of 50 percent of these same activists would express tolerance of liberal opposition speaking, demonstrating, or running for public office in their communities.[22]

New Christian Right Movement Leadership

With only a few exceptions, the importance among rank-and-file New Christian Right members of respect for minorities in a plural society seems to have been lost on the political leaders of the movement. Since the early 1970s, movement leadership has consistently emphasized using the political process to reshape American society around conservative Christian morals and values. They have attempted to fulfill the goal of "reclaiming America"[23] by placing primary importance on working within those bastions of majoritarianism in American politics—the U.S. Congress, state legislatures, and the electoral process. In particular, legislative lobbying has held the position of primary importance within the New Christian Right's overall strategy—the organizations that represent conservative Christian interests in Congress have always been the best funded, best organized, most highly visible, and most aggressive of all the many and varied institutions that compose the far-flung movement.

The history of the New Christian Right since the 1970s illustrates this emphasis, which is ultimately at the heart of the disconnect between the attitudes of its leadership and their followers. As the movement gained political influence and momentum immediately preceding the election of Ronald Reagan to the presidency, its first order of business was to organize for electioneering and legislative lobbying. The movement generated a set of organizations with a Washington, D.C., presence, extraordinary levels of funding, the ear of congressional leadership, and a vast grassroots membership. Prominent organizations included the National Christian Action Coalition, the Religious Roundtable, Christian Voice, Concerned Women for America, and (perhaps the most influential among the set during the early 1980s) the Moral Majority.

New Christian Right rhetoric during this time was associated most closely with Jerry Falwell and the Moral Majority, who engaged in "spiritual warfare" against "godless secular Humanism" and sought a return to "moral sanity." This return would be characterized by the writing of Protestant Evangelical Christian principles into policy after electing handpicked candidates to office.[24] The Moral Majority not only set the legislative agenda for the movement (and at times even for Congress), but created its overall strategy as well. The organization exerted extraordinary pressure on Congress and its members by combining heavy-handed Capitol Hill lobbying tactics with massive member mail and telephone networks to get the grassroots involved in national issues. Its primary strategy was to "[b]ring an avalanche of [grassroots] Christian opinion down on Congress at critical points in the legislative process"[25] by flooding congressional offices with letters and telephone calls. It used these tactics with some success. The Moral Majority pressured Congress to hold hearings on overturning *Roe v. Wade* and forced several unsuccessful floor votes on constitutional amendments banning abortion. Furthermore, it successfully lobbied for major legislative packages limiting or halting federally funded abortions.

Despite its political muscle, the New Christian Right found victory elusive, in part because such tactics ultimately reduced its influence.[26] By the late 1980s, the movement was rethinking its model for legislative lobbying in the U.S. Congress when the struggle over abortion policy moved to state legislatures. State affiliates experienced a series of bitter and politically bloody battles across the nation. Following the Supreme Court's decision in *Planned Parenthood v. Casey*[27] (in which the Court allowed some state regulation of abortion, but refused to overturn the right to abortion itself), the movement had to deal with a policy stalemate. It had failed to deliver victory at the national or state levels on the issue it had defined as its single most important.[28]

Even after the demise of the Moral Majority and the disappointments at the state level, legislative lobbying continued to be the most prominent and problematic aspect of New Christian Right strategy. By the early 1990s, the Christian Coalition had replaced the Moral Majority as the movement's leader lobbying Congress, and other organizations either retooled or disbanded. However, if the model for lobbying legislatures changed, the emphasis on achieving political

victory by exerting influence on majoritarian policy-making institutions remained consistent. New Christian Right legislative lobbyists continue to experience extreme dissatisfaction with the results of their efforts to influence both
electoral politics and policy making. Steven P. Brown notes the discouragement
of movement stalwarts at the end of the twentieth century.[29] He quotes Paul
Weyrich (a founder of the Moral Majority and a longstanding leader within the
New Christian Right) as making the following extraordinary admission.

> I no longer believe that there is a moral majority. I believe that we probably
> have lost the culture war. That doesn't mean the war is not going to continue
> and that it isn't going to be fought on other fronts. But, in terms of society in
> general, we have lost.[30]

Other New Christian Right leaders followed with similar statements suggesting
that their involvement in politics and policy making had not only failed to
achieve the expected results, but would never achieve their goal of cultural
transformation.

These admissions are extraordinary for two reasons—leaders of the New
Christian Right were conceding defeat[31] on the dominant front, and they did so
in absolutist terms. Since the 1960s, political and theological leaders of the
movement had defined the central mission of the movement as routing the forces
of secular humanism that were perverting the foundations of American society.[32]
To admit that the strategy failed was tantamount to challenging the theological
and intellectual groundings of the movement. Furthermore, experience in politics seems to have had very little effect on the way movement leadership thought
about the goals of political influence. After several decades of experience lobbying legislatures, participating in the process of policy making and electing candidates to office, they still defined success in terms of absolute victory. Ration-
ally, it would seem that, as the New Christian Right moderated its message in
the 1990s, it would begin to see the value of political compromise, regardless of
what the logic underlying theological tradition suggested. Instead, it appears that
the 1990s rhetoric of inclusion and moderation did not supplant the overall goal
of dominating the society morally and politically. These elite leaders viewed
politics as a zero-sum game in which complete triumph was the only satisfactory
scenario and any compromise an unacceptable form of defeat. As a eulogy to the
Moral Majority, one scholar noted, "with the Moral Majority . . . the mission
was defined so broadly that absolute, ultimate success was elusive."[33] It appears
that more than a decade later, New Christian Right leaders had not resolved this
tension so central to defining the success of the movement's legislative agenda.

New Christian Right Public Interest Litigation

Not all this may come as a surprise to those who see ideology as more important within the New Christian Right than political realities. However, it is

ironic that there is a branch of the movement, coming into being approximately a decade before Weyrich and his colleagues made their remarks, that more closely mirrors the attitudes of modern Protestant Evangelical intellectuals and grassroots. This branch is composed of public interest law firms making up the litigating arm of the New Christian Right. In fact, movement leaders recognized the importance of litigation to the conservative Christian agenda very early.[34] In particular, Robertson encouraged the development of high-powered public interest law firms. With the support of leaders like Pat Robertson and Jerry Falwell, conservative Christian litigating firms proliferated during the late 1980s. Their influence upon the movement has been profound. Above all, they have shifted the movement's logic in court away from casting Christian claims as part of majoritarian politics and have provided courts with arguments presenting Christians as a protected minority rather than a majority asserting its will.

They have also come to respect court norms such as compromise, incremental policy change, and the evolving nature of law; and they have applied these norms to the broader movement. Leaders of dominant litigating firms see the voice of the church as one among many in a pluralist society. They approach litigation with the idea that religious convictions are appropriate for social discourse—society should welcome religion as one valid perspective. Thus, their recent efforts in the courts center on themes of equal access for Christians in public, freedom to express religious opinions, and securing a place for the church in public life and civic discourse.

The most profound contrast to New Christian Right legislative lobbyists has come from the rhetoric that some conservative Christian litigators employ. Jay Sekulow, general counsel of the American Center for Law and Justice (ACLJ), consistently refers to the power of courts to set policy on religious rights in the United States. Stephen McFarland, former general counsel of the Christian Legal Society, also notes the centrality of the Supreme Court to policy making and its place as the protector of minority rights. He goes so far as to claim a preference for the court-based civil rights protections of a William Brennan over an Antonin Scalia who places primary reliance on majoritarian institutions as the first bulwark for civil rights protections. "But that is contrary to the oath he took," says McFarland. "As long as the Bill of Rights is still enforced, he [Scalia] doesn't have the luxury to minimize the role of the courts."[35] On the topic of majoritarianism, Sekulow notes that he and many of his compatriots reject the image of Christians excluding the ideas of others. In fact, his position is quite the opposite—Christianity, as with any other religion, must be given the same protection as any other minority view. Clearly, at some point, Christian litigators departed from the old movement mantra that claimed deference to majoritarian interests when it came to religion in public life.

Perhaps we can account for this shift in logic as simply being in the interests of New Christian Right litigators—they want policy influence, and the only way they can get it is by playing the game correctly. Their rhetoric simply reflects their adoption of certain values that they do not truly endorse and would shed as soon as they offered no benefit in court. Their strategies for using the courts simply amplify their influence rather than revealing a newfound respect for legal norms and practices. This is the standard critique of New Christian Right litigation offered by their opponents in court. The problem with this account is not that it assigns sinister motives to New Christian Right litigators. Rather, it assumes too much about motivations while offering us little in the way of explanation for behavior. It is a fact that some movement litigators have adopted liberal arguments and some have not done so. It is a much more interesting question to ask why this is so. The motivations of New Christian Right litigators are complex and flow from a defined belief system. Any attempt to account for the differences among them must explore the source of these beliefs, that is, the internal organizational culture of interest group litigators.

Cultural Theory and Politics

> Although it is eminently reasonable to study—as most of us, including myself, have throughout our professional lifetimes—how people try to get what they want through political activity, it is also *unreasonable* to neglect the study of why people want what they want.[36]
>
> —*Aaron Wildavsky*

This book explores the connections between the internal culture of conservative Christian litigators and the structure of their behavioral choices. I examine the culture and behavioral choices of a small set of conservative Christian lawyers—elite individuals who lead small public interest law firms that litigate the conservative Christian agenda for social action within the court system. To apply the concept of culture to the study of a particular set of interests begs the question: What is culture? How does culture structure choice and why use it in the study of a small set of attorneys?

In applying a cultural theory of politics to conservative Christian litigating interest groups I am inspired by the work of Aaron Wildavsky on culture as a determinant of political preference. According to Wildavsky, political culture is a useful tool in identifying the source of political preferences. He argues for locating that source within social life and defines culture as "shared values legitimating social practice."[37] Political culture consists of social meanings attached to objects through interaction with others. As he says, "[P]references come from the most ubiquitous human activity: living with other people."[38] Within Wildavsky's theory of culture, shared values provide a filter for analyzing politics and cues for developing a set of coherent responses to political environments. These responses, based in a preconfigured set of values and socially viable options,[39] provide structure for individuals and organizations when selecting what Wildavsky calls "second-level choices (which of the available ways of life do I prefer) and third-level choices (which policies do I believe are efficacious in supporting my preferred way). . . ."[40]

Thus, the process of selecting among second- and third-level choices exists within a socially derived context. A central tenet of a culture theory of politics is that preferences are not formed outside of or independent from social constraints.[41] Furthermore, an examination of culture tells us much about what goals truly lay behind political action and why a group has selected certain goals over others. As Laitin notes in his analysis of Yoruba religious and political conflict,

> [Political] action implies goal-oriented behavior; but only a theory of culture can tell us what goals are being pursued. One cannot understand . . . political action until one understands the cultural cues that give substance to abstract goals.[42]

The importance of cultural theory is not restricted to a comparative examination of cultures that are relatively or completely foreign to Westerners. Promoting understanding of subcultures within American society demands insight into the motivations that lie behind the adoption of goals and the tensions that surround those decisions. Furthermore, Wildavsky's perception of interest group politics is particularly insightful when analyzing the values of elites and the goals they pursue. He says, "[B]eneath mundane political struggles were battles between ways of life. . . . Beneath discrete individual choices people were choosing between ways of life or types of rule." On this view, people playing interest group politics are not simply playing a game to determine a tax code or human services policy, or even a code on student-led prayer in public schools. They are fighting over values they define as fundamentally constituting a way of life and the survival of those values in society.

It seems then, when we find politics being acted out at this level, we must make *both the motivations and goals* of groups intelligible in their own terms— in the terms employed by the actors themselves. Besides simply characterizing a particular set of groups and their goals for shaping policy, as we would characterize any other set of interests vying for influence, this book attempts to explore political action systematically in terms of core group values as well as broad group goals. This is not a new practice to political science, nor is it new to the study of conservative Christianity. Fritz Detwiler notes the benefits of a cultural and social movement emphasis in the study of the New Christian Right. To truly understand conservative Christian vision for reform of American society, he says,

> [W]e must be conversant with the basic presuppositions that give the movement its identity, purpose, and coherence. Only then can we comprehend the scope and the depth of the Christian Right. These fundamental ideas also define the goals and strategies of the movement.[43]

Many of these fundamental ideas are worked out by "cultural elites" that engage in a wide variety of pursuits providing the movement's intellectual background and the mechanisms for political and social action.[44] However, culture is not a static concept, nor is it hegemonic. Developments in society can influence values and beliefs. They can also multiply the number of valid responses available within a culture to those developments. Thus, we might expect differences among New Christian Right litigators in primary motivations behind the strategies they pursue and the arguments they make. We should also expect even more fundamental differences to exist at the level of values, especially in the importance of religious belief and professional norms within various firms. If these differences do exist, it is reasonable to suppose that they have expression in the preferred strategies and behavior of New Christian Right litigators.

Culture as a Determinant of Behavior

Religious Ideology

The New Christian Right is as well bounded a segment of American society as one can find. It includes a core of constituents, elites, institutions, fundamental (even Fundamentalist) beliefs, and preferences for living that can and do translate into political action. However, the movement, like other subcultures that develop into social movements,[45] is characterized by decentralization and diffusion of institutions and ideas. As Steven P. Brown notes,

> [T]he movement is strongly rooted in the conservative evangelical Protestant tradition. Evangelical Protestantism is highly decentralized, embracing not only large denominations, such as the Southern Baptist Convention, but also thousands of independent Baptist, Reformed, Pentecostal, Churches of Christ, and nondenominational evangelical churches, among others. Those within this diffuse grouping affirm the inerrancy of the Bible, the divinity of Jesus Christ, the need for personal conversion, and the necessity of religious activism, or "witnessing" to bring about conversion of others.[46]

Within this vast array, a variety of opinions exist on how best to achieve movement goals, sparking disputes that cause dissent, conflict, and even schism. For example, violent protest against abortion and advocacy of killing abortion doctors caused considerable upheaval within the New Christian Right during the late 1980s and early 1990s.

For much of the twentieth century, the New Christian Right directed political action toward mainstreaming the cultural perspectives and goals of the movement. As with any social movement seeking adoption and ratification of its preferences by the wider society, efforts to mainstream have come through the creation of institutions. The movement has developed a wide array of educational institutions, media networks, and policy institutes.[47] It has also assembled a wide-ranging set of organizations seeking political influence in party and electoral politics, government, and the bureaucracy. In creating these institutions, the

New Christian Right has identified three broad goals—reinforcing the preferences of movement members, broadening the appeal of the movement across the
country, and shaping governmental policy. One facet of this mainstreaming has
been the development of a legal arm to ratify the broader movement's objectives
in court. The conservative Christian bar reflects many of the traits apparent in an
examination of the broader movement. Within the bar, there are a variety of perspectives on, approaches to, and goals for litigation as a tool for achieving influence. It is to an examination of these groups' internal culture to which this book
is devoted.

When we speak of internal group culture, we refer to that underlying and reinforcing set of values that define group preferences and beliefs. An exploration
of internal culture can tell us much about a group, its internal functions, and why
it seeks influence. Understanding the culture of a group seeking political influence requires that we know something about those values a group defines as
fundamental and worth promoting internally, that is, values defining, constructing, and affirming a way of life and a worldview. Knowledge of this worldview
is particularly important for understanding the behavior of elite leaders who
guide and direct a group. It can provide the sort of information that Wildavsky
found so important for the study of politics—the source of elite preferences and
the reasons why elites who manage interest groups want what they want.

Few bother to ask the question why groups want what they want. For example, we know that conservative Christians oppose gay marriage and abortion on
moral grounds. However, the structure of the belief systems that generate such
opposition are rarely explored or understood. Furthermore, knowledge of the
influence of such opposition on the behavior of elites who represent the movement is underdeveloped. For example, is it safe to assume that the conservative
Christian movement is monolithic in its adherence to a particular belief system,
or is there a range of beliefs that result in subtly shaded variations in behavior?[48]

In this volume, I pay close attention to the importance of one aspect of
group internal culture in determining the general strategies that groups will
adopt and the arguments they will make in court. I define this aspect of organizational culture as religious ideology. Religious ideology encompasses the importance of religious values when seeking to influence the world outside the
group—how strongly religious values limit, shape, or determine what is appropriate behavior when attempting to influence policy outcomes.

Religious values have expression beyond internal group functions. They influence the behavioral choices a group makes when it attempts to effect political
outcomes, that is, when it attempts through political action to map its values
onto public policy as closely as it is able. When interest groups select from
among behavioral options they are choosing from specific strategies of litigation
activity. Scholars have identified various litigation strategies include sponsoring
(i.e., bearing the cost of) litigation, assisting in preparation of a case, and
submitting supporting briefs.[49] The sphere of interest group litigation strategy
also extends to the arguments that a group repeatedly uses when approaching the
courts. These arguments must be at some level congruent with internal values.

Goals

In exploring the influence of group culture and how it structures behavioral choices, we find that culture mixes with political realities to shape not simply what a group wants or is willing to do, but what it can feasibly do. The behavioral choices a New Christian Right litigating firm makes are not simply a product of its religious ideology, but are a reflection of the limitations of its political environment as well. Some of the environmental features effecting group behavioral choices concern the institutions a group hopes to influence. For a litigating group these include the state of current precedent, the willingness of appellate courts to hear and decide cases raising particular issues, and their willingness to listen to certain arguments. Other external features involve a group's constituency—their willingness to fund group activities and their preferences for policy outcomes.

The influence of political environment finds its expression in the goals a group adopts for political action. Goals are blueprints for political action designed to carry a group's values into the policy arena. They embody the influence a group hopes to exert on its external environment—changes that it may create in the limitations imposed on it by an external reality such as policy or legal precedent. These plans reflect the realities of the political environment and help a group establish a general plan of action for achieving its goals.

Interest group scholars identify three broad categories of goals that organizations pursue through litigation.[50] These are policy-oriented, reputation-oriented, and media-oriented approaches to litigation. Each category requires different group features including funding, expertise, and organizational complexity. Like other organizations, conservative Christian groups generally litigate for the purpose of influencing court-crafted policy. Groups pursuing policy-oriented goals influence policy by building precedent favorable to their preferred policy position. Groups generally achieve policy influence through sponsoring cases (bearing the cost of litigation) and through the test case strategy, or bringing cases up through the court that raise particular policy questions in ways that may allow for a favorable outcome. This goal places the highest demands on a group in terms of time, energy, and monetary resources. The goal of influencing policy is certainly not an innovation of New Christian Right litigators. Liberal groups, such as the NAACP and ACLU, pioneered a policy-oriented approach and developed goals to affect policy nationally, rather than pursue court cases in jurisdictions that had lesser impact

A group pursuing reputation-oriented goals seeks the benefits of an increased reputation among its fellow organizations and among members of its broader movement. It seeks the public perception that it is a leader among its fellows. Finally, a group pursuing media-oriented goals will strive to elevate its status regionally or nationally, to bring media attention to its cause, and to increase the saliency of certain issues to the public. Epstein notes that groups identifying media-oriented goals anticipate an unfavorable outcome in court and seek to limit their losses by drawing attention to their plight in the media.[51]

Outline of the Book

There appear to be two factors that define and limit the behavioral choices of interest groups. Their influence on group behavior is broad and overlapping. Internal culture defines the vision of policy that the group hopes to promote, while at the same time limiting the range of potential arguments and actions a group defines as legitimate. Goals reflect the limitations of what a group can realistically do given the current state of policy, available resources, and its place within its movement. Goals address the "how" of interest group litigation (generally, how a group will approach the courts, and what strategies it will favor). Internal culture influences the "what" of interest group litigation (what arguments will a group present when it finally arrives in court, and what strategies best allow it to present those arguments). This book focuses on the culture, goals, and behavioral choices of interest group litigators, specifically conservative Christian litigators. It explores the ways in which internal culture and group goals interact to define group litigation strategy.

In the present instance, it is important to consider religious principles as part of an explanation of group behavior, that is, religion as a cultural determinant of behavior. There are many ways conservative Christian attorneys can conceive of religion and its proper influence on litigation. Conservative Christian litigators come from diverse backgrounds and identify cultural roots that differ in important ways. These differences create distinctions among them in the role religion should play in their profession and lead them to the selection of alternative strategies for achieving their goals in court. In this case, religious ideology defines what the group means when it identifies a goal and a range of legitimate behavior. Ultimately, I conclude that we can only understand the nature of the goals a group has identified when we consider the internal perspective of those establishing those goals.

In the following chapters, I explore the internal features of three leading conservative Christian law firms and how these features create external differences in their strategic behavior and legal arguments. Included in the analysis are the American Center for Law and Justice (ACLJ), the Liberty Counsel, and the American Family Association—Center for Law and Policy (CLP). I selected these three groups using a non-random technique that is appropriate for the goals of descriptive analysis and theory building, and to the research question at hand. When engaging in a process of theory building, concern for randomness in sampling may give way to other research strategies.[52] I employed four criteria for inclusion in the study. First, each group identifies the same primary goal—policy influence. I do this to test of the proposition that all litigators seeking policy influence will pursue similar litigation agendas. While all three groups articulate the same goal, their behavior is quite different. Thus, I keep variation in primary goals constant to explore other explanations for variation in behavior.

Second, I selected groups that are influential within the litigating arm of the New Christian Right. In the 1990s, each group assumed a leadership role and a position of importance in defining the broad sweep of movement emphases. Third, data was readily available to analyze the groups. Each agreed to on-site interviews and allowed me limited access to internal documents. Finally, each is an interesting case in itself. The ACLJ has participated in a huge number of cases since its inception (including sixteen before the U.S. Supreme Court), has a highly developed internal structure, and a large funding base. From its origins as the movement's litigator in the southeast, the Liberty Counsel has developed into a well-funded firm with a national litigation agenda and ties to one of the most prominent movement leaders—Rev. Jerry Falwell. Finally, the CLP is a grassroots-oriented law firm established by one of the prominent crusaders against pornography and gay rights — Rev. Donald Wildmon.

To facilitate comparison among them, I first present case studies of each group. In the core narrative chapters (chapters 2 through 4), I explore the internal culture of each organization. I employ a diverse set of data drawn from the public record, from in-depth personal interviews conducted at the law offices of each firm, phone interviews, and empirical data on the litigation agendas of each group. I present data gleaned from the Lexis/Nexis Legal Database on all reported cases brought before courts in which each group participated as case sponsor, Counsel on Brief, or as *amicus curiae*. The study characterizes groups on a broad set of variables including resource acquisition, internal developments, litigation emphases, development, and implementation of organizational goals and other features of internal organizational life. I sketch founding periods, dominant characteristics of litigation behavior, and organizational development and change. These variables become the basis for comparison among the groups in the final chapter of this work, especially a comparison of litigation agendas.

Chapter 5 begins with a comparison of the litigation-driven behavior of the three organizations. It then turns to a discussion of religious ideology among the groups as an explanation for differences in behavioral preferences. I introduce the concept of religious ideology, reconsider data in light of this cultural theory-based explanation, and introduce responses from members of the three groups to explicit questions about the importance of religion for their organizational mission. I find that both a consideration of religious ideology and attention to the process of goal setting within groups explains differences in litigation behavior. I conclude the chapter and the book with a discussion of the implications for the study of interest-group behavior deriving from the study of internal group characteristics. Commonly, researchers assume the goals of an organization from its behavior. However, where groups with similar resources and goals differ in the character of their litigation agendas, religious ideology can help us explain why these differences exist. Furthermore, behavior is a function of organizational maturity and context. While religious ideology limits the range of acceptable behavior, the context in which a group sets goals can place limitations on behavior as well. To function fully, a group must develop a full agenda that includes pursuing multiple goals and identifying objectives for building its reputation, its presence in the media, and its influence on policy.

Chapter Two

A Place at the Table

Jay Sekulow and the American Center for Law and Justice

Jay Sekulow is not the type that would come to mind if most people were to think of the leading attorney of the New Christian Right. He is in almost every way precisely what one would not associate with that social and political movement. That he is the founder of the New Christian Right's most successful law firm, the American Center for Law and Justice (ACLJ), is surprising. That he is the de facto attorney general to the New Christian Right's de facto president, the Reverend Pat Robertson, is even more so. In the first place, Jay Sekulow is Jewish. He has never converted from Judaism to Christianity. He worships as a Messianic Jew,[1] a sect so far outside the mainstream most Jews usually deny its existence as an impossibility. In the second place, Sekulow, once a registered Democrat in the state of Georgia, often finds himself on the wrong side of issues at the heart of modern conservatism. He supports gun-control measures, is adamantly opposed to the death penalty as a matter of principle, and had high praise for the Clinton administration's guidelines for religion in public schools. Not to mention the worst of his sins—he supported Jimmy Carter for president over Ronald Reagan.

Other attorneys speak of him with grudging respect and a baffled shake of the head—after all, he has taken twelve cases to the United States Supreme Court over the last fifteen years and participated heavily in four more. Of those sixteen, he has won ten, with two of those coming before a unanimous court. To the popular media he is "the Supreme Court's go-to guy on God matters."[2] Congress has convened to pass legislation because Jay Sekulow managed to convince a majority of Supreme Court justices that abortion protesters could not be prosecuted under a hundred-year-old statute aimed at stopping the Ku Klux Klan.[3] He speaks of Justice Thurgood Marshall with deep respect and admiration. He likes one of the most liberal members of the current Supreme Court, Justice Ginsburg, because in his words she reminds him of his mother.[4] Quite simply, Jay Sekulow is one of the most influential legal minds in the country. His work reflects the complexity of his logic, often placing him at odds with his compatriots.

At first glance, Jay Sekulow's association with the New Christian Right is somewhat bewildering. But, his place within the movement is the key to understanding how Christian litigators have developed a high degree of legal sophistication over the past decade. This refinement has vastly increased their influence on the formulation of court-crafted policy. For almost two decades, Sekulow has been among the vanguard that uses the courts to secure a role for the Christian church in society. His genius has been in defining goals for Christian litigation that assimilate and reflect the norms of the judiciary—respect for precedent, argument couched in legal terms, and an incremental approach to changing law and policy. This chapter is dedicated to understanding Sekulow's influence on Christian litigation, how he redefined the central aims of Christian litigators in the 1990s, and how he has struggled to carry those aims to fruition through his organization, the ACLJ.

Jay Sekulow: Legal Eagle, Legal Bulldog

How different is Jay Sekulow from his fellow Christian litigators? In 1999 while Paul Weyrich was complaining that the New Christian Right had lost the culture war, Sekulow went on record saying that there has never been a better time to be Christian and Protestant in America. As an example, Sekulow points to a case he litigated that brought prayer back into public schools.[5] But, it came back in the form Sekulow wanted, not the form endorsed by the New Christian Right's leadership. "Student-led prayer is what we want," says Sekulow, "not state-led. If we thought about it for a minute we'd realize that!"[6] He has fired an associate from the American Center for Law and Justice who wanted to argue that killing abortion doctors is justifiable homicide.[7] He pioneered the free-speech defense for public display of religious belief and protest. He follows his logic into legal conflicts with the Small Business Administration over loans to a day-care center using a Christian curriculum.[8] He has grappled with the IRS over a church's tax-exempt status after campaigning against Bill Clinton,[9] stating, "Dr. King spoke in Selma about the tactics of Bull Conner and nobody revoked First Baptist's tax-exempt status."[10]

And, he has done battle with public schools. The ACLJ's central victories in court have involved recasting public schools as public forums for student expression of faith-based belief. The organization has defended students who wanted to use facilities for a student-led Bible club[11] and hammered the public school that phoned police when its principal saw students praying around a flag-pole on the National Day of Prayer.[12] But, Sekulow says he supports religious freedom, not simply Christian freedom; he cringes when he hears colleagues call for an American return to the values of a Christian nation. The ACLJ's stated policy is that it is "committed to defending the First Amendment free-speech rights of all people of faith."[13] He has in fact defended Jews for Jesus, and by association Hare Krishnas and Scientologists,[14] against government-imposed restraints on free speech.

Sekulow's influence is broad, extending from the courts into the U.S. Department of Justice where he acts as an adviser to Attorney General John Ashcroft.[15] In court, he has framed legal issues in a way that greatly expanded the potential of victory for the New Christian Right. From a policy standpoint,

Sekulow has displayed consistent influence over the formulation of policy alternatives on hot-button issues ranging from the Defense of Marriage Act and the Bush administration's policy on partial birth abortion to the Patriot Act, which Sekulow authored.[16] Sekulow had lasting influence over the 1990s and into the new century, even when other conservative leaders managed to destroy the religious grassroots network they developed so carefully during the 1980s and even when conservative Republican leadership in Congress managed to squander their political capital in the mid-1990s. In an era when the New Christian Right and conservative congressmen appeared to be writing the rules so that they lose, Sekulow showed amazing staying power, and his organization thrived and developed into an important player across the broad spectrum of policy making.

Art Spitzer of the National Capitol Area American Civil Liberties Union (ACLU), one of Sekulow's archrivals, describes his influence: "Jay has had a real impact on the development of the law. He's been successful in his crusade to say that religious speech is just another form of speech. He's someone who enjoys intellectual exercise."[17] It is Sekulow's intellectual approach that has changed the face of Christian litigation in the United States. However, his intellectualism, liberalism, and tolerance are not always well received by his compatriots. He states that "[a] Jewish liberal is not the same as a gentile liberal."

> I bring a uniquely Jewish perspective to the cause of Christian liberties in America. I always frame these cases as a question of free speech, not church versus state. That means you tolerate speech you don't like, which not everyone in the Christian conservative movement is willing to do. I often surprise some of my Christian friends on issues like flag burning. If you can't burn it, the liberty behind it is meaningless.[18]

While Sekulow's views on religious freedoms often place him at odds with other Christian litigators, his views on appropriate behavior, inside and outside the courtroom, have stunned his adversaries. He is not what others had come to expect from Christian litigators. "People say I'm rude and aggressive," he notes. "The Supreme Court was used to Christian lawyers being meek, mild, and manageable. I'm a reasonable fanatic."[19] Sekulow is a passionate speaker, aggressive debater, and a commanding presence. He has demonstrated his rhetorical skills and solidified his position as the mouthpiece of the New Christian Right in court during various appearances on CNN's *Crossfire*, ABC's *Nightline*, CBN's *700 Club*, and other broadcasts. He is a highly sought after guest in the age of confrontational journalism mainly because he refuses to back down under heavy fire. The heavy fire began almost as soon as Sekulow emerged as a movement leader for the New Christian Right. Consider the following exchange that took place between co-host Harry Smith, Sekulow, and Barry Lynn of Americans United for Separation of Church and State during the July 13, 1995, broadcast of *CBS This Morning*:

> **Smith**: We're talking about President Clinton's speech yesterday in Virginia about religious expression and prayer in schools. . . . If you look at the presi-

dent's speech yesterday and look at the Supreme Court decisions of the last several years, you're still not going to get a prayer at a graduation ceremony, are you—Barry Lynn?

Lynn: No, you're not. . . .What the president did yesterday was not to play politics with this issue. The persons who played politics with this issue—people like Jay Sekulow and his boss, Pat Robertson, who have insisted that we get a vote on a completely unnecessary constitutional amendment on this issue so that they can bash any member of Congress who doesn't vote for it as being anti-religious and anti-God. So, when Jay Sekulow has the nerve to say the president is playing politics with prayer, he better look at his own house first.

Sekulow: Well, let me say, Harry I respectfully disagree with my friend Barry Lynn. Let me make it real clear. Here we are in the middle of July, the president of the United States goes to a public high school. High schools don't meet generally in the middle of July. This one, for some reason, students are there, and he is discussing these things as the religious liberty equality amendment is already in field hearings and—about to take place in Washington, DC, two weeks after the Supreme Court, much to the dismay of my friend Barry Lynn, rules overwhelmingly in two cases for religious expression . . .

Smith: Both of you guys hang on a second. Is this something we should be mud-wrestling about on television right now or at any point . . .

Sekulow: Sure—

Lynn: No, if the—if the—

Sekulow: It's politics, Barry.

Lynn: Jay, let me finish. He's doing this in the middle of the summer because he wants to give the Department of Education an opportunity to issue guidelines before the next school year opens so that you don't have the possibility . . . of all these threats of litigation.

Sekulow: Hold it. Here's what—here's what you've got in reality at bottom. You've got an attempt to politicacize [sic] the issue because fifteen months ago the president said he could not send out a directive. Now he can.

Lynn: Maybe he just didn't want to send out Pat Robertson's directive.

Sekulow: But he just did.

This is one of many instances in which Sekulow has willingly stepped before the cameras to debate issues with rivals on neutral ground. His passion for confrontation and his confidence in the clarity and rationality of his arguments have stood him in good stead and frustrated his opposition. A refusal to allow his position to be radicalized (e.g., the flurry of exchange toward the end of the above excerpt) is a hallmark of his rhetorical style. Furthermore, Sekulow's emphasis on free speech as the crucial First Amendment freedom is clear when he defends student-initiated prayer at public school functions. Consider this exchange between Michael Kinsley, Bob Peck of the ACLU, and Jay Sekulow on CNN's *Crossfire*:

> **Kinsley**: Is it totally unimaginable to you, Jay, that a nonbeliever or a believer in a minority religion would be made . . . to feel like an outsider and unwanted at an official graduation ceremony at a public high school where there was a prayer?
>
> **Sekulow**: An eighteen year-old at a graduation, or a seventeen year-old, in America better get used to speech they disagree with or feel uncomfortable with. This is a free society.
>
> **Peck**: It is not the offense of the speech. It is the fact that government said this is an event you are going to have to attend and you are going to have to sit through it.
>
> **Sekulow**: Oh, you are going to have to sit through this 30-second prayer that you find repugnant. Well, tough. This is America . . . this is what I love: I'm sitting next to Bob Peck from the ACLU, whom I respect, who's saying "Let's censor speech."[20]

Today, he remains a highly visible spokesperson for the ACLJ, for the New Christian Right, and in defense of Bush administration policies. In 2004 alone, he appeared on over fifty programs including guest appearances on MSNBC's *Scarborough Country*, NPR's *Morning Edition* and *Talk of the Nation*, ABC's *World News Tonight with Peter Jennings* and *Nightline*, NBC's *Nightly News*, and Fox News Network's *The O'Reilly Factor* and *Special Report with Brit Hume*.[21] He has also testified on the Federal Marriage Amendment before the House Constitutional Subcommittee.[22]

Founding the ACLJ

Sekulow began to litigate First Amendment issues at the behest of Moishe Rosen, the head of Jews for Jesus, Inc. Rosen was looking for an attorney to defend Jews for Jesus evangelists who were arrested under a city ordinance declaring First Amendment free speech rights were in abeyance at Los Angeles International Airport (*Board of Airport Commissioners of Los Angeles v. Jews for Jesus, Inc.* 1987). Sekulow, in the middle of dissolving his law practice and filing for personal bankruptcy in Georgia, claims to have been pulled in the direction of defending people of faith, but never acted on that instinct. When approached by Rosen, Sekulow had little desire to take the case and felt that the airport directors would settle before proceeding too far through the federal courts. They did not do so.

The pivotal event in this case (and perhaps in Sekulow's career) came while preparing for oral argument before the Supreme Court in 1987. According to Sekulow, during a conversation immediately before entering the Court chambers for oral argument, he asked the Los Angeles district attorney why he continued to appeal his case and why he chose to interfere with Jews for Jesus evangelists when so many other groups went unhindered in their efforts to proselytize. The Los Angeles DA responded that the airport commissioners "did not think Christians would put up a fight. They had a regulation to test, so why not pick on the pious, placid Christians . . .?"[23]

This answer contributed to the ferocity of his onslaught during oral argument that day.[24] The perceived challenge to his faith evoked a response that raised Sekulow's consciousness about the legal profession's tolerance of faith-based public expression. In any event, despite presenting aggressively and interrupting the chief justice, Sekulow won his first case before a unanimous Supreme Court. He went on to found a public law firm called Christian Advocates Serving Evangelism (CASE) and committed his career to litigating First Amendment speech, free exercise, and establishment claims. He led CASE for three years until a growing friendship with Rev. Pat Robertson resulted in his association with the ACLJ.

Around 1990, Rev. Pat Robertson began to implement plans for a high-powered Christian litigating organization affiliated with Regent Law School and his Christian Broadcasting Network. Following the unraveling of the grassroots movement in the mid-1980s and the Reagan administration's reluctance to support the agenda of the New Christian Right, there was widespread lack of enthusiasm among movement leadership for relying solely on their political influence within Congress and the presidency. Moreover, victories in Congress and at the White House were often hollow, given early conservative losses when those policy victories were challenged in federal and state courts.

Robertson appears to have acted on two goals when initiating the founding of the American Center for Law and Justice. First, he hoped to restore "fundamental religious freedoms in America."[25] His concern that religious freedoms were being undermined extended far beyond the case Jay Sekulow had just argued before the Supreme Court. He envisioned an organization that would litigate the New Christian Right's position in a vast array of issue areas including religious expression and abortion policy. Robertson has also cast the role of the ACLJ as leveling the playing field for people of all faiths to express that faith in public forums, regardless of the issue at hand. Second, he wanted to create an organization that would counter the efforts of liberal public law firms, specifically the ACLU.[26] To accomplish both goals, Robertson needed a sophisticated legal machine that respected the dictates of the legal profession for reasoned argument and an incremental approach to policy change.

It is almost legendary at the ACLJ that when Robertson formed the organization, his first move was not to hire a general counsel[27] to develop a litigation strategy and build the organization, but to hire a top-flight fundraiser. However, after being introduced to Sekulow by the dean of Regent University Law

School, Robertson knew he had found his chief litigator. Sekulow had developed the rudiments of his litigation strategy at CASE and was busy testing it in the courts. Furthermore, his recently published book[28] outlined his general principles for litigating First Amendment cases. His fierce defense of Christian rights in public spaces struck a chord with those in the Christian Right, like Robertson, who wanted to see courts endorse their policies. As Robertson intended, the ACLJ emerged in 1990 fully formed with a clearly defined mission, an already proven litigation specialist with a tested litigation strategy, and a well-developed fundraising system completely distinct from Robertson's other enterprises.

Sekulow has been called Rev. Pat Robertson's consigliore, and there is a general impression among the public and the media that Robertson runs the ACLJ. There is no doubt that ties between the ACLJ and Robertson are strong. Sekulow delivers regular legal updates on the *700 Club* (Robertson's flagship television program), and the ACLJ keeps its headquarters on the campus of Robertson's Regent University. However, there is a sense that, if called upon to do so, the ACLJ could break free and "go it alone." In fact, Sekulow notes tremendous autonomy to take the cases he chooses. He runs the organization the way he sees fit.

> Pat Robertson has without a doubt a vision to be a counterpoint to the American Civil Liberties Union. There's no doubt about it. He's talked about it since the 1970s. He waited and waited, and he and I got to know each other over a number of years, and a friend of mine (Keith Fournier) became the executive director of the ACLJ. We were friends and we got along so I was doing the legal work. Saying I'm "Consigliore" to Pat Robertson is I think another way of saying that Pat Robertson is the founder of the ACLJ. Does he run its day to day affairs? No. Could he tell you the top five cases we have? Probably not. I'm not sure that he cares to know.

Sekulow's assertion was tested after the 2000 election when he radically altered the structure of the organization to pursue a broader policy focus. Robertson wholly supported the move. These changes are taken up in detail below.[29]

Goals and Religious Ideology

The primary reason for the existence of the ACLJ is to influence policy and build precedent favorable to the expression of religious faith in social, political, and cultural contexts. When asked to describe the goals of the organization, Sekulow replied, "I made a statement a long time ago that the only books we wanted to write were books that ended up in those [book]cases right there [pointing to shelves holding the Supreme Court Reporter]. And we've had good success there." That is certainly an understatement. In addition to its successes before the Supreme Court, the ACLJ has brought numerous cases before lower federal and state courts, and has always aimed to establish favorable precedent of national scope. Sekulow himself has expanded his interests into areas beyond litigation encompassing the whole of policy making, policy revision, judicial selection, and oversight by the judicial branch.

The all-encompassing nature of Sekulow's involvement in policy making points to an important and enduring emphasis within the ACLJ. The organization is committed to religious ideological positions, but these commitments are tempered and adapted in important ways to the realities of being an inside player within the policy process. Thus, Sekulow tends to discuss religion in legal and social terms, rather than treating the law as a reflection of religious ideology. While this may appear to be a subtle nuance in organizational culture, the distinction is crucial for understanding the place of the ACLJ within the New Christian Right, and its broad influence on court-crafted policy.

Making the Box Bigger: Legal Policy Goals and Religious Doctrine

Sekulow sees part of the ACLJ's mission as educating the leadership of the New Christian Right on how to approach the courts and appeasing them when their efforts do not end in a positive outcome before the Supreme Court. Conservative leaders have used Supreme Court decisions to "rally the troops," or bring the attention of membership to their cause. This had resulted in rather negative rhetoric directed at the Court[30] and fueled a desire to win at all costs in the political process. In contrast, Sekulow's approach to the courts flows from lessons he learned in early litigation efforts and implicates a more liberal understanding of rights doctrine that is in part at odds with the position of New Christian Right leadership.

Two issue areas stand out as particularly galling to movement leadership. The first is in church-state litigation. In ruling that public schools may not require students to participate in teacher-led times of prayer, that public schools may not post the Ten Commandments in classrooms, and that cities may not display a crèche depicting the birth of Christ, the Supreme Court has acted to flesh out the constitutional provision that government may not take any action "respecting an establishment of religion." However, movement leadership says that these decisions go beyond the spirit of the law to demonstrate hostility toward expressions of religious faith both public and ceremonial. They cite such discrepancies as policies that disallow the display of the Ten Commandments in public schools and courtrooms, and those that provide funding for artists who defame sacred religious symbols. The second area is abortion policy. In ruling that states have authority to tailor abortion restrictions unless those restrictions "unduly burden" the abortion rights of women, the Supreme Court has acted to revise the standards of permissible state intervention in abortion policy. However, the trend in the reluctance of state legislatures to enact restrictions on abortion after the Supreme Court's ruling in *Webster* continued after it handed states more discretion in *Casey*. State legislatures still introduced regulatory proposals, but calls for outlawing abortion outright disappeared. Successful regulatory measures guaranteed abortion rights while enacting only Court-sanctioned restrictions. One might think that the pro-choice side had carried the day both in the courts and legislatures. However, New Christian Right leaders have reassessed their role in abortion policy, shifted focus as the abortion debate moved on to other issues, and acted to preserve the expressive rights of abortion protestors.

In both of these issue areas, the ACLJ has become the leading organization making the New Christian Right's position known in the courts. But, it is an organization that appears to be significantly more pragmatic and less prone to conservative angst than leading Christian organizations of the past several decades. For example, in the past other conservative Christian organizations have exploited specific instances of abuse perpetrated by public officials—especially where those officials inappropriately curtailed freedom of religious expression in public places or schools. However, when assessing the overall state of religious freedoms, the ACLJ finds much to be positive about, rather than dwelling on particular abuses.

The organization's stance on issues of First Amendment rights as they relate to secular and other religious expressions stems from its early victory in *Board of Westside Community School District v. Mergens*.[31] Sekulow refers to this case as "foundational." It is the case that for Sekulow defined the ACLJ's mission and character. Joel Thornton, ACLJ senior counsel, notes the significance of Sekulow's victory in establishing the ACLJ's approach to First Amendment litigation and its key merger of religious doctrine with legal goals.

> One of the questions that the justices asked Jay in *Mergens* was "if we open this up to Bible groups does this mean we are going to have to let the Satanists and the Nazis into the schools as well?" And his answer was "Freedom is freedom." The price of freedom is that sometimes we hear things we do not want to hear.

This continues to be a theme in ACLJ rhetoric. The case established the "place at the table" approach that has been the ACLJ's bread and butter in all equal access and religious expression cases to follow.

For Sekulow, *Mergens* was also a challenge to encourage Christians to make use of their access to public schools. Both Sekulow and Thornton referred to Sekulow's response after the Court released its opinion in *Mergens*. Sekulow was on hand when the opinion came down, and as he left the Supreme Court building, he says he swore not to "put the victory up on the shelf like a trophy." He would work to encourage students to start Bible clubs in their local schools. Shortly after, the ACLJ started a sister organization called Ripe for the Harvest. It has assisted in establishing Bible clubs in more than 700 high schools in the United States by 2000.[32]

However, the ACLJ's position is not widely held within the New Christian Right, by the rank-and-file membership or by its leadership, whose efforts to change policy often include limitations that would undermine First Amendment freedoms. The ACLJ, recognizing Christian leaders' frustration with policies that appear to reject or curtail mainstream Christian moral views, also recognizes that the New Christian Right's response is often beyond the constitutional pale. Sekulow sees this as a general lack of faith in the efficacy of the church's Gospel message (as if an immortal God might need a little help ensuring that his message received full consideration). Thornton notes the Christian Right's limited view in light of Sekulow's own legal and religious mission.

> Jay has said that his mission is "to make the box bigger for people," to make the box that they place God in bigger. We all place God in some kind of framework for understanding him. It is defining and confining. Perhaps the church's box is too small.

Goals for Litigating

When questioned about the goals of his organization, Sekulow often refers to the power of the courts in making and interpreting policy as the basis for litigating high-profile cases. He has noted publicly that "it is ultimately the courts which decide the scope of religious liberties in America."[33] His descriptions in the media of the ACLJ's litigation goals are peppered with civil rights–era rhetoric. "They can't change the rules because it happens to be religion," he says. "Whether you agree or don't agree with it, you don't want religion treated as a second-class citizen."[34] The Supreme Court has exhibited much sympathy with that argument and with Sekulow's efforts to reframe church-state issues in terms of free expression.

Friends and foes alike note the centrality of influencing court-crafted policy to the ACLJ's mission. In an article on public interest law firms litigating religious liberty cases, one author compares the role of the ACLJ in the court system to that of the Christian Coalition in electoral politics, and notes its ultimate goal of "arguing cases up to the Supreme Court."[35] Tom Jipping of the Free Congress Foundation says the ACLJ

> [has] had an enormous impact. By winning cases in the Supreme Court, they send a message. . . . Just like the ACLU has been able to discourage religious practice through the threat of litigation, the ACLJ has been able to encourage [it] by winning.[36]

Bob Peck of the ACLU notes how the ACLJ pursues its goals using a planned litigation strategy. "They've been successful in part because they are careful in choosing their cases. They have a good advocate in Jay because he is able to attract high-visibility cases . . . and because he thinks about long-term strategy. He does build on cases."[37]

On the litigation side of the ACLJ's agenda, bringing cases up to the Supreme Court is the central goal. While Sekulow is content to take what comes his way, he has a clear notion that the goals of the organization fit with an array of cases representing a variety of issues so long as they include one important feature. "We look at cases that are going to set a national precedent," he notes, "or at least a state precedent." He made that statement in 1998, when one of the firm's primary emphases was intervening on behalf of rank-and-file New Christian Right supporters. But, as with all things at the ACLJ, this was secondary to the goal of national policy influence. There is a clear congruence here between the ACLJ's legal goals and its spiritual mission. But, Sekulow makes it clear that he is not aiming to proselytize or force the God on the culture (an accusation that could be directed at the broader movement). His mission is quite different. He speaks of religion in legal terms that emphasize the place of the church within a diverse and plural society.

> We want to open the avenues, one for the proclamation of the Gospel, two . . . to make sure that a Christian worldview can be accepted in the marketplace of ideas as legitimate expression. . . . I want to see the day where the Christian worldview is welcome at the table and anticipated because there's something valid here to offer.

The ACLJ's issue-area emphases have changed over time. In recent years, the ACLJ has scaled back participation in issue areas that were its primary concern during the 1990s, in part because it has moved on to other concerns.[38] These new concerns are those of its constituency, and include litigating the Defense of Marriage Act and the partial birth abortion ban. Within its broad mandate to represent the interests of the church in society, the ACLJ follows trends in what cases capture the public's attention. In 1998, Sekulow noted the changes in the types of cases his constituents brought to him, while emphasizing the overall sameness of the ACLJ's goals as a litigating organization. "When we started in 1987, (formally I was doing cases for Jews for Jesus and other ministries) everything was evangelism access. Those were the cases in the 1980s. In the 1990s, its not."

> Part of that is because [after] the Jews for Jesus cases in the Supreme Court and a couple of other ones we litigated, you don't have those cases anymore. Now it's establishment clause cases, it's the voucher cases. We are right now involved in one of the leading voucher cases in the country in Maine. We took the case knowing we would lose in the lower courts with the idea we would go to the Supreme Court. I told our law clerks yesterday that's where I suspect it's going to go, and it *will* go there.

In point of fact, it didn't. *Zelman v. Simmons-Harris*,[39] a case out of Ohio in which the ACLJ participated as *amicus*, made it there first. But, the emphasis on national policy making is consistent across all of the ACLJ's interests.

By 2004, the ACLJ's agenda had changed and adapted to the political realities of the times. Sekulow states that he could continue to litigate free expression
and equal access cases if he chose, but he does not. "We don't do much of that
anymore because in the area of equal access, the school cases, Bible clubs,
we've won that," he stated when explaining the shifts in litigation and other emphases. "I don't like spending a lot of money on something we've won three
times before. I don't feel like wasting our resources that way. When we get
cases like that we try to get them resolved." With the ACLJ about to become a
victim of its own success, Sekulow began examining ways to develop the organization beyond its focus on litigation. When the opportunity arose to move
into the policy sphere, he took it.

The ACLJ's Organizational Structure and Resources

The resources of the American Center for Law and Justice qualify it as one of
the best-funded public interest law firms in the country. Presently it boasts a
budget over $30 million per year, 100 support staff, and forty-four full-time at-
torneys employed around the country. By any objective standard, resources have
never been a problem for the ACLJ. In 1990 it came into existence with a $6
million budget and a small, capable, and experienced leadership team in place.
Yet, the ACLJ's executive director, Keith Fournier, referred to the ACLJ as an
organization in its adolescence.[40] How does an organization with such financial
power and legal talent mature after such extraordinary beginnings? Traditionally, scholars have examined a number of resources that impact the efficiency of
group capabilities and their maturation over time. These resources include
monetary budget, acquisition of legal expertise, adequate staff and facilities, a
well-developed organizational system, and support from sister organizations in
sharing the costs of litigation efforts. In this section I examine the resources of
the ACLJ as they have developed inclusive of its existence as an organization.
The analysis is complicated by a dramatic change in organizational structure that
occurred in 2001. But, there has been a unifying theme to the ACLJ's organizational development. As an analytical framework, I use this section to explore
how the ACLJ has adapted its resources and organizational structure in pursuit
of its ambition for national policy influence.

Organizational Structure

The events of September 11, 2001, resulted in significant modifications to
the ALCJ's mission that are ultimately reflected in its structure. Sekulow had
been involved in crafting legislation, writing the Defense of Marriage Act
(DOMA) signed into law by President Clinton. But, after the World Trade Center disaster, he began modifying the ACLJ's prior emphases by taking its inter-

est in policy making to an entirely different level. The organization still maintains its core services, such as resolving religious liberties disputes for clients through the demand letter approach. However, "we send out probably twenty a week, but it's not like the 100 a week in the old days," he said in 2004. When Republicans in Congress and the Bush Administration came calling, Sekulow began to reformulate the ACLJ's organizational emphases toward policy making by enlarging the Washington, D.C., branch. He created the ACLJ Governmental Affairs Office and began working closely with the Department of Justice as a primary author of the Patriot Act. Currently, the organization appears to have a dual structure reflecting its continued commitment to litigation and its new role as a key consultant in the policy process. Below, I examine how both of its emphases are reflected in its organizational arrangement.

The ACLJ is often referred to as the conservative counterpart to the American Civil Liberties Union (ACLU). Its name was chosen to encourage that comparison. However, significant differences emerge when viewing organizational structure and management styles. The ACLU is noted for the autonomy of its regional offices. ACLU chapters make their own decisions concerning their litigation agenda. The national office often only becomes involved in cases developed by regional affiliates when those cases come before higher courts, or courts of last resort. Occasionally, regional affiliates end up on different sides of the same case. One example of the consequences of ACLU decentralization occurred in a case litigated by the ACLJ. In *Schenck v. Pro-Choice Women's Network*,[41] three state affiliates filed *amicus* briefs in support of the ACLJ's position, while the national office filed an *amicus* brief against.

Unlike the ACLU, the ACLJ is clearly centered on a particular personality. This might suggest to some that the influence of New Christian Right litigators is unstable and likely to evaporate after Sekulow's career ends. While the ACLJ is a very important player among movement litigators, it should be noted that the New Christian Right has simply taken a different route toward institutionalizing a conservative presence in court. Rather than developing one dominant organization with local chapters that function as partially autonomous law firms, the movement has developed a network of small firms of which the ACLJ is the most visible. Others include the Liberty Counsel, Thomas More Law Center, Alliance Defense Fund, American Family Association's Center for Law and Policy, Christian Legal Society, and the Rutherford Institute. These sometimes cooperate together to achieve overlapping goals in much the same way that ACLU local chapters combine forces. The development of these firms has been a conscious decision among New Christian Right litigators who experimented with more formal coordination in the 1990s. However, the most significant attempt to coordinate funding, litigation, and merge legal talent at a national level was particularly unsuccessful.[42]

The ACLJ has developed a flexible organizational structure that supports the broad array of issues in which it participates legally or legislatively. While the affiliate offices handle the many requests for intervention in religious disputes brought to the organization each year, the governmental affairs office, based in Washington, D.C., manages legislative and policy docket. At any given time the ACLJ represents between seventy and ninety members of Congress. Sekulow notes that they often do not employ legal staff and so retain the ACLJ "to assist with legal issues related to legislation, or the need for legislation."

Organizational arrangements on the legal side reflect Sekulow's dominance of the organization. Generally speaking, the ACLJ can resolve 99 percent of the religious liberties disputes brought to its attention through the use of demand letters. However, when this process produces cases with greater policy implications, ACLJ regional directors and Sekulow's senior staff closely manage them from the trial stage onward. Sekulow contrasted the ACLU's organizational structure and affiliate autonomy to that of his firm.

> That autonomy will never happen at the ACLJ. We're not going to do that. The ACLU has this model where their regional offices are very autonomous, where they can file against each other in positions. That's not going to happen here— that's toppling the upright.

Joel Thornton, Sekulow's senior lieutenant, notes that the effect of this centralization of authority on case selection is not always positive.

> Good facts and good clients make good cases. That's the hardest part—picking a good client, particularly when you pick from all over the nation and you don't have time to go spend three days with somebody and get a feel for it. You have to do a lot of this over the phone and you have to go spend an hour with somebody and make a determination if this is a person that really has the vision to see this thing through and understand how tough this could become.

The top-down organizational structure of the ACLJ began to take shape in 1992. Early on, Sekulow realized that the organization needed a first-rate stable of experienced litigators to develop the national prominence and impact that he hoped. But, rather than finding that talent through recruiting efforts, the talent found him. At a November 1992 meeting of all the major Christian public interest law firms held in Washington, D.C., the ACLJ stole the show. Its combination of aggressive litigation and attorney-led organizational structure appealed to many of the senior counsel of other New Christian Right firms. "In the history of Christian public interest law firms, this meeting is momentous," Sekulow recalled.

> I don't think we realized the significance of it until five years later. All of the lawyers for all of the legal groups got together at the Willard Hotel in Washington, D.C., for a day in a very informal setting. And from the meeting, relationships started developing with senior counsel. Everyone liked the ACLJ's structure better than their own to some extent. In the other firms you had non-lawyers as the head of the organization. They do a great job, but they're not lawyers. The ACLJ was led by Keith Fournier and me—both lawyers. Keith did the administrative stuff and I did the litigation. It was very attractive to these guys and over a period of time the head of Free Speech Advocates, Pat

Monaghan, which was a pro-life group, came over. He and I had been friends for years, but he came on as our senior counsel. Ben Bull from the American Family Association came on as senior counsel. Jordan Lorance who was the senior counsel at Concerned Women for America, joined us, as did Mark Troobnick, who was a deputy at Concerned Women of America, and Jim Henderson. All these guys from different organizations, joined us. It created a little bit of tension in the beginning.

As a result of that meeting, Sekulow and Fournier acquired top-flight legal talent with an array of experience in First Amendment litigation. That corps of talent remains largely intact.[43] The core of legal talent resembles partners in a law firm. They are responsible for managing the ACLJ's caseload, training the junior staff, developing long-term strategies to expand the organization, and litigating its most prominent cases. The original goal of the ACLJ was to have an office within each federal circuit's geographic jurisdiction. Currently, it has regional offices in the Northeast (Connecticut), West (Arizona), and Southeast (Alabama). Additionally, there are state offices located in New York City and Dallas, and an office in the hills of Kentucky. Despite the top-down management style of the ACLJ, each office exhibits its own style and regional interests. Sekulow is proud of the differences, noting that the Dallas office reflects the sophistication and polish of the North Texas legal culture, and the Kentucky office has been aggressively defending Appalachian churches. Each state office is closely supervised by a regional office, which in turn reports to the ACLJ headquarters in Virginia Beach, Virginia.

There is an upside to this arrangement that has an important influence on the organization's policy influence. Micro-managing the ACLJ's national caseload has produced considerable consistency in the arguments it presents across jurisdictions. The benefits of such an arrangement were apparent during the 1990s as the ACLJ dominated New Christian Right litigation and exerted significant influence at the appellate level. Currently, other groups are attempting less formal arrangements by sharing ideas and entering into partnerships to litigate cases nationally that fall into specific policy areas.[44]

Acquiring Resources: "There's Never Enough"

The acquisition of financial resources is vital to the life of a litigating organization. The ACLJ has been particularly successful in acquiring the money it needs to litigate, to implement a long-term litigation strategy, and to sustain its base of financial support. Beginning with a budget of $6 million, the organization increased its financial resources by about $2 million a year until 2001. Currently, its budget (estimated at $12 million in 1998) has increased to over $30 million in 2004. The ACLJ is a donor-supported organization, funded mainly by direct-mail solicited contributions. In 1998, the average amount contributed from direct mail solicitations was $24. That figure was revised upward after the

ACLJ completed its campaign to attract larger individual contributions from major donors. According to Joel Thornton, the ACLJ has a very aggressive program for acquiring new donors that has been bolstered by Sekulow's radio program, his appearances on the *700 Club,* and the organization's high profile. "In the Christian marketplace, we are a slice," says Sekulow. "Not everybody's interested in Christian litigation. You have a lot more support for organizations like . . . Focus on the Family than you can get for a litigation group. We're willing to deal with that. That's fine." However, as part of the public perception that the ACLJ is run by Pat Robertson, there is also the perception that Robertson's money funds the litigation activities of the ACLJ. Such speculation was bolstered by the 1997 sale of Robertson's media interests to Rupert Murdoch's Fox Network. Sekulow was quick to dispel the notion that Robertson still contributes, or that the ACLJ profited from that multi-billion dollar sale. "We were independent from the word go."

> The first year we had a very close economic relationship with CBN [Robertson's media network]. They helped seat us. But once we got past that first year, we have not received a dollar from CBN unless there was money raised on the air [specifically] for the American Center for Law and Justice.

The ACLJ has been extremely effective in increasing its donor base. Sekulow is closely involved in soliciting for donors. "Moneying this thing is a full time job," he says.

> Doing the cases I do is a full-time job, so I get two full-time jobs. I have a great administrative staff, I have a great support staff. I have a good structure here in my office. We're really set up for this, so it works out very well.

Despite the recognition that money is an ever present need if the ACLJ is to carry on its work, very little of Sekulow's air time is taken up with asking for money, and there is no "hard sell" characteristic of other religious organizations. Listeners are encouraged to donate money only twice during a half-hour broadcast, and only if they are interested in the ACLJ's work. Although Sekulow has little concern about the stability of his donor base (the ACLJ even has its own endowment), seeking out monetary support remains a large part of what he does. Significant organizational resources are directed toward acquiring and processing the donations that support the central mission of the organization.

Inevitable comparisons arise between the budget of the ACLJ and the ACLU. In 1998, the ACLU's budget of approximately $30 million per year dwarfed that of the ACLJ. However, in recent years the mission of the ACLJ has become much like that of its liberal foe. Both pursue a diversity of policy-related projects. Although the ACLU funds a number of projects related to civil liberties while the ACLJ primarily directs its money toward litigating establishment clause and free exercise claims, the emergence of a legislative policy component has filled out the ACLJ's mission. Thus, the ACLJ in a few short years has developed into an organization that is monetarily equipped to meet the challenges of its foes in court and in Congress.

A Mission to the World

The ACLJ is an organization focused on long-term policy influence. However, from the discussion above, one might conclude that the ACLJ is entirely focused on influencing policy in the United States. This is not entirely true. The ACLJ is expanding into other countries and demonstrating a profound concern for impacting policy on an international level. Perhaps the role the ACLJ played in securing the rights of a host of international missionaries during the 1996 Atlanta Olympics prompted an interest in expanding internationally. When discussing that event and the ACLJ's foray into international law, Thornton noted the influence of the Atlanta Olympics on the ACLJ's international mission.

> That's an example of an international event, and international situations arising that will affect other events in the future all over the world. What happens here effects what happens over [in Europe]. What happens over there has influence here. That's why we ultimately want to have international centers all over the world.

In recent years the ACLJ has opened two international centers—the European Center for Law and Justice (ECLJ) based in Strasbourg, France, and the Slavic Center for Law and Justice (SCLJ) based in Moscow. What motivates the ACLJ to open international centers is the same motivation that underlies its mission in the United States—protecting the capacity of Christians to present their faith as a viable and reasonable alternative in the marketplace of ideas. Moreover, the ACLJ believes that it can do its job more effectively in the United States if it extends its mission internationally. Thornton made this point when discussing what effect opening the ECLJ will have on the ACLJ's work.

> If we don't fight the fight in America against same-sex marriages, if we don't fight the fight to preserve Christians' right in public places in Europe, then we'll have to fight that fight again here or over there. The ultimate goal is to have an international objective. There is a group that wants to set up an Australian Center for Law and Justice. We want to have as many international centers as possible.

Strategizing a Place at the Table:
The ACLJ's Litigation Agenda

I turn now to a discussion of the means that Jay Sekulow and the American Center for Law and Justice use for carrying their goals to the courts—the litigation agenda. A litigation agenda consists of specific actions taken by a group to pursue litigation in the courts, and it implicates both methods for achieving policy sue litigation in the courts, and it implicates both methods for achieving policy (e.g., selecting cases, pursuing a national agenda across jurisdictions) and the general logic (i.e., legal rationale and arguments presented in court). I begin with a general overview of the ACLJ's litigation agenda and its methods for pursuing its goal of policy influence in the court. Next, I consider the major contribution of the ACLJ to New Christian Right litigation—the equal access argument. I explore its use of equal access in various issue areas in which the ACLJ has been actively litigating, highlighting specific and important cases in which it participated. Finally, I turn to an in-depth analysis of the ACLJ's litigation participation, examining in particular its long-term commitment in devoting organizational time, energy, and resources to protracted litigation.

The Glorious Tip of the Iceberg

The types of cases coming to the ACLJ from its supporters have changed since it began its work in the early 1990s. According to Sekulow, by 1998 free expression seemed to have run its course as an issue of saliency to the courts. They still appear less willing to consider such cases (although there are always important exceptions, the sheer number of cases has diminished) as other issues have risen to prominence. This lull, and changing interests of its supporters, produced changes in the types of cases the ACLJ litigates. Additionally, the organization found other ways to use its energy. Joel Thornton noted the change in cases and issues over time. In its infancy, the organization's smaller size and budget allowed it to focus on "defending the right to proclaim the gospel in public places." It emphasized litigation on schools as public places (e.g., *Board of Education of Westside Community Schools v. Mergens*), then expanded its agenda to include streets and public buildings (*U.S. v. Kokinda*,[45] and *Lamb's Chapel v. Center Moriches Union School*[46]), including a line of cases involving public protestation (*NOW v. Scheidler*[47]). As the ACLJ's resources grew, its capacity to respond to its clientele expanded as well. Supporters have increased the number of complaints about gay rights ordinances in particular—an area in which the ACLJ became active during the lull in free expression litigation. Thus, the ACLJ's resources have developed over time, even as the type of cases it takes has changed due to legal environmental factors and supporters' changing concerns. On a related point, the general lull in litigation allowed the ACLJ to pursue its interests in founding international affiliates. In 1998, the ACLJ established a European Center for Law and Justice and assigned a senior staff member to oversee its operations.[48]

On the other hand, Thornton noted that the change in the ACLJ's litigation agenda was as much a product of its own success before the Supreme Court as it was the courts' unwillingness to accept cases defining the issue area further. Even an incremental approach to litigation eventually culminates in an endgame scenario. "The strategy has always been to . . . chip away at a law as much as you can," he says.

> It's step by step, precept upon precept, until you get the interpretation you want. But, we are not doing much of that anymore [in the area of free expression]. We've defined what it means to have a Christian club in schools. Does it mean we can come on campus, participate in announcements, hold fundraisers like every other club? We've worked all that through.

As a result, the ACLJ finds itself litigating for enforcement of established principles at lower jurisdictional levels and cultivating cases in various issue areas with unique fact patterns in the hope that some will find their way up for review by the high court. "A Supreme Court case is the tip of the iceberg . . . the glorious tip of the iceberg," Thornton stated. "But there is much more to do besides just that."

> Influencing policy in the long term means filing in a number of cases that clarify issues raised in previous ones. Arguing before district courts, courts of appeal . . . we have cases all over the country. Any one of them could go to the Supreme Court if the time was right.

Thornton noted that the organization's success has required it to identify new issue areas while remaining true to its overall goals.

> Back when we started, same-sex marriage wasn't an issue. Had it been there, if it had been a crucial issue, we would have addressed it. I think all of the cases we take on are in keeping with that initial mission. And this issue is the same as the others. It's about the right to believe and act on that belief.

Even in light of new issue concerns such as disputes over gay rights ordinances, clients still bring the ACLJ claims falling under policies it helped to craft through litigation. These disputes, although rarely involving litigation, qualify as educating the public about religious freedoms. For example, senior ACLJ staffers identify and handle disputes generally resolved with a letter or call. But some of these disputes can involve a high-profile stage for expressive freedoms. Thornton conveyed an example of the ACLJ's activity during the 1996 Atlanta Olympics. Sekulow and Thornton met with city and Olympics committee officials to ensure that evangelists received access to public places, including streets around Centennial Park. Their presentation at that meeting referenced the Supreme Court's decisions in *U.S. v. Kokinda* and other cases the ACLJ litigated concerning public access. As a result, the city, its private organizing committee, and the United States Olympics Committee agreed not to interfere with the activities of evangelists during the games. Thornton noted how easily breaches in that policy were resolved as a result of his contacts with Olympics organizers.

There [are] 8,000 missionaries arriving in Atlanta for two weeks. There are going to be so many you can't ignore them. As a result of that meeting, I have the
contacts. We had Jews for Jesus missionaries there. I was playing tennis with
my father. My phone rings. "I'm on public property. I have security guards here
that work for Congress Center, they are hassling me." I call the lawyer of that
organization, and said, "Hey we talked about this. We don't want to sue." I call
the missionary back, and he says, "There is no one hassling me anymore."

The Equal Access and Free Expression Arguments

Although the ACLJ refocused its goals on national policy issues following
the World Trade Center disaster, it remains influential within the litigating wing
of the New Christian Right. Sekulow is largely responsible for shaping the central logic of its legal arguments and providing some of its greatest victories in
court. Although the venue for policy influence has shifted (de-emphasizing
cases at the trial level and conflicts solved by a demand letter), Sekulow remains
the champion of equal access for religion in public life. As Brown notes, the
"forging of a new jurisprudential relationship between the free speech clause
and religion is a legal contribution that has left a distinct impression on contemporary church-state litigation."[49] Sekulow continues to make that impression,
litigating cases such as *Locke v. Davey*[50] that clarify particular aspects of the
equal access doctrine.

Conventional wisdom suggests that New Christian Right litigators have a
negative impact on fundamental freedoms in the United States. After all, the
Conservative Right has been fighting a culture war based on majority values for
years. One would expect their representatives in court to do the same. The position of the movement's critics does much to bolster this view. Arthur J. Kropp of
People for the American Way has stated that "[the New Christian Right's]
agenda is having a corrosive impact on public education, on civil liberties and
on the fundamental principles of tolerance and pluralism." "Ultimately," says
another critic, "their agenda [in court] is about limiting freedoms, not expanding
them."[51] Some scholars have suggested that at the heart of social conservative
litigation is a desire to return to majoritarian values and practices of the past.[52]

Clearly, New Christian Right litigators maintain much more complex motives than the above statements suggest. The struggle between majoritarian and
minoritarian values within the New Christian Right is a significant theme within
this work. In particular, I argue that New Christian Right litigators represent a
minoritarian offshoot within the movement. In large part, Sekulow's preference
for a "place at the table" approach to litigation has prompted a rethinking of traditional conservative Christian themes among movement litigators. His influence has led others to endorse attitudes more tolerant of diverse ideas and
speech. All these changes can be considered under the rubric of equal access.

At the heart of the equal access argument is the view that religious convictions are appropriate for social discourse. Society should welcome religion be-

cause it offers a valid moral, cultural, and social perspective. On this view, the voice of the church is one among many in a plural society. It is a voice to be welcomed in public life and civic discourse, and protected if democratic society is to flourish. By linking religion with free speech, New Christian Right litigators have shifted the movement's logic in court away from casting Christian's claims as part of majoritarian politics (a strategy that allowed their opponents to define the terms of debate). Instead, they provide courts with arguments presenting Christians as a protected minority rather than a majority asserting its will in the form of policy. Thus, in the courts New Christian Right attorneys aggressively assert Christians free expressive rights in a variety of contexts, having reframed the debate and moved it away from separation of church and state.

Equal access, then, means that contributions to discourse based on a religious worldview cannot be excluded from public life simply because of their religious content. Conservative Christian litigators argue that free exercise of religion often involves an expression of faith and that the Constitution protects religious expression as free speech. As Sekulow has noted, "I'm not concerned about competing worldviews. The danger is in keeping any of them out of the forum."[53] The arguments presented by the movement in court have integrated strains of liberalism and legal sophistication. Even traditional opponents have endorsed the position taken by New Christian Right attorneys on equal access and free expression. For example, Kent Willis, director of the Virginia chapter of the ACLU, has publicly endorsed the free expression argument made by Sekulow in *Mergens* and other cases.[54]

As noted in chapter 1, recent cases have brought into question whether New Christian Right litigators will continue to consistently employ equal access and free expression arguments. Sekulow argued many of these recent cases himself. In *Hill v. Colorado*[55] and *Locke v. Davey*,[56] Sekulow stuck to his guns, making the equal access and free expression case. In *Hill*, Sekulow argued against the use of legislatively mandated speech-free zones (called "bubble zones") during public protests at abortion clinics. In both his brief and during oral argument Sekulow contended that courts were best suited to institute and monitor government regulation during protests, and that the rights of protesters to be heard outweighed government's power to regulate speech. On most of the controversial policy provisions, Sekulow won his point. In *Locke v. Davey* Sekulow argued unsuccessfully that denial of tuition money for a graduate degree in theology under a state-funded inclusive scholarship program singled out religion for unfavorable treatment in violation of free exercise. The Court held that such support was permitted under the religious establishment clause, but not required by the free exercise clause. The decision, while certainly a defeat, does not undermine previous decisions of the Court more favorable to religious expression in the public square. In *Good News Bible Club* the ACLJ participated as *amicus* in support of the equal access argument adopted by other New Christian Right attorneys who handled the case. In keeping with the ACLJ's example in previous cases, they argued successfully that schools must provide access to religious clubs supervised by community religious leaders and that granting such access did not excessively entangle government with religion.

In contrast to these cases stands *Santa Fe v. Doe*,[57] the football prayer case. It should be noted in all fairness that Sekulow agreed to take the case only after the Supreme Court accepted it for review.[58] However, the case left the impression that movement attorneys had gone beyond the logic of equal access to endorse government sponsorship of religion. It is also important to note the support the ACLJ gave other attorneys in cases like *Board of Regents v. Southworth*[59] in which conservative Christian attorneys argued that Christians should have the right to opt out of supporting minority groups whose ideas or values they find offensive. In supporting this position, the ACLJ created the perception that it was seeking to undermine the very groups it had hoped to find at the table when the church took its seat.

These and other cases present a cloudy picture for the future of the equal access argument. The 1990s were a period of relative success in the courts for Jay Sekulow and the New Christian Right. More recent decisions have shown that the Supreme Court can and will reject their claims. It is also clear that Sekulow is unlikely to undermine his long-term strategy before the courts or to limit his influence on policy because of strict adherence to religious principle. However, he faces several barriers to influence in the courts, not the least of which is the increasing conflict surrounding gay rights.

Beginning with the Supreme Court's decision in *Boy Scouts of America v. Dale*,[60] gay rights has assumed an increasingly important position on the New Christian Right litigation agenda. Recognizing the long-term importance of the issue (both legally and to its constituency), the ACLJ began litigating gay rights cases as part of its appellate agenda.[61] Following the Court's decision in *Lawrence v. Texas* (a case in which the ACLJ participated as *amicus curiae*), the gay rights issue achieved extraordinary national attention as well. In that case, the Supreme Court struck down a Texas statute criminalizing certain homosexual conduct as "deviant sexual intercourse." The Court overturned its earlier decision in *Bowers v. Hardwick*,[62] finding that the statute attempted to control a personal relationship and thus violated substantive guarantees of personal liberty and privacy contained in the due process clause of the Fourteenth Amendment. The Court also ruled that criminalizing the conduct of one class (homosexuals) and not another (heterosexuals) violated the equal protection of the laws.

The decision in *Lawrence* was the impetus for a series of clashes at the state and local level over gay rights and gay marriage. In November 2003, the Massachusetts Supreme Judicial Court ruled in *Goodridge v. Department of Public Health* that the state violated the Massachusetts constitution when it denied "the protections, benefits, and obligations conferred by civil marriage to two individuals of the same sex who wish to marry."[63] Then in February 2004, the Massachusetts court ruled that proposed state legislation formalizing the legal status of gay couples by creating civil unions violated its earlier decision. At about the same time, city officials around the country began to force the issue of gay marriage.

Both the *Lawrence* and *Goodridge* cases prompted a flurry of activity around the country to which New Christian Right law firms responded. The ACLJ's response was to take a different approach than other firms. Sekulow, who helped draft the federal Defense of Marriage Act (DOMA), has focused on cases in which that law is challenged. The ACLJ also represents states that have passed defense of marriage acts. Currently, it is defending such acts for the state of Nebraska and is involved in cases in New Jersey, Connecticut, and Florida. However, the issue itself presents a logical conundrum for those who have made the equal access argument in the past. Remaining consistent with the previous stance on minority rights and the church would require at least toleration of efforts to recognize some aspects of gay rights under law. But, that is unlikely given the nature of the conflict—a conflict sometimes as intense as that over abortion rights. If recent history gives any indication, the New Christian Right will likely reevaluate its most recent strategies and adopt practices more consistent with court norms and with rights doctrines. However, portraying those who support heterosexual marriage as a minority to be protected presents a logical problem that Sekulow and his compatriots must overcome if they are to remain successful in court.

The ACLJ's Litigation Participation

In this section I examine trends within the ACLJ's litigation agenda. I begin with a general examination of litigation participation over time, jurisdiction, preferred litigation method, and issue area. Next, I examine ACLJ litigation in federal court—the ACLJ's dominant arena for participation. Finally, I examine a particular feature of ACLJ litigation—its use of case sponsorship and the test case strategy, or sponsoring the same case across jurisdictions until its final adjudication, sometime before a court of last resort.

Participation by Year, Jurisdiction, and Strategy Type

Table 2.1 displays the frequency of ACLJ litigation, defined as instances of participation in cases in which a court issued an opinion. Here (and throughout) I examine instances of participation, not simply cases themselves. A group may generate several instances of participation in each case depending on whether it continues to appeal that case to a court of last resort (such as a state supreme court, or the U.S. Supreme Court). In table 2.1 results are displayed by year and jurisdiction. Row totals for this table reveal the raw amount of litigation conducted by the ACLJ in each year (i.e., the amount of litigation per year without regard to jurisdiction or issue area). The data indicate that, after climbing steadily from 1987 through 1993, participation rates stabilize for a time beginning in 1995. This leveling off lends credence to Sekulow's assertion that the organizational growth of the ACLJ slowed for a period of years before picking up again moving into the 2000 election year. In 2000 (the year in which Sekulow began to reshape the internal structure of the ACLJ), the organization litigated more than at any other time. However, beginning in 2001, litigation participation fell back to levels in the mid-1990s.[64]

Table 2.2 displays the litigation conducted by the ACLJ according to year and type of participation. Scholars use various methods to categorize litigation participation types. O'Connor explores the participation of women's litigating groups using a typology of participation that includes direct sponsorship of litigation, participation as *amicus curiae*, and intermediate behaviors.[65]

Sponsorship is defined as an action that usually involves serving as attorney of record and bearing the cost of litigation. *Amicus curiae* intervention is a court-sanctioned form of participation in which a group submits a brief supporting one party or the other, and urges the court to adopt its rationale for arriving at a decision favoring that party. Finally, intermediate behaviors involve participation as Counsel on Brief. Here, a group assists in the preparation of submissions to the court and may even bear part of the cost of litigation, but does not sponsor litigation or participate in oral argument.

I examine category totals for type of participation, trends in type of participation over time, and other characteristics of ACLJ litigation involvement. As table 2.2 reveals, in 124 of the 193 instances of litigation involvement (nearly two-thirds of its litigation activity), the ACLJ served as case sponsor. Furthermore, the data demonstrate a trend over time toward higher levels of participation as case sponsor, a revelation of the organization's deep involvement in influencing court-crafted policy. Instances of case sponsorship trend upward from 1990 (the official date of the ACLJ's formation) to a period of intense litigation beginning in 1997. Moreover, a quick look ahead to table 2.5 reveals that the large bulk of the 124 instances of participation as case sponsor occur in cases filed in federal court—twelve instances of case sponsorship in Supreme Court cases, fifty-one in courts of appeal, and fifty-two in district court. These data reveal that the actions taken by the ACLJ reflect its overall mission—to effect a profound impact on the shape of policy at the national level.

Table 2.2 also shows that the ACLJ made use of two other types of litigation participation. The organization participated as *amicus curiae* in fifty-six instances, and this rate of participation is linked to its overall interest in case sponsorship. Since 1996, *amicus* participation has dropped considerably, even as case sponsorship reached its highest levels. Much like case sponsorship, the vast majority of the ACLJ's *amicus* participation occurred in the context of federal cases. It is noteworthy that over 55 percent of the ACLJ's *amicus* submissions were in Supreme Court cases (see table 2.5). ACLJ emphases on *amicus curiae* participation at jurisdictional levels are the opposite those for case sponsorship. Two complementary explanations present themselves. First, it is significantly easier to prepare and file an *amicus* brief in a Supreme Court case than it is to sponsor a case. Financial costs for shepherding a case through the courts are high, and the chances are low that a particular case will be granted *certiorari* review. Thus, even a group such as the ACLJ, one that focuses on deeply influencing policy at the national level through case sponsorship, will find it efficacious to file a significant number of *amicus* briefs. Second, arguments presented to higher courts, even those arguments contained in *amicus* briefs, have a much higher chance of influencing policy outcomes. Therefore, a group such as the ACLJ has every reason to submit an *amicus* brief in important cases in which it does not act as sponsor. Finally, the ACLJ appeared as Counsel on Brief in thirteen cases over its lifetime. There does not appear to be any particular trend for this intermediate participation. Sekulow has stated that the ACLJ will assist sister organizations where it is able to do so, but providing this assistance is not his foremost concern. Thus, intermediate behaviors do not figure prominently in the ACLJ's overall litigation strategy.

Trends in Participation Rates Across Issue Areas

Tables 2.3, 2.4, and 2.5 explore the ACLJ's litigation agenda by issue emphases. Construction of categories involved an inductive determination of case attributes—categories were created to reflect what the groups included in this study do as much as any other defined decision rule. Thus, church/state cases were divided between those involving displays of religious faith in public places and those involving religion in schools, reflecting the emphases within the litigating arm of the movement. As with many cases involving constitutional law, categories are not entirely discrete. Decisions to place cases in one category or another required a careful analysis of both the issue at stake in the case and the predominant understanding of those issues within the movement. For example, there is considerable overlap among those cases involving use of public school facilities for after-hours worship or religious instruction by churches. Such cases were coded as Church/State: Public Places because they did not involve a conflict over religious expression and curricular or extracurricular activities so typical in the Church/State: Schools issue area. Furthermore, groups participated in a large number of cases defending abortion protesters or challenging laws limiting protestation rights. I have created a separate category for these cases since the substance of the governmental action at issue differs significantly from those cases involving the right to obtain an abortion. Various other categories were created out of references to the importance of particular kinds of cases to organizations.

In this discussion of tables 2.3, 2.4, and 2.5, I examine category (column) totals to uncover trends in issue-area involvement across time, type of participation (case sponsorship, etc.), and jurisdiction. Table 2.5 displays ACLJ litigation by issue area over time. Column totals provide a picture of what issue areas have been most emphasized by the ACLJ. The ACLJ is most heavily invested in three issue areas: Church/State: Schools, Church/State: Public Places, and Abortion: Protestation. As a testament to their importance, the ACLJ litigates in the Church/State: Schools or Public Places issue areas more than one-half of the time. When interviewed, Sekulow noted their importance to the organization, and the ACLJ web site and documents refer to defending the church as the primary purpose of the organization. On the other hand, Sekulow also noted the importance of flexibility and responsiveness to the needs of the ACLJ's constituency. Examination of litigation in the categories of Abortion: Protest and Abortion: Rights over time shows that it took up a considerable percentage of the ACLJ's resources in the mid-1990s. The category Abortion: Protestation has the second highest column total of all categories and was the most significant area of ACLJ issue participation in various years. For example, in 1994 and 1995, the ACLJ was involved in eighteen abortion protestation cases, as compared to twelve cases in the two church/state categories combined. From 1994 through 1998, the most aggressive period of ACLJ litigation, abortion protestation accounted for twenty-six instances of litigation involvement. The combined categories of church/state litigation account for an equal amount during this period. However, the table clearly reveals that it is diminishing in importance. Rates of participation in Abortion: Protestation drop off significantly beginning in 1998.

Other categories represent newer or less central areas of concern to the ACLJ. Family Policy is of notable size. Composing less than 10 percent of the ACLJ's litigation involvement, this area is an amalgam of legal issues said to influence the family, including regulation of television and entertainment, and parents' rights. In 1998, Sekulow and Thornton noted the importance of the issue as an emerging area of concern. However, the organization clearly has poured its resources into other concerns. The data reveal that Sexual Orientation is relatively minor, but an emerging area of interest at present. Certain cases that do not fall clearly into one issue area or another make up the Other category. One example of such cases includes three bankruptcy cases the ACLJ litigated in the mid-1990s. At that time, Sekulow noted the aggressiveness of the IRS in revoking churches' and conservative organizations' tax-exempt status, as well as intervening in bankruptcy proceedings where individuals have contributed money to religious enterprises. The ACLJ launched into these areas as the need arose.

The discussion above provides a more detailed examination of the frequency of ACLJ's litigation participation. However, raw amounts of litigation involvement do not provide a complete sense of the significance of each category of participation to the overall goals of the organization. Tables 2.4 and 2.5 attempt to explore instances of litigation participation providing a richer sense of how the ACLJ expends its energy and to what ends. Table 2.4 examines only instances of participation in federal litigation. As noted above, the ACLJ's participation in federal court litigation makes up the vast majority of litigation participation (more than 86 percent). Each level of federal jurisdiction is examined in terms of type of participation and issue area. Table 2.6 explores participation by type and issue area for the years 1994 through 1998, a period of intense growth as well as participation for the organization.

Table 2.4 provides an examination of types of participation by issue area. The table reveals that an important synergy exists within the ACLJ overall agenda between strategy preferences, and issue area emphases. The ACLJ uses case sponsorship as its overall dominant strategy, and it prefers to use that strategy almost exclusively within its three preferred issue areas. For example, at no time has the ACLJ sponsored an Abortion: Rights case, preferring to employ the *amicus* strategy in this issue area. The same trend is apparent in all other issue areas except Sexual Orientation. Here, the ACLJ is primarily interested in case sponsorship. Perhaps, because of the saliency of the issue for its constituents, the ACLJ becomes much more deeply involved.

Finally, table 2.5 groups the 179 instances of ACLJ involvement in federal court litigation by jurisdiction. Comparisons of row totals (participation type) across jurisdictions demonstrate that case sponsorship remains the preferred method of participation for the ACLJ, except in instances of Supreme Court participation where *amicus* participation is more pronounced. Given the difficulty in obtaining review by the Supreme Court, not to mention the stellar record of the ACLJ in doing just that, it is not surprising that *amicus* participation at this level would be higher. Differences in issue-area emphases within the ACLJ's Supreme Court and overall agendas become apparent upon comparison. While the least emphasized in its overall litigation agenda, ACLJ participation as sponsor and *amicus* in Church/State: Public Places is pronounced. These differences may be explained as reflecting the exigencies of appealing cases to the Supreme Court and denial of *certiorari* review. However, church/state and abortion categories remain most important, involving all instances of case sponsorship and intermediate participation.

Participation at trial and appellate levels may provide a more precise picture of the type of ACLJ participation in litigating specific issues. Trends in litigation revealed during analysis of table 2.4 continue here. The church/state categories and the Abortion: Protestation category remain important in the overall litigation efforts of the group. Furthermore, they overwhelmingly represent the categories in which the ACLJ has participated as case sponsor. There appears no trend in participation as Counsel on Brief, and *amicus* participation at the trial and appellate levels is attenuated. Overall, these data tend to confirm trends in issue area participation, while confirming the ACLJ's interest in effecting policy on a national level.

Deep Influence on Policy

It has already been noted that the ACLJ's litigation participation is directed primarily at federal courts. Moreover, the analysis illuminates trends in ACLJ litigation participation and issue-area emphases across jurisdictions. In exploring these trends, the analysis touched on the scope of ACLJ litigation participation, noting that the ACLJ is deeply committed to influencing policy in three primary issue areas. Table 2.6 explores the depth of ACLJ participation in federal and state courts. While the ACLJ's emphasis on case sponsorship indicates that it might emphasize depth of involvement, an examination of continuing participation across jurisdictional levels will reveal how deeply committed the ACLJ is to effecting court-crafted policy. Continuing litigation refers to what is commonly called the test case strategy.[66] Groups employing this strategy will sponsor a case across jurisdictions to its final resolution before a court of last resort. Recognizing that groups sometimes make a long-term commitment to a case, but after the trial phase of litigation, I note various kinds of continuing litigation within table 2.6.

The depth of the ACLJ's litigation participation is noteworthy. Of those 193 instances in which the ACLJ participated in federal court litigation, sixty-eight were part of a strategy of continuing participation across jurisdiction levels in twenty-five cases. Of those twenty-five, the ACLJ participated in seven that moved from trial court to the U.S. Supreme Court and one that moved from state trial court to state supreme court. In two more cases that made their way up to the Supreme Court, the ACLJ began its participation after appeal from the trial court. Fourteen of the twenty-five cases ended in a U.S. court of appeals after the ACLJ participated at the trial and appellate levels. Four of these were denied *certiorari* review by the Supreme Court after the ACLJ requested (and in one instance defended against) a grant of review. These data reflect the ACLJ's depth of commitment to litigation as a means for policy change, yet they represent only a small segment of what the ACLJ does. However, it is exceedingly difficult to bring cases up through the judicial system to the Supreme Court, to find cases with appropriate facts and clients who are willing to sustain the litigation through to the high court. In spite of these difficulties, the ACLJ demonstrates a strong commitment, not simply to litigation, but to sustained and continuing litigation that has the potential for lasting impact on policy formulation.

Conclusion: Organizational Life and Change

This chapter has been devoted to analyzing the American Center for Law and Justice. I have developed an understanding of characteristics of organizational life within the ACLJ that will provide the basis for a closer comparison of litigating firms in later analyses. To that end, I have explored the internal organizational culture, goals, structure and resources, litigation emphases, and behavior of the ACLJ from its founding. The study of the ACLJ's internal culture reveals a firm commitment to achieving longstanding objectives for national policy influence through protracted appellate litigation. Jay Sekulow has developed a highly responsive organization that has continuously developed to meet new challenges from its environment. Having crafted the central logic of legal arguments made by many conservative Christian litigators, Sekulow suddenly reconstructed the ACLJ around a broader vision of policy influence on a national level. Furthermore, Sekulow pioneered an approach to organization building that combines his broad interests in media and reputation oriented goals as a means toward achieving that ultimate aim.

I have also explored the influence of the ACLJ on New Christian Right litigation. Of the three firms included in this analysis, the ACLJ is perhaps most influential and most distinct from the movement of which it is a part. It has pioneered a philosophy of litigation that is oftentimes at odds with the dominant worldview of the New Christian Right. Its leader is a powerful force within the movement, and yet he takes positions that are often at odds with those who offer the ACLJ financial backing and support. Furthermore, he has extended his influence into government, assuming policy-making functions and advising roles that broaden the influence of the ACLJ far beyond that of most New Christian Right lobbying firms. At the same time, both Sekulow and the ACLJ face a complex legal and political environment in which new challenges emerge regularly. The future of the ACLJ's dominant philosophy based on Sekulow's "place at the table" approach to religion in public life remains uncertain, especially as other conservative Christian firms begin assuming a prominent role. In particular, as other firms litigate the gay rights issues, it is not entirely certain that they will remain consistent in applying this approach. Thus, in following chapters, I use the ACLJ as the basis for comparison among other firms and explore ways in which they differ from the standard-bearing New Christian Right law firm in commitment to religious principle, approach to litigation, and strategic emphases.

Table 2.1. ACLJ Litigation by Year and Jurisdiction

Year	USSC	SSC	USCA	USDC	SCA	SCO	Other	Total
1987	1	0	0	0	0	0	0	1
1988	0	0	0	1	0	0	0	1
1989	0	0	2	0	0	0	0	2
1990	4	0	0	0	0	0	0	4
1991	0	0	2	3	0	0	0	5
1992	5	0	3	0	0	0	0	8
1993	2	0	5	1	0	0	0	8
1994	3	0	5	3	1	0	0	12
1995	2	0	6	5	2	0	0	15
1996	5	1	3	4	2	0	1	16
1997	3	3	4	4	1	0	0	15
1998	1	1	4	9	0	0	0	15
1999	2	1	7	8	1	0	0	19
2000	7	0	6	8	0	0	0	21
2001	2	0	12	2	0	0	0	16
2002	2	0	6	6	0	0	0	14
2003	5	0	4	6	0	0	0	15
2004	3	0	3	0	0	0	0	6
Total	47	6	72	60	7	0	1	193

Source: Lexis/Nexis Legal Database

Note(s): *USSC* =United States Supreme Court; *SSC* =State Supreme Court;
USCA =United States Court of Appeal; *USDC* =United States District Court
SCA =State Court of Appeal; *SCO* = State Court of Origin

Table 2.2. ACLJ Litigation by Year and Type

Year	Sponsorship	On Brief	Amicus	Total
1987	1	0	0	1
1988	1	0	0	1
1989	2	0	0	2
1990	2	0	2	4
1991	3	1	1	5
1992	2	4	2	8
1993	6	0	2	8
1994	8	1	3	12
1995	9	1	5	15
1996	7	0	9	16
1997	10	2	3	15
1998	9	2	4	15
1999	16	0	3	19
2000	15	0	6	21
2001	11	1	4	16
2002	9	1	4	14
2003	10	0	5	15
2004	3	0	3	6
Total	124	13	56	193

Source: Lexis/Nexis Legal Database

Table 2.3. ACLJ Participation by Year and Issue Area

Year	Church/State Schools	Church/State Public Places	Abortion Protestation	Abortion Rights	Sexual Orientation	Family Policy	Other	Total
1987	0	1	0	0	0	0	0	1
1988	1	0	0	0	0	0	0	1
1989	1	1	0	0	0	0	0	2
1990	1	1	0	1	0	1	0	4
1991	0	3	2	0	0	0	0	5
1992	2	3	1	1	0	0	1	8
1993	2	3	3	0	0	0	0	8
1994	1	0	10	1	0	0	0	12
1995	3	2	8	0	0	3	0	16
1996	2	3	2	1	1	5	2	16
1997	1	4	5	1	0	3	1	15
1998	2	8	1	0	0	0	4	15
1999	5	8	3	0	1	1	0	18
2000	7	9	1	2	1	0	1	21
2001	2	5	5	0	4	0	0	16
2002	4	5	1	0	1	0	3	14
2003	6	3	3	0	1	2	0	15
2004	2	1	1	0	0	0	2	6
Total	42	60	46	7	9	15	14	193

Source: Lexis/Nexis Legal Database

Table 2.4. ACLJ Participation, 1987–2004, by Type and Issue Area

Type	Church/State Schools	Church/State Public Places	Abortion Protestation	Abortion Rights	Sexual Orientation	Family Policy	Other	Total
Sponsorship	26	46	38	0	6	2	5	123
Counsel on Brief	2	3	5	0	0	1	1	12
Amicus curiae	14	11	3	7	3	11	8	57
Other	0	0	0	0	0	1	0	1
Total	42	60	46	7	9	15	14	193

Source: Lexis/Nexis Legal Database

Table 2.5. ACLJ Federal Court Participation by Type and Issue Area

Type	Church/State Schools	Church/State Public Places	Abortion Protest	Abortion Rights	Sexual Orientation	Family Policy	Other	Total
Supreme Court Participation								
Sponsorship	5	3	4	0	0	0	0	12
Counsel on Brief	1	2	1	0	0	0	0	4
Amicus curiae	8	2	1	3	3	7	7	31
Total	14	7	6	3	3	7	7	47
U.S. Court of Appeals Participation								
Sponsorship	12	18	17	0	3	0	1	51
Counsel on Brief	0	1	2	0	0	1	1	5
Amicus curiae	5	7	2	2	0	0	0	16
Total	17	26	21	2	3	1	2	72

Continued on next page

Note(s): Sponsorship is determined by the name of the ACLJ or attorney employed by the ACLJ listed as Attorney of Record within the published court opinion. Similarly, Counsel on Brief is determined by the name of the ACLJ or attorney employed by the ACLJ listed as On Brief within the published court opinion, and *amicus curiae* by the same listed as *amicus*, or preparer of an amicus brief (e.g., for another organization) within the published court opinion.

Table 2.5—Continued

Type	Church/State Schools	Church/State Public Places	Abortion Protest	Abortion Rights	Sexual Orientation	Family Policy	Other	Total
U.S. District Court Participation								
Sponsorship	9	25	11	0	3	2	2	52
Counsel on Brief	1	0	2	0	0	1	1	5
Amicus curiae	0	1	0	1	0	1	0	3
Other	0	0	0	0	0	0	0	0
Total	10	26	13	1	3	4	3	60

Source: Lexis/Nexis Legal Database

Table 2.6. ACLJ Litigation across Jurisdictions by Type, Issue Area, and Appearances

Participation	Jurisdiction	Issue Area	Appearances in Court
Case Sponsorship:			
	Trial to CLR[a]		
	1) *Locke v. Davey (2004)*	Church/State: Schools	3
	2) *Scheidler v. NOW (2003)*	Abortion: Protestation	4
	3) *Campbell v. St. Tammany Parish Sch. Bd. (2001)*	Church/State: Schools	6
	4) *Hill v. Colorado (2000)*	Abortion: Protestation	4
	5) *Chandler v. Siegelman (2000)*	Church/State: Schools	4
	6) *Kaplan v. Prolife Action League of Greensboro (1997)*	Abortion: Protestation	2
	7) *Lamb's Chapel v. Center Moriches School District (1993)*	Church/State: Public Places	3
	8) *Westside Community Schools v. Mergens (1990)*	Church/State: Schools	3
	Intermediate Appellate to CLR		
	9) *Schenck v. Pro-Choice Network (2003)*	Abortion: Protestation	4
	10) *U.S. v. Kokinda (1990)*	Church/State: Public Places	2

Continued on next page

[a]CLR = Court of Last Resort

Table 2.6—Continued

Participation	Jurisdiction	Issue Area	Appearances in Court
Case Sponsorship—Continued:			
	Trial to Intermediate Appellate (petition for higher review[b] denied)		
	11) Full Gospel Tabernacle v. Community Sch. Dist. 27 (1999)	Church/State: Public Places	3
	12) Edwards v. City of Santa Barbara (1998)	Abortion: Protestation	2
	13) Hoffman v. Hunt (1997)	Abortion: Protestation	2
	14) United States v. Terry (1994)	Abortion: Protestation	3
	Trial to Intermediate Appellate (no petition for higher review)		
	15) ACLU Neb. Found. V. City of Plattsmouth (2004)	Church/State: Public Places	2
	16) ACLU v. Capitol Square Review & Advisory Board (2004)	Church/State: Public Places	2
	17) United States v. Alaw (2003)	Abortion: Protestation	2
	18) S.D. Myers, Inc. v. City and County of San Francisco (2001)	Sexual Orientation	2
	19) Altman v. Minnesota Dept. of Corrections (2001)	Sexual Orientation	2
	20) Mahoney v. Lewis (2001)	Church/State: Public Places	2
	21) Branch Ministries, Inc. v. Rossotti (2000)	Church/State: Public Places	2
	22) Henderson v. Stanton (1998)	Church/State: Public Places	2
	23) In re Hodge (1998)	Bankruptcy	2
	24) Women's Health Servs., P.A. v. Operation Rescue (1994)	Abortion: Protestation	2

Continued on next page
[b]Petition for higher review: Includes requests for rehearing *en banc* and petition for *certiorari*.

Table 2.6—Continued

Participation	Jurisdiction	Issue Area	Appearances in Court
On Brief Participation:			
	Trial to CLR		
	25) *NOW v. Schiedler (1994)*	Abortion: Protestation	3
Amicus curiae Participation: *(No cases fall into this category)*			
		Total Particpation:	68

Source: Lexis/Nexis Legal Database

Chapter Three

Educating for Equal Access

Mathew Staver and the Liberty Counsel

Mathew Staver is perhaps the most educated among those who lead New Christian Right law firms. He holds a master's degree in theology, obtained a law degree from the University of Kentucky Law School (where he was captain of the National Moot Court Team), and is fluent in four ancient languages. He is published in the areas of workers' compensation and First Amendment litigation, including a series entitled "Faith and Freedom: A Complete Guide to Defending your Religious Rights," a book entitled *Equal Access: Guidelines for Student Groups on Public School Campuses*, and a law journal article entitled "Injunctive Relief and the *Madsen* Test."[1] He is uniquely qualified to write on the subject of *Madsen*, as he argued that case before the Supreme Court of the United States.

While his business interests extend into areas of law not related to civil rights litigation[2] and into areas not at all related to law,[3] he has also founded one of the leading conservative Christian litigating organizations in the nation—the Liberty Counsel. The Liberty Counsel, describing itself as a "non-profit litigation, education and policy organization,"[4] has litigated cases throughout the United States, and especially in the Southeast. The firm handles First Amendment cases almost exclusively and is especially drawn to disputes involving abortion protestation, church/state issues in public schools, and gay rights. The Liberty Counsel has enjoyed considerable success in litigating issues on the Religious Right's agenda, especially before appellate courts. Initially, Staver managed to do all this almost completely on his own without any support from a parent organization or the benefit of partners among whom to divide tasks.[3] He has built the Liberty Counsel from the conservative Christian litigating arm of the Southeast to a firm with a national presence and a movement player in establishing long-term goals and strategies. He has also taken on a very public role as a representative of the movement. Staver is the subject of frequent interviews and has discussed his positions on abortion protestation and religious expression on national television programs, including *Nightline, The News Hour with Jim Lehrer,* and *Politically Incorrect with Bill Maher.*

Staver is among those attorneys that pioneered the most significant legal contribution of the new breed Christian litigators—the free expression defense in religious establishment cases. But, reflecting his intellectual background and cautious approach, his contribution had its genesis in a candid evaluation of religious tolerance. Staver came to the realization very early on that the issue of religious expression was becoming clouded by the way the central questions in such cases were framed. Traditional religious establishment jurisprudence structured the issue as state sponsorship of religion, or as a negative right rather than a positive grant of personal freedom. Through his early litigation experiences, Staver came to the personal realization that government endorsement of religious beliefs was not really at issue, but that a lack of tolerance of free speech rights existed on all sides of the debate, including (and perhaps especially) within the New Christian Right.

He has embraced a set of goals founded on a willingness to play the policy game as courts have defined it. His approach emphasizes respecting precedent and providing courts with the legal rationale that will serve their efforts to develop policy incrementally. However, Staver's Liberty Counsel differs from other conservative Christian firms in important respects, including goals, mission, and issue-area emphases. In particular, the Liberty Counsel's central goal is to educate both its membership and public officials about the role of religion in public life. At one time the Liberty Counsel was much slower to resort to litigation than other groups. Today it pulls the trigger on litigation much sooner in the process (especially citing resistance among administrators to equal access), but it still identifies a slightly different vision for the role litigation plays in public policy making. Unlike other firms, it identifies an educational component to its litigation efforts.

Furthermore, Staver takes perhaps the most consistently liberal view of expressive freedoms among all New Christian Right attorneys, applying these views in a variety of unlikely contexts. He has opposed a flag-burning amendment to the U.S. Constitution. While litigating several cases involving student-initiated prayer in Florida schools, he publicly opposed the 1995 Florida State School Prayer Bill, provoking harsh criticism from the American Family Association.[5] He has argued for free expression within public schools, including student advocacy of atheism, secular humanism, and gay marriage, as well as Christianity. His views on expressive freedoms have at times made him the unlikely ally of the ACLU. Additionally, he has expanded his notion of the appropriateness of such expression into little-noted contexts, including the workplace.[6] He also praised the Clinton administration for its presidential directive clarifying federal policy on public religious expression, calling it "a very positive step forward."[7] Staver has had a pronounced effect on the logic of his movement and on court-crafted policy. This chapter is dedicated to exploring the sources of this influence and the internal culture of his organization, the Liberty Counsel.

Out of the Ministry and into the Law: Founding the Liberty Counsel

After receiving his bachelor's and master's degrees in theology, Staver began his career as pastor of a Seventh-Day Adventist church in Lexington, Kentucky.[8]

He states that the law was of no concern to him at that time, nor had he envisioned a career as a litigator, to say nothing of the appellate specialist he has become. The events that brought about such drastic changes occurred while attending a local ministerial meeting where he was shown a film on abortion.[9] "[A]t the time," notes Staver, " I really had no conviction one way or another on abortion."

> If you asked me I probably would have been more in favor of it than against it. [The ministerial association] showed this video. I was pretty shocked by it. They obviously mentioned *Roe v. Wade* in the video. So I began going to an organization called Central Kentucky Right To Life to get information from them. They gave me the *Roe v. Wade* opinion, and I began to read it. So I began gaining interest in some of the legal aspects of the issue.[10]

Staver noted two other factors, which contributed to his decision to leave the ministry and attend law school.

> [During that time] our church was becoming more involved in the community, more activist oriented. And I began to realize that there were [differences in law] that either allowed you or prohibited you from engaging in religious expression. Also, for the previous two to three years, every time the Christmas season would roll around, I would read another headline about government being sued. It seemed to be very big back then, suing the government over nativity scenes. And I would look at that and become frustrated about the whole situation. I felt the need to go into law school, so I applied. I was pretty naïve actually. I didn't even take the LSAT prep course. I took the test, applied to law school and I only applied to the University of Kentucky, which is close by.

Staver's ideas about the very issues that prompted him to attend law school have changed radically. "Going to law school has not changed my view of religious freedom, but I have radically changed my idea of free speech."[11] On various occasions, he has compared his early views on expression to his current notions, stating that "[w]hen I was a pastor in Kentucky, I favored censoring *The Last Temptation of Christ* because I thought it was blasphemous. Christians and the liberals fall into the same hole—free speech is great as long as it is something we agree with."[12] In fact, Staver's ideas about free expression did not completely evolve during law school. One of his first cases after founding the Liberty Counsel was a lawsuit filed to block Seminole Community College from showing that very film to its students, a suit he regrets filing. "Now, I would not advocate that they ban it. Clearly, that is one of those areas where my First Amendment free speech understanding has evolved."[13]

In 1987, during his third year in law school, Patrick Monaghan, at that time general counsel for the Christian litigating group Free Speech Advocates,[14] approached Staver about a job. Monaghan needed an able assistant to help defend abortion picketers from prosecution in California. Staver, already interested in constitutional law, got his first taste of religious liberty litigation and brief writing outside of moot court sessions in law school. He was hooked, and began planning a way to, as he says, "combine aspects of both my careers." Graduating from law school, he moved to Orlando, Florida, began working for a private firm specializing in workers' compensation, and represented abortion protesters on the side. Two years later, and after tangling with ACLU National in a suit against the City of St. Cloud, Minnesota, over a religious symbol attached to a public water tower, Staver resigned. He started his own workers' compensation practice and founded the Liberty Counsel six months later.

Staver stepped into workers' compensation private practice with no clients, but with a desire to assist the Religious Right in Florida and the Southeast. Six months after starting his private practice, Staver founded Liberty Counsel and began plans to do pro-life litigation almost exclusively. But, because of the demands of Staver's supporters and his own broad interest in religious liberties, the Liberty Counsel has developed into a First Amendment public interest law firm, taking a variety of cases involving public expressions of religious conviction.

Until very recently, the Liberty Counsel was distinctive among Christian public interest law firms in that it had no parent organization or foundation that supported it financially. Former Liberty Counsel staff attorney Nicole Arfaras-Kerr states that "the firm [Staver's private practice] is the closest thing to that."[15] Staver has used his private practice to make up the funding deficiencies that the Liberty Counsel has had since its inception. For example, in 1994 the Liberty Counsel took in just over $200,000 in donations. Staver's private practice made up the over $1 million dollars per year extra required to conduct the litigation on the Liberty Counsel's agenda. Through 1999, all employees working on Liberty Counsel–related litigation were paid fully by Staver and Associates (Staver's private practice), and all of their time was designated for work in the Liberty Counsel. Furthermore, many of the assets of the Liberty Counsel were donated by the private practice—the two entities shared office space, computer systems, and personnel. Neither Staver, nor any of his staff attorneys or Liberty Counsel Board members, received any compensation directly through the Liberty Counsel. All acted either in a volunteer capacity or were designated employees of the private practice. Such a complicated financial arrangement had its benefits. The Liberty Counsel was not beholden to any outside party or foundation, and its initial goals formed apart from the influence of a parent organization. Staver maintained complete control over the organization's focus and direction and had complete discretion over the Liberty Counsel's litigation agenda. Staver had a degree of freedom that only a few leaders within the Religious Right enjoy.

On the other hand, this kind of arrangement had negative consequences for both firms. The demands of running a full-time private practice and conducting complex First Amendment litigation took their toll on Staver. He shut down the private practice in 1999, sold all its assets in 2000, and entered a partnership arrangement with Rev. Jerry Falwell that provides the Liberty Counsel with backing and the credibility of Falwell's name within the movement. Staver has become very involved with Falwell's organizations, especially Liberty University. He sits on the university's Board of Trustees, is the university's vice-president for law and policy, and oversees the law school steering committee. In return, the Liberty Counsel uses the law school as a pipeline for personnel and resources. This new arrangement corresponded with a redefinition of the Liberty Counsel's goals,[16] new leadership on its board, and the opportunity for Staver to devote all of his time to his cause.

A One-Man Army for Equal Access

Staver's experiences in law school and as a young lawyer added to the concern for religious liberties that he experienced as a pastor. As a result of this personal revelation, and in collaboration with his fellow Christian litigators, Staver helped develop a philosophy for litigating religious establishment cases based on a heightened tolerance of speech. As discussed above, this new philosophy is characterized by various attributes that encourage and support use of the courts to achieve policy aims—a willingness to chip away at unfavorable precedent, to change policy slowly, and to forego pursuing every conflict into the court system. The approach appears to have particular currency with Staver. As Jay Sekulow has noted, "Mat has not been one of those who resisted it kicking and screaming. He saw the strategy, he understands and has implemented it."[17] Despite initial resistance from within the movement,[18] Staver has clung tenaciously to the overall litigation strategy he helped define, emphasizing the importance of picking the right cases and the benefits of an incremental strategy for effecting policy change.

> Sometimes the law has been pretty much set against you. We would prefer to negotiate a reasonable resolution without going to court, instead of going to court on a particular issue. Sometimes it is better to resolve something than to litigate it, or even to litigate a small area of an issue. Instead we try an incremental approach, because you can only eat the elephant one bite at a time. Sometimes people think because they can't swallow the elephant whole they don't want to have any of it.

Staver followed his newfound view of the First Amendment into conflicts over religious expression in a variety of contexts. He has been at the forefront of Christian litigation to test the tension between religious establishment and free expression rights. A large segment of the Liberty Counsel's litigation agenda is composed of cases involving religious expression in public schools, but Staver's most prominent cases have been in an area where Christian litigators have made related expressive freedom arguments—abortion protestation. He points to his performance before the U.S. Supreme Court in *Madsen v. Women's Health Clinic* as the defining case for the Liberty Counsel. Although *Madsen* was a setback, Staver's arguments for protecting the free speech interests of abortion protesters did not deviate from the core rationale that has become the hallmark of Christian litigation. On the other hand, Staver takes a very activist stance when the Supreme Court does not support his policy goals. After the Supreme Court rendered its decision in *Madsen*, Staver accused the Court publicly of turning zones around abortion clinics "into a type of Tiananmen Square."[19] "This is the McCarthyism of the nineties," he said, "where speech is censored before it can be spoken, where peaceful protests must first be permitted by those of the opposing viewpoint."[20]

Yet, Staver is certainly not in the same category as other Christian attorneys that see their litigation activity as frontline guerilla warfare against the forces of a godless society. He recognizes a general tension in society over religious expression and is frustrated by it. But, unlike his compatriots, Staver has not made the leap from the specific instances of intolerance he cites to a more comprehensive view of socially endemic religious oppression. Staver's attitude translates into an institutional emphasis within the Liberty Counsel on education as part of its mission. The Liberty Counsel defines this goal as providing information about current policies on religious expression to all sides in a dispute. Thus, for the Liberty Counsel the goal of education extends to its supporters and to the public officials who may be the root cause of actions taken adversely against Christians in public places. Below, I explore the primacy of education within the organizational culture of the Liberty Counsel and its importance as an extension of its liberalized view of social policy and Christians' free speech claims.

Goals and Religious Ideology

Like so many other New Christian Right litigating firms, the Liberty Counsel exists for the purposes of influencing policy and building up precedent favorable to faith-based expression in social, political, and cultural contexts. However, Staver and the Liberty Counsel began thinking about goals in much broader terms than this. When interviewed in 2004, Staver noted that the organization and its board of directors had refined the Liberty Counsel's mission as "restoring [American] culture by advancing expressive freedoms, the sanctity of human life and the traditional family." The statement reveals several important elements of the Liberty Counsel's internal culture. Although the mission does not identify education per se as the organization's central aim, Staver only discusses what he means by restoration of the broader culture in terms of educating his clients, supporters, and policy makers. This is a significant break with the traditional language used within the New Christian Right to characterize a society viewed as godless, adrift and immoral.

The mission statement also reveals the three broad policy areas in which the Liberty Counsel is most often active in advancing American culture toward its optimal position—expressive freedoms, sanctity of human life, and matters impacting the traditional American family. For example, the Liberty Counsel has litigated extensively for student and abortion protesters' expressive rights. Although these two case groupings differ significantly, Staver thinks of them in the related terms of restoring a culture of expressive freedom. Moreover, he lumps abortion rights, patient rights, aging, and other medical issues into the category sanctity of human life. He also notes overlapping considerations. His concerns for the traditional American family extend to student expression and the gay rights/same-sex marriage issue discussed more fully below. Staver goes on to identify three areas of activity that are primary for achieving the Liberty Counsel's mission, only one of which involves going to court. Of the mission statement he notes that "[it] is an exceptionally broad and long-term strategy."

> And we have identified three methods for achieving it—education, litigation and policy making . . . writing policy into law. While policy will actually become more important over the next several years, I think our education effort is continuing to be emphasized.

Goals for Litigating

Among Staver's preferred methods for achieving policy influence, education is listed first. The Liberty Counsel is an organization committed to educating the public and public officials about the rights of people of faith to express their beliefs in public contexts. "Our goal is to solve problems," says former staff attorney Nicole Arfaras-Kerr, "and education is the best tool for doing that."

> We have an education mandate to correct misconceptions about things like separation of church and state. We want to provide adequate information to people. Usually [the cause of the conflict] is just misinformation about what the law is. For example, I have a call in to the human resources director of a [Orlando, Florida] company that restricted people from reading their Bibles and discussing in the lunchroom. I said, "This is a form of discrimination. I would be happy to send you a statute or some court decisions outlining the state of policy in this area." That usually solves the problem. That is the most efficient approach. If this does not resolve things, then we will resort to litigation. Only then.

Staver even thinks of litigation in terms of its educational impact. "We look at litigation as an extension of our educational mission," he notes. "Education resolves 95 percent of the situations with which we are involved."

> Litigation has an educational aspect to it—the printed cases or the media presentation of a particular situation. That's an educational aspect [to litigation]. Basically our goal is to be able to provide education rather than purely litigation. This could be through printed materials or through having to litigate something. . . . That's why we called it Liberty Counsel, not Council. And the reason is that most of our cases evolve through education. We don't go into the

courtroom all the time, nor should we. In those 5 percent of cases that don't re-solve, either someone has a latent hostility to a religious viewpoint, or they have dug their heels in because they have set themselves in a particular direc-tion. Even then, we try to settle them out, and it's through education, not litiga-tion. We are not afraid to litigate, and we will litigate if we have to. But, we prefer to give somebody the opportunity to see if it's an information problem or something else.

Thus, the Liberty Counsel, while focused on litigating for policy change, also focuses on resolving tensions associated with those policies, providing informa-tional resources where those resources might mean the difference between toler-ance and suppression of public expressions of faith.

Goals are only as good as the cases that potentially achieve them. So, shift-ing popularity among issues could present some problems for an organization seeking to contribute to policy by encouraging religious tolerance. The Liberty Counsel is responsive to developments in issue saliency, but the goals of the organization and strategies for carrying those goals forward remain constant. Staver is conscious of issue developments. "A lot of what we do is an attempt to be responsive to what is in the culture," he says.

The abortion protest cases emerged out of conflicts in the culture. The gay rights issue is emerging as an issue because of the mandatory sensitivity issues these ordinances raise for Christians and other citizens. It seems like a lot of our agenda is what is going on in the culture. We are always going to have First Amendment cases and school issues. And I think we are just trying to be here to address those concerns.

The Liberty Counsel's Organizational Structure and Resources

The Liberty Counsel appears to do more with fewer resources than any of the other groups examined in this research. Of the three organizations in this study, it has the smallest budget and the fewest attorneys. Yet, the Liberty Counsel has managed to leave an indelible mark on court-crafted policy on a national level and in its regional sphere of influence. The fact that the Liberty Counsel achieved its current status as a leading Christian litigating organization before it began its serious efforts to develop and grow is important to note. In this section I explore the current state of the Liberty Counsel's internal organizational struc-ture in terms of efficiency, capabilities, and maturation over time.

Organizational Structure

The Liberty Counsel is distinguished from other leading Christian litigating firms by its relative lack of organizational complexity. For years, the firm conducted business from the office that it shared with Staver's private practice in Orlando. The Liberty Counsel relies heavily on its general counsel to litigate cases on its agenda. Its few staff attorneys process between twelve and fifteen thousand requests for information and intervention in First Amendment–related disputes per year while also handling often complex litigation around the country. Furthermore, many of the Liberty Counsel's other projects are conducted from its Orlando office, including Staver's radio program and publication of the Liberty Counsel's monthly newsletter, *The Liberator*. While the Liberty Counsel has opened two regional offices and an educational center at Liberty University, the organization still remains small and intimate. Staver has controlled organizational growth for years, carefully selecting a few talented attorneys from an ever-expanding pool. The Liberty Counsel has employed various associate counsel over the course of its life, but the number of those junior attorneys never exceeded three until 2001. Currently, the Liberty Counsel employs six attorneys (including Staver and his wife), with plans to add a seventh.

The Liberty Counsel utilizes both staff attorneys and local volunteer counsel in an arrangement that has become more typical of New Christian Right litigating firms. Often, media reports and scholarly studies claim that conservative Christian firms have a vast army of volunteers all around the nation that they use aggressively. This arrangement is becoming very rare because of the difficulties managing volunteers and maintaining consistency in approach and arguments. Most New Christian Right firms have had to deal with local attorneys who, while having little experience litigating public law cases, insist on maintaining control over the case. Staver's experience working with the Alliance Defense Fund and its pro bono training program convinced him that volunteer local counsel could be used only in a very limited fashion. The Liberty Counsel does maintain a network of volunteer attorneys and will refer disputes to them where the probability of litigation is low. However, Staver and his staff attorneys keep tight control over the actions of volunteer attorneys and the arguments they make in court. No Liberty Counsel volunteer has ever litigated a referred case alone. "Working with them [local counsel] has been problematic," says Staver of the volunteer attorney network.

> In the Liberty Counsel training program offered as part of the continuing education curriculum at Liberty University School of Law, we are not concerned so much about volume, but about the quality of the litigation. Other kinds of arrangements used by other firms have created pressure to take cases that might not be so good for their overall strategy and could produce bad precedent.

This arrangement is typical of all New Christian Right litigating firms with one grand exception. As Nicole Arfaras-Kerr notes, the Liberty Counsel's "litigation agenda is much more centralized than, say, the Rutherford Institute."

> We are lead counsel in all our cases and we litigate them from here [in Orlando]. We do have affiliates who help us, and serve as local counsel when we

have not been admitted to a particular district . . . but, they would never be considered lead attorneys in a case, unlike the Rutherford Institute that gives a case
to one of its volunteers.

Thus, the Liberty Counsel uses its corps of volunteer attorneys in much the same
manner as the other groups in this study. Volunteer attorneys serve as local
counsel, assist in preparation of briefs and depositions, handle filing documents,
assist in preparation for trial or oral argument, and provide a base of operations
within a court's jurisdiction. At no time has Staver allowed a volunteer to serve
as lead counsel in a matter, nor has he hired a volunteer attorney to a staff position within the Liberty Counsel.

Acquiring Resources

While acquiring resources is a vital concern for any litigating interest, it is of
particular importance to the Liberty Counsel, an organization with limited time
and energy to devote to litigation, let alone to acquire resources from private
sources. Like other Christian litigating groups, the Liberty Counsel attempts to
balance its fundraising activities with more crucial mission-oriented activities.
The Liberty Counsel is a donor-supported organization. Its private contributions
come from its membership and those who respond to direct-mail solicitations for
contributions. The average contribution from these private sources is approximately $17. However, direct-mail contributions are not the Liberty Counsel's
only, or even primary, source of financial support. The Liberty Counsel enjoys
an arrangement with Rev. Jerry Falwell that provides it with significant monetary resources. Staver has also pursued a mixture of sources including foundation grants and contributions, donations from churches, and court-ordered compensation of fees incurred through litigation. Foundation grants were largely
channeled through the Alliance Defense Fund. While the relationship between
the Liberty Counsel and the Alliance Defense Fund is treated elsewhere, it is
important to note that in 1998 Staver believed the Alliance Defense Fund was a
vital tool for acquiring resources and focusing them for the benefit of a movement-wide strategy in the courts. Today, Staver has severed all ties with the Alliance Defense Fund, and the reasons for doing so were not simply financial.
Staver came to believe that it had strayed from its original mission and became
too concerned with acquiring money, rather than using it to advance the movement's goals in the courts.

When interviewed in 1998 (before the Liberty Counsel and Liberty University entered into their arrangement), Staver noted the effect of resource limitations on the work of the Liberty Counsel. Compared to the other groups, the
Liberty Counsel has had to make many more choices about which cases it could
afford to take, given its limited resource base. "It has been frustrating in certain
situations where there aren't the resources," said Staver candidly.

We have never turned away anybody that we feel has a legitimate case. We try to help them, and we have never actually neglected to take a case that we feel should be taken. But, there are situations where there is just more to do than you will have time and resources to do. And that's just a hard reality. We have found ourselves with situations that are emergencies. You have to figure out which one of, say, these three emergency situations are we going to take.

We've never had to really turn away somebody but we haven't been able to do everything we wanted to do.

Furthermore, when faced with a potentially significant case that would overwhelm the staff and other resources of the firm, the Liberty Counsel will pass because "We just don't have a huge battalion of attorneys to do that kind of research."

That situation, characterized by such frustration, has completely changed. The financial support of Jerry Falwell Ministries has reduced the stress of dealing with limited funding and of investing time and energy into fundraising. "We are able to bring a lot to the table for Dr. Falwell," Staver says, "and he has been able to bring a lot to the table for Liberty Counsel." Yet, the Liberty Counsel's budget remains relatively small,[21] reflecting Staver's desire to keep the organization lean and aggressive.

Strategizing for Equal Access: Liberty Counsel's Litigation Agenda

In this section I turn to a discussion of the Liberty Counsel's litigation agenda, that is, the specific actions taken by the Liberty Counsel to pursue its policy goals in the courts through litigation. I begin with a broad overview of the Liberty Counsel's litigation agenda and its overall approach to litigation as a means for achieving policy aims. Next, I consider the various areas in which the Liberty Counsel has been actively litigating issues, highlighting specific and important cases in which the Liberty Counsel participated. Finally, I turn to an indepth analysis of the Liberty Counsel's litigation participation, examining in particular its long-term commitment in committing organizational time, energy, and resources to protracted litigation.

Internal and External Limitations

The Liberty Counsel's web site describes its organizational mission as "restoring the culture one case at a time by advancing religious freedom, the sanctity of human life and the traditional family."[22] In pursuit of these goals, it has become involved in a wide array of cases and disputes, ranging from abortion protestation to religious discrimination in the workplace. While Staver began the

Liberty Counsel with the intention of providing legal support to pro-life elements in Florida, he has branched out into many other areas, counting many of
the important religious issues of the day among the Liberty Counsel's primary
concerns. The Liberty Counsel is most clearly involved in religious liberties
cases (public places and public schools) as well as cases involving abortion
protestation and rights. A new and expanding area of concern to the Liberty
Counsel's supporters is the gay rights issue. The Liberty Counsel is currently at
the forefront of New Christian Right litigators in addressing gay rights issues in
court. It has partnered with the American Family Association to coordinate their
response in court to gay rights policy nationally, and it maintains the largest
active docket of litigation in the gay rights issue area. Below, I outline the Liberty Counsel's litigation agenda. I provide a general summary of its litigation-
related activities and emphases and an overview of its approach to litigation.
Further, I explore specific cases that provide examples of the Liberty Counsel's
influence on policy through litigation.

The Liberty Counsel's general approach to litigation is to avoid entering the
courts where possible. The primary reasons for it to avoid litigating disputes are
twofold—the Liberty Counsel exercises care in selecting cases it will bring up
through the courts, and it prefers to use education as a tool to identify and target
institutions particularly resistant to respecting religious liberty. As noted above,
the Liberty Counsel does not actively pursue litigation in cases it knows it can
settle through mediation and education. However, while the Liberty Counsel
cites education as one of its primary goals, Staver also employs it as a means for
identifying those parties that require a more combative approach. Stanley noted
that in recent months the Liberty Counsel has encountered more resistance to its
effort to mediate disputes, particularly from public schools. Counsel for public
schools have been active in exploiting the information the Liberty Counsel provides by using that information in legal pleadings to counter Liberty Counsel
arguments. Such subterfuge has convinced the Liberty Counsel to pursue its goal
of education in initial attempts at dispute resolution but to move toward litigation more quickly where parties demonstrate little desire for a negotiated settlement. Still, Staver views education and mediation as the preferred and initial
method for dealing with conflict.

This approach works in favor of the Liberty Counsel given its resource
base. Despite its stable financial situation, the Liberty Counsel is a goal-driven
organization with a limited capacity to pursue those goals. While its agenda
spans a number of issue areas, its relatively small resource base and its desire to
foster legal precedent favorable to religious liberties have encouraged Staver to
exercise care when selecting cases to litigate. "No matter how big you get you
have to limit some of the cases you take," he says.

> Because you can't simply take everything, nor do you want to take everything,
> especially things that just simply shouldn't be in court. There are the cases that
> you may want to take, but because of resources . . . you are unable to take them.
> The Rutherford Institute has a motto that they take anything. Well, . . . we don't

take anything and we don't intend to. If you take everything you're going to make bad precedent. You've got to select the cases that are going to make the good precedent.

While the Liberty Counsel settles the vast majority of the disputes brought to it by its supporters before they reach the courts, Staver scans these potential cases for those that are best suited to achieving the Liberty Counsel's goals for effecting policy change. "By and large what we do is look for a situation that has good facts," he notes, describing what he looks for when selecting a case from a pool of disputes.

> One that would either reaffirm existing law, would clarify [law], or push the envelope on law to expand some area of liberty. And we look at the fact pattern. It's hard to explain what that would involve but we look for something that would develop good clean facts where the issues can be presented. For example, there are certain things you would like the Supreme Court to clarify.

The Liberty Counsel has neither the time nor the resources to devote to cases with anything less than clear legal arguments and case facts unclouded by extraneous factors. The value of this approach became clear during the Supreme Court's 2001 term when it decided *Santa Fe I.S.D. v. Doe. Santa Fe* was a case with poor case facts, and a case that no conservative Christian litigating firm was willing to argue at trial or on appeal. Jay Sekulow, who ultimately agreed to argue the case before the Supreme Court, much preferred that the Court hear another case first—*Adler v. Duvall County School District II* (discussed in detail below), which Staver was litigating in Florida. In this instance the lack of control over which case reached the Court first short-circuited Staver's carefully planned agenda while pointing to the benefits of such an approach.

Second among the Liberty Counsel's distinguishing characteristics is a propensity to act as an intervener to defend governmental polices that affirm a religious liberties position. For example, the Liberty Counsel has repeatedly offered its service to local governments threatened with litigation for implementing such policies. In 1997, the Liberty Counsel agreed to advise the Ozaukee (Florida) County Board on the legality of its official Good Friday holiday and represented it free of charge in a suit brought by the Freedom from Religion Foundation. That same year, Staver joined Florida Attorney General Robert Butterworth in defending the Women's Right to Know Act, the Florida abortion consent law. The Liberty Counsel filed a motion for intervention on behalf of two women, a Christian pregnancy care center, and a fictitious Jane Doe representing the women of the State of Florida. In 1999, the Liberty Counsel represented the city of Marshfield, Wisconsin, in a suit brought by the Freedom from Religion Foundation.[23] The city maintained a public park in which stood a statue of Christ. The statue had been donated to the city forty years previous to the filing. After the Liberty Counsel intervened in support, the city deeded the public property to a private group that has agreed to maintain the statue for a period of time.

At trial, the Liberty Counsel obtained a summary judgment in favor of the city, and the association appealed to the Court of Appeals for the Seventh Federal Circuit where the Liberty Counsel prevailed again.[24] Thus, the Liberty Counsel has participated in some significant litigation in which it attempted to assert itself on behalf of government.

Early in its history, the Liberty Counsel litigated primarily in the Southeast. However, Staver has built a national docket of cases and acquired enough resources to pick up any case he deems important anywhere in the country. Thus, the Liberty Counsel has litigated cases in various jurisdictions, including state appellate courts. Currently, some of the most significant cases on its docket originated in state courts. For example, in 2004, the Liberty Counsel participated in *State of Kansas v. Limon*, a case in which the Kansas court of appeals upheld a state law criminalizing certain forms of homosexual conduct. The Liberty Counsel's *amicus curiae* brief figured heavily in the outcome,[25] and the majority opinion was strongly critical of the Supreme Court's recent decision in *Lawrence v. Texas*. Several important cases have originated in state courts, including some involving abortion protestation,[26] religious expression in public places,[27] and student expression in public schools.[28] Furthermore, the Liberty Counsel has acted as counsel of record in federal district court cases originating in Wisconsin,[29] Iowa,[30] Kentucky,[31] and North Carolina.[32] It is currently litigating gay rights cases on both coasts, including the cases against Mayor Jason West of New Paltz, New York, and Gavin Newsome of San Francisco.[33]

Equal Access in Public Schools

During the early 1990s, the Liberty Counsel became deeply occupied with litigation involving free expression of religious views in public schools. As stated above, Staver did not found the Liberty Counsel with the intent to act on behalf of students attempting to represent their religious views in the context of public schools. However, students holding religious views (and Christian students in particular) have called on him time and again to defend them from actions by school administrators deemed to adversely effect free expression. Equal access cases involving public school students continue to be very common, finding their way onto the Liberty Counsel's agenda with regularity despite the emergence of other issues. In its most promising case in this policy area to date, the Liberty Counsel intervened, taking over representation on behalf of public school students and in support of a school board policy.

Recently, the Liberty Counsel has litigated several important cases with the potential for Supreme Court review. The most prominent of these is *Adler v. Duvall County School District*, a case that has experienced a multitude of procedural twists and turns. The case, begun in 1994 and concluded in 2001 following the Court's decision in *Santa Fe I.S.D. v. Doe*, involved a dispute over the graduation message policy of the Duval County School Board. The board initiated a policy allowing graduating seniors to vote to have a two–minute pre– or post–graduation message, and to select a member from their own graduating class to deliver that message. The school board agreed not to censor that message, regardless of its sacred or secular content. The ACLU, representing a student who objected to the potential religious content of the class message, sued the school board on grounds that the policy violated the First Amendment prohibition of state sponsorship of religion. The first *Adler* case was dismissed for mootness when the plaintiff school-age child graduated. It was reinitiated later when the ACLU substituted a sibling as plaintiff.

In both *Adler* cases, the ACLU argued that the graduating senior delivering the message was acting as an agent of the state, that the school board should only censor the religious content of such a message, and that religious leaders should be excluded from delivering graduation messages. When queried by the trial judge, the ACLU applied its rationale to exclude religious leaders such as Billy Graham and Jerry Falwell because, based on their occupations, they were likely to say something religious. On the other hand, the ACLU would permit the school board to invite Jane Fonda (the example supplied by the judge) because "it is likely Jane Fonda would not say something religious."[34]

The Liberty Counsel intervened on behalf of the students of Duval County supporting the school board's policy (since the students were party to the suit, the Liberty Counsel took over the case with the consent of the school district). Staver argued in both *Adler* cases and prevailed at every stage until May 1999 when the case began to ping-pong between the Eleventh Circuit and the Supreme Court.[35] Many in the New Christian Right would have preferred that the Supreme Court hear this case instead of the one it ultimately reviewed (*Santa Fe I.S.D. v. Doe*). After the Court's decision in *Santa Fe*, the Eleventh Circuit reviewed *Adler* again, deciding that the policy was constitutionally permissible because students acted as individuals and not agents of the state under the policy. However, the impact of the decision is limited to the Eleventh Circuit, and a case that could have had national import ended when the movement lost momentary control of its strategy.

Regardless, the Eleventh Circuit's decision in *Adler* has important policy implications. Using a rationale that supported Staver's position, the court considered the establishment clause implications of the policy as well as the religious expression element, noting that "[a]t the core of Establishment Clause jurisprudence is the notion that the state may not favor, endorse, or oppose the propagation of religious doctrine by its citizens."[36] Using this classic rationale, the Eleventh Circuit concluded that a school policy that is neutral as to the content of speech cannot be challenged on the grounds that some of the speech might contain religious content.

In 1998, Staver noted that *Adler* was the logical next step in testing the bounds of student religious expression in public schools after the Court's decisions in *Lee v. Weisman* and *Westside Community Schools v. Mergens*. In *Weisman* the Court struck down a policy allowing school officials to offer prayer at school-sponsored activities, determining that support for such a practice amounted to state sponsorship of religion. However, the Court in *Mergens* refused to categorize student-led religious organizations as part of state religious sponsorship. The question presented in *Adler* raised a unique factual question representing a concern the Supreme Court had not addressed in the collision between *Weisman* and *Mergens*. As Staver notes above, he would like to see the Court clarify the legality of student-initiated religious messages, and *Adler* appeared to present the purest factual situation among those cases in the courts. Staver had been particularly aggressive in shepherding *Adler* through the courts. Furthermore, the school board's policy was unencumbered by the extraneous legal concerns present in the *Santa Fe* case—there was a minimum of involvement by school officials in the process of selecting and presenting the message. School officials did not review or censor the message before it was presented, and there were no content restrictions of any kind placed on the student selected to present. The policy represented a pure form of neutrality on the part of a school board toward the presentation of a potentially religious message. The neutrality of the policy was exactly the element that Staver valued most in *Adler* as a test case. Yet, his hopes for a policy of national application emerging from the courts were dashed.

Another example of Liberty Counsel litigation in the policy area of religion and public schooling is a highly publicized case involving a student-led Christian club. This case has brought the Liberty Counsel into conflict with school districts in Florida and around the country. Early in 1999, Staver began a campaign aimed at school districts that refused to knuckle under after repeated attempts to mediate disputes over equal access for Christian clubs. In January 1999, the Florida ACLU publicly supported the Liberty Counsel in a suit against the Manatee School District under the Equal Access Act of 1984. The school district refused to allows Christian students to meet on school grounds and utilize other school resources available to other student-led clubs. Staver filed the lawsuit and called a press conference in Tallahassee. In a statement widely reported in the press, he blasted the school district and put others on notice that the Liberty Counsel was planning much more aggressive litigation. "This is the first in a series of lawsuits that we'll be doing around the state of Florida and the country," said Staver.

> If you have one student club on campus, you must treat all student groups equally. Schools do not have the right to restrict clubs because of their message or content. They are not trying to disrupt the school. They are just trying to meet.[37]

Staver followed up with a press release entitled "Florida High School, School Board and Principal Sued for Discrimination against Christian Student Club; Liberty Counsel States, 'All Schools Are On Notice.'" In it, Staver is quoted as saying, "We have run out of patience with schools refusing to comply with the law on this issue."

For years, when we were contacted about Equal Access issues we would contact school personnel, give them the benefit of the doubt, and offer to resolve the situation short of litigation. Those days are gone . . . we will no longer hesitate to file suit when violations arise. This suit marks the beginning of a national campaign by Liberty Counsel to ensure public schools abide by the Equal Access Act.

The school district settled with the Liberty Counsel in April 1999 and revised its policy on equal access.

The Liberty Counsel continues to pursue a policy of litigating against public schools that are slow to respond to equal access demands. For example, during the spring of 2004, the Liberty Counsel initiated something it calls "'Friend or Foe' Graduation Campaign" in which it promises to educate administrators, but holds out the threat of litigation. Staver's public proclamation of the campaign includes the following explanation.

> Earlier this year, Liberty Counsel announced a "Friend or Foe" Graduation Campaign, meaning that Liberty Counsel will either be a friend by providing free legal representation to schools that take a neutral position toward students' graduation messages, or will be a foe of schools that censor the religious viewpoint or content of student speakers. [38]

Many complaints brought to the Liberty Counsel are settled out of court, but others make their way onto the Liberty Counsel's litigation agenda. These include some egregious violations of the federal Equal Access Act of 1984. The *Hall v. Seminole County School Board*[39] and the *Hinderly* case decided in Ohio federal district court[40] are early examples of the Liberty Counsel's current campaign. The Liberty Counsel is targeting the worst offenders. Yet, these cases are what Staver refers to as mopping-up operations. The policy in the area of equal access for student-led religious clubs is fairly settled. The Liberty Counsel is litigating to achieve compliance with the law by school districts and is not aiming to innovate new policy concerns. However, these cases remain a significant part of the Liberty Counsel's mission.

Equal Access in Public Places

As the case involving Manatee High School was winding down, Staver's erstwhile comrades, the Florida ACLU, filed suit in federal court against the same school district in an attempt to evict churches that rented school buildings for Sunday worship services. The Liberty Counsel intervened on behalf of the approximately ten churches that rent facilities from Manatee County School District, representing them in court free of charge. While the case highlights the impermanence of coalitions between New Christian Right and liberal litigating firms, it also reflects the Liberty Counsel's longstanding commitment to promote equal access in public places. Staver's first case, as a third-year law student, involved a dispute over display of a religious symbol in public, and the Liberty Counsel continues to take cases involving expression in public places.

The Liberty Counsel has represented Jews for Jesus in disputes over literature distribution in a variety of cases. Notably, the Liberty Counsel has litigated disputes over distribution at Florida airports, including Tampa International Airport in 1995. (*Jews for Jesus v. Hillsborough County Aviation Authority*, 1995) The Aviation Authority had banned any and all distribution of pamphlets by groups seeking to proselytize. This dispute garnered some publicity for the Liberty Counsel during its infancy, and Staver was quoted as saying, "This one here is pretty elementary. Tampa simply can't do what they're doing."[41] As in similar suits against the Fort Lauderdale and Orlando airports, the Liberty Counsel prevailed and obtained compensation for legal costs. Just before the 1998 Superbowl, the Liberty Counsel filed suit on behalf of Jews for Jesus when the National Football League attempted first to prevent religious groups from handing out leaflets and then relegated them to a space far from most major entrances to the San Diego stadium. The Liberty Counsel's efforts resulted in both the city of San Diego and the NFL agreeing to set up free-speech zones that allowed more effective access to ticket holders.

Perhaps the most celebrated equal access in public places case brought by the Liberty Counsel is *Christ's Bride Ministries v. Southern Pennsylvania Transit Authority*.[42] The case blurs the lines distinguishing abortion policy and equal access in public places. Here, a Christian pro-life organization purchased advertising from the transit system. Its ads, placed on the sides of city buses, noted a recent medical study establishing a link between abortion procedures and breast cancer. After fielding a large number of complaints from the public and pro-choice groups, the city removed the signs from its buses. The Liberty Counsel filed suit in federal district court alleging that the city violated the right to free expression by censoring the content of the advertisement. The district court ruled in favor of the transit authority, and the Liberty Counsel appealed. In 1998, the Third Circuit Court of Appeals ruled in favor of Christ's Bride Ministries, stating that the transit authority had allowed pro-abortion speech to be displayed in ads placed on its buses. Thus, the actions of the transit authority constituted viewpoint discrimination.[43] While Staver says that litigation for equal access to public places has peaked, and even declined as a percentage of the Liberty Counsel's overall litigation agenda, clients continue to bring disputes to the Liberty Counsel. These are largely settled outside of court, a reflection of the uneasy truce that appears to have settled over the policy area in recent years.

Abortion Rights and Protestation

While Staver initially envisioned the Liberty Counsel as a pro-life legal advocacy group, litigation activity in other areas has eclipsed abortion policy in importance on its overall agenda. However, the Liberty Counsel continues to litigate abortion rights and protestation cases and remains involved in supporting governmental policies placing restrictions on abortion rights. Significantly, when asked to point out the single case that defined the Liberty Counsel, Staver noted his participation in *Madsen v. Women's Health Clinic* as a pivotal case for the Liberty Counsel.[44] He also noted its importance for the Supreme Court's later decisions on abortion protestation, particularly *Hill v. Colorado*, where the Court ruled against the use of floating bubble zones based on arguments Staver had made in *Madsen*.

The Liberty Counsel has a long history of interest and impact in the area of abortion. However, while the Liberty Counsel has defended abortion picketers since the late 1980s, it did not go to court in an effort to shape abortion policy until 1993. In that year, as a result of an injunction issued by a Florida Circuit Court judge, Staver launched challenges to such restraints in both state and federal court. In *Operation Rescue v. Women's Health Center*,[45] Staver asked the Florida Supreme Court to overturn the ruling of Florida Circuit Judge Robert McGregor. McGregor had issued an order restraining abortion protesters from coming with thirty-six feet of abortion clinics in the counties of Brevard and Seminole. Thus began the long involvement of the Liberty Counsel in the case that ultimately became *Madsen v. Women's Health Clinic* (1994). In federal court, Staver filed suit against McGregor, challenging the same injunction as a violation of the First Amendment's free speech clause.[46] Staver's tactic of filing in state and federal court paid off when the Eleventh Circuit Court of Appeals struck down the use of buffer zones as an unconstitutional abridgement of free expression, while the Florida Supreme Court sustained the injunction. As a result of the inconsistency across jurisdictions, the Supreme Court consolidated these cases and accepted Staver's petition for *certiorari* review from the Florida Supreme Court.

In oral argument, Staver adopted the position that limitations on the activities of pro-life protestors based on a perceived governmental interest[47] are inconsistent with the First Amendment's guarantee of freedom of speech. The Court dispensed with Staver's argument that the injunction censored anti-abortion speech and not criminal activity, deferring to the findings of the state court that activity around the clinics demanded many (but not all) of the limitations imposed. The Court's decision turned on the nature of an injunction and how narrowly the state judge tailored provisions of the injunction at issue to achieve governmental objectives, rather than free expression concerns.

Interestingly, Staver's client, Judy Madsen, had never appeared on an anti-abortion picket line at the clinics in question. However, as Staver noted, if she did happen to appear after this decision, her speech would be curtailed under the provisions of the injunction upheld by the Court. While Staver did win on several points (the consent provision for personal interaction, the image-observable provision, and the restrictions on picketing around workers homes were all struck down as overreaching legitimate governmental objectives), the overall result of *Madsen* was seen as damaging to the pro-life position.

In spite of the outcome in *Madsen*, the Liberty Counsel has been successful in defending pro-life organizations in the courts. Staver's efforts have been in defense of protesters arrested under court-ordered injunctions, as well as challenging municipalities that sought to limit protest through licensing and other bureaucratic means. Other cases have involved related issues. For example, in 1996 the Liberty Counsel represented a pro-life organization in a dispute with the Florida Health and Rehabilitation Services Department.[48] The department had issued a ruling prohibiting pro–life groups from engaging in adoption counseling. Staver garnered a victory in federal court and full reimbursement of his $105,000 legal fees from the state.[49] Thus, while the Liberty Counsel does not litigate as much in the area of abortion policy, it has handled significant cases and achieved major victories for the pro–life movement in the Southeast.

Gay Rights: No Longer an "Emerging Issue Area"

The Liberty Counsel is noted for its responsiveness to the issues its supporters identify as salient. Over the years it has added issues to its list of policy concerns when the interests of free expression demand. Staver has tracked cycles of cases brought to the firm, and he notes that the waves of cases brought to the Liberty Counsel have changed over time. Beginning in the early 1990s, disputes over abortion protestation made up the largest and most visible cases on its agenda. This changed in the mid-1990s to religion in public schools, then to religion in public places in the late 1990s, and finally to the present stage in the cycle—gay rights. Overarching all of these disputes is the defense of religious expression in public life. To understand the Liberty Counsel's position on gay rights, one must view it from the standpoint of religious expression.

In 1998, Staver forecast the emergence of gay rights as a dominant component of the Liberty Counsel's agenda. In fact, the Liberty Counsel has experienced an explosion of gay rights disputes and litigation. By the end of 2003, pending gay rights litigation made up approximately 13 percent of its litigation agenda, placing it in the top three most active issue areas. Staver notes that this belies the reality of time spent. He estimates that he spends between 40 and 50 percent of his time negotiating or litigating gay rights disputes. Furthermore, the Liberty Counsel is involved in key gay rights issue cases, including serving as counsel in a Georgia case challenging a state defense of marriage act.[50] The Liberty Counsel has also supported the state in a case challenging Florida's ban on homosexual adoption,[51] helped challenge a gays-only public school in New York City,[52] and attempted to intervene in support of Florida's Defense of Marriage Act.[53] Below, I outline the policy concerns of the Liberty Counsel regarding gay rights and explore a few instances of conflict in which the Liberty Counsel has become involved.

Gay rights policies that create conflicts with Christian groups, as well as rank-and-file sentiment, involve three related issues—partner health insurance ordinances, anti-discrimination ordinances, and mandatory on-the-job sensitivity training. Anti-discrimination ordinances, directed at businesses and public institutions contain a threat of criminal penalties for churches and private individuals that discriminate against gays based on personal moral concerns over homosexuality. One of the most significant early disputes in the area of gay rights on the Liberty Counsel's agenda involves an anti-discrimination ordinance put into effect in Dade County. Arfaras-Kerr commented on the significance of the dispute and the Liberty Counsel's involvement.

> We just became involved last week with challenging the Dade County discrimination ordinance. We have been approached about what kind of response we should make. The challenge may go to litigation, but we try to work through the system in other ways—referendums, etc. Those tactics usually work because average citizens are against such ordinances. There is a possibility of taking Dade County to court because the ordinance contains no provision protecting individuals. It exempts religious organizations, but it doesn't religious individuals. So, if you are a private citizen, and you don't want to rent your apartment to individuals, gay couples, couples living together, you do not have that option. You have no protection under those circumstances [in Dade County].

Thus, the primary concern among New Christian Right groups is not that such ordinances perpetuate a social harm through the legitimization of homosexual conduct (which, of course, is also their concern). They are mainly concerned that those who wish to discriminate for reasons of moral conviction may find themselves punished under the law. Arfaras-Kerr commented on that possibility under the Dade County ordinance.

> There is a lot of unhappiness and concern about its effect on individuals, because Dade County is such a tolerant and progressive place. There is a Gay Chamber of Commerce there. There is not much discrimination. There is a fear that the ordinance will be used as a weapon against the ideological opponents of some more radical gay activists.

Gay rights issues also crop up in religion in the workplace disputes through mandatory sensitivity training or diversity training seminars put into place by employers. The Equal Employment Opportunity Commission (EEOC), rather than federal or state courts, adjudicate these cases, and the Liberty Counsel has been involved in such disputes, most notably a claim of religious discrimination brought against Wal-Mart. In this case, Wal-Mart disciplined an employee who read his Bible throughout a mandatory sensitivity training class. The case was ultimately settled after the EEOC filed suit in federal court. Staver has also drawn attention to the religious discrimination in the workplace through comments made in the press that "religious discrimination is the forgotten discrimination . . . often overlooked in the workplace."[54]

While firms like the Liberty Counsel are able to cast these disputes in terms of free expression, or the right of the religious to object to homosexuality and its broad acceptance within society, gay rights disputes represent a particular philosophical challenge to the New Christian Right. On occasion, the Liberty

Counsel has litigated cases where it acts to protect the interests of the dominant majority's conception of morality, family, and tradition. When it makes these arguments, it begins to lose the credibility of its minoritarian position. No longer can it claim status as a minority to be protected when it sometimes works to limit the legal impact of another minority population. While not every case presents the Liberty Counsel or its sister firms with this difficulty, such cases are becoming more common. Thus, the gay rights issue threatens years of work within the New Christian Right developing a position in court on religious freedom that resonates with judges.

The Liberty Counsel's Litigation Participation

In this section I examine trends within the Liberty Counsel's litigation agenda. I begin with a general examination of litigation participation over time, jurisdiction, preferred litigation method, and issue area. Next, I examine Liberty Counsel litigation in federal court, which makes up the bulk of the instances in which it participates. Finally, I examine a particular feature of Liberty Counsel litigation—its use of case sponsorship and the test case strategy, or sponsoring the same case across jurisdictions until its final adjudication, sometimes before a court of last resort.

Participation by Year, Jurisdiction, and Strategy Type

Table 3.1 displays the frequency of the Liberty Counsel's litigation by year and jurisdiction. Here, I define frequency as instances of participation in cases in which a court issued an opinion. It is important to note that the Liberty Counsel has not litigated 106 cases since 1989. Rather, it has gone to court 106 times in eighty-one cases. Thus, a case that is appealed from the trial level to a court of last resort will generate a minimum of one instance of participation per court. Row totals for table 3.1 represent the raw amount of litigation conducted by the Liberty Counsel in each year, that is, the number of instances of litigation by the Liberty Counsel, without regard to jurisdiction, issue area, or type of participation.

Table 3.1 reveals several general characteristics of the Liberty Counsel's litigation agenda First, although the Liberty Counsel has existed since 1987,[55] Staver did not begin to implement his litigation agenda in earnest until the 1993 term. During that term the Liberty Counsel filed the lawsuits in both state and federal court that ultimately converged on the Supreme Court as *Madsen v. Women's Health Clinic* in 1994. Of the seventeen instances of participation during 1993 and 1994, seven of them were part of the challenge to the injunction issued by the Florida Circuit Court against Operation Rescue and Judy Madsen.

Second, in 1995 (the term following its participation in *Madsen v. Women's Health Clinic*), the Liberty Counsel's litigation activity increased significantly. This mirrors an increase in revenue experienced by the Liberty Counsel in 1994.[56] Thus, there was a quite normal lag from the time that the Liberty Counsel acquired significantly more resources to the time that it brought those resources to bear in the form of an expanded litigation agenda.

Additionally, the column totals for table 3.1 display instances of Liberty Counsel litigation by jurisdiction. Staver's interest in influencing policy on a national scale is borne out by the data. The 106 instances of Liberty Counsel litigation participation include 89 instances in federal courts. However, the Liberty Counsel has been unable to overcome the bottleneck presented by federal courts of appeal. In three instances, the Supreme Court rejected the Liberty Counsel's petition for *certiorari* review. In a fourth instance, the Liberty Counsel opposed a grant of *certiorari* review.[57] All of these *cert* denials occurred after the landmark *Madsen v. Women's Health Clinic* (1994). Clearly, Staver and the Liberty Counsel have made a commitment to provide federal courts with arguments supporting the policy positions of the Religious Right, and that commitment is supported by a desire to influence policy of national scope. However, the Liberty Counsel is plainly working toward achieving that goal, but has not realized it yet.

Table 3.2 displays litigation conducted by the Liberty Counsel according to year of participation and type. Here, I examine category totals for type of participation, trends in type of participation over time, and other characteristics of Liberty Counsel litigation involvement. As the column totals of table 3.2 show, the overwhelming preference of the Liberty Counsel in litigation participation is case sponsorship. The organization served as case sponsor in 75 percent of the 106 instances of Liberty Counsel litigation participation. Instances of participation as Counsel on Brief and *amicus curiae* account for just over 23 percent of all participation. An examination of instances of case sponsorship by year reveals that, beyond the expansion of the Liberty Counsel's litigation agenda in 1995, there is no clear trend of increasing use of case sponsorship. Rather, levels of sponsorship decline significantly after 1995. Turning briefly to table 3.5, an examination of row totals for instances of case sponsorship reveal that the large bulk of these occur in cases filed in federal court—one being a Supreme Court case, twenty-four cases in courts of appeal, and forty-seven in district courts. Clearly, the Liberty Counsel's mission is to effect court-crafted policy at the national level, but this mission has not been fully developed in the courts.

Trends in Participation Across Issue Areas

Tables 3.3 and 3.4 examine Liberty Counsel participation by separating instances of litigation participation into issue area categories. Table 3.3 reveals issue participation over time. Column totals provide a glimpse of where the Liberty Counsel invests its time, resources and energy. The Liberty Counsel, while initially established to support pro-life groups, has branched out to cover the majority of issues areas salient to the movement. Moreover, the church/state issue areas appear to have supplanted abortion as an organizational emphasis. Church/State:Schools and Church/State: Public Places represent the top two column totals, with 66 percent of all Liberty Counsel cases involved disputes in those issue areas. Abortion disputes made up only 25 percent of all Liberty Counsel litigation participation. This disparity becomes greater when one considers that of the twenty-two instances of participation in Abortion: Protest disputes, eight of these involved the cases that ultimately culminated in *Madsen v. Women's Health Clinic* (1994).

Table 3.4 demonstrates the importance of case sponsorship among the top issue-area emphases, but it also provides a more textured understanding of those emphases. While the Church/State:Schools issue area represents the second most active category for the Liberty Counsel, it also demonstrates that it uses *amicus curiae* participation most fully here, far and beyond its use in other issue areas. Perhaps this reflects the significance of the issue (Staver notes that a significant percentage of all disputes reported to the Liberty Counsel involve religion in the schools). Clearly, religion in public schools is of prime importance to the organization. Staver spent considerable time discussing the topic when interviewed, used specific disputes to illustrate typical Liberty Counsel work, and noted that it provides a large pool of disputes from which to draw. Yet, the importance of *amicus* activity here is pronounced, perhaps indicating that when the Liberty Counsel cannot participate (because it does not represent parties to the suit) it uses *amicus* participation to demonstrate to its supporters that it remains active and engaged in important cases.

Staver does not downplay the important impact of church/state–related disputes on the agenda of the Liberty Counsel. The organization is aware that its issue emphases shifted relatively early in its existence. Finally, church/state disputes, particularly regarding schools, remain a consistent fixture on the Liberty Counsel's agenda over time, while the majority of Liberty Counsel abortion litigation occurred between the years of 1993 and 1996. Thus, the Liberty Counsel is an organization that has consistently invested its time and resources in church/state disputes, allowing it to refine its free expression approach to church/state litigation. On the other hand, the abortion issue area served to establish the Liberty Counsel's early reputation as a leading New Christian Right firm, fading in importance as the Liberty Counsel's agenda expanded.

The discussion above attempts to provide a more precise examination of the raw amount of Liberty Counsel litigation over time, broken out by type of participation. Table 3.5 provides a more complete sense of the significance of each issue category in light of jurisdictional emphases and type of participation. This table examines instances of Liberty Counsel litigation in federal courts. Liberty Counsel federal court participation accounts for the vast majority of all Liberty Counsel litigation participation (as noted above), and the table allows comparison of the significance of issue areas and participation type across federal jurisdiction. Comparison of row totals (i.e., participation type) across jurisdictions demonstrates that (naturally) case sponsorship is the Liberty Counsel's preferred method of participation in federal courts. To put a finer point on this result, the Liberty Counsel participated as *amicus* in six instances outside of its Supreme Court participation and not at all as Counsel on Brief. Plainly, the Liberty Counsel does not countenance alternative modes of participation in lower courts, participating largely in an intermediate role to express its views to the Supreme Court. Thus, the Liberty Counsel uses an *amicus* strategy to compensate for lacking a long-term presence before the Supreme Court.

When comparing Liberty Counsel participation in federal district courts and federal courts of appeal, one finds that trends revealed in table 3.4 continue here with only minor differences. While the analysis of table 3.4 showed that the Liberty Counsel emphasized both church/state issue areas, and the public places sub-issue in particular, table 3.5 reveals a slightly different picture. In church/state disputes, the Liberty Counsel participates at the trial stage more often in cases involving disputes over religion in public places than in those involving public schools. However, at the appellate level, this emphasis is reversed. Almost one-half of all Liberty Counsel participation in courts of appeal litigation is in the area of Church/State: Schools. Moreover, in three of the nine instances of appellate participation as case sponsor in that issue area, the Liberty Counsel had participated at the trial-level, either appealing the federal district court decision or defending its victory at the trial level. It did so only once when litigating the Church/State: Public Places issue area. Furthermore, its participation as *amicus* at the intermediate appellate level occurs almost exclusively in Church/State: Schools disputes. Thus, despite more participation in Church/State: Public Places litigation at the trial level, the Liberty Counsel demonstrates commitment to influencing policy on religious expression in public schools at the appellate level.

Deep Influences on Policy

The above analysis reveals that the Liberty Counsel's litigation participation is directed primarily at federal courts. Moreover, the analysis illuminates trends in Liberty Counsel litigation participation and issue-area emphases across jurisdictions. In exploring these trends, the analysis touched on the scope of Liberty Counsel litigation participation, noting that the Liberty Counsel is deeply committed to influencing policy in the Church/State: Schools issue area through participation across federal jurisdictions. Table 3.6 explores the depth of Liberty Counsel participation in federal and state courts. While the Liberty Counsel's emphasis on case sponsorship indicates that it might emphasize depth of involvement, an examination of Liberty Counsel's continuing participation across jurisdictional levels will reveal how deeply committed the Liberty Counsel is to effecting court-crafted policy.

The Liberty Counsel's commitment to depth of litigation participation is noteworthy. Of the 106 instances of Liberty Counsel litigation participation examined, 42 (39 percent) were part of continuing participation across jurisdictional levels. I examine the 42 instances and the cases that generate them in table 3.6. They represent Liberty Counsel participation at different jurisdictional levels in sixteen separate cases. Of these sixteen cases, the Liberty Counsel participated in two that moved from a state or federal trial court to the Supreme Court.[58] Eleven cases ended in a U.S. Court of Appeal after the Liberty Counsel participated at the trial and appellate levels. In three of these eleven cases the Supreme Court denied *certiorari* review. The Liberty Counsel has made significantly less use of a continuing litigation strategy as Counsel on Brief or *amicus curiae*. It participated as Counsel on Brief in a state-level case. It also participated as *amicus* across jurisdictions in *Campbell v. St. Tammany Parish School Board*, a case sponsored by the ACLJ. This case was granted *certiorari* review by the Supreme Court and then immediately remanded to the U.S. Court of Appeal. It also participated as *amicus* in *Santa Fe v. Doe* on appeal—even before Sekulow stepped in to argue that case before the Supreme Court.

These data reflect the advancement and development of the Liberty Counsel's litigation agenda over time—it has made a strong commitment to deep policy influence and has worked to effect national policy even as its position within the movement became more prominent. It is apparent that, while Staver exercises great care in selecting appropriate cases with good case facts and clients willing to sustain litigation through the appeals process, the Liberty Counsel has been relatively unsuccessful in bringing its most important cases to the Supreme Court. Instead, the Liberty Counsel's policy influence has been limited largely to federal circuit and state court decisions. However, this is a reflection of its emerging status as one of the top three litigating firms within the movement. The Liberty Counsel demonstrates a strong commitment, not simply to litigation, but to sustained litigation efforts through its participation in the appellate process. This participation demonstrates the Liberty Counsel's potential for exerting a lasting impact on policy formulation—it is an organization with a distinctive character, moderate and growing resources, clearly established goals, and methods for achieving those goals through an active litigation agenda.

Conclusion: Organizational Life and Culture

This chapter has developed an understanding of those characteristics of organizational life that will provide the basis for a closer comparison of New Christian Right firms in later analyses—internal organizational culture, goals, structure and resources, litigation emphases, and behavior. The study of Liberty Counsel's internal culture reveals certain unique and established patterns of viewing the structure of the social conflicts that it litigates and a firm commitment to achieving longstanding objectives in court. Staver and the Liberty Counsel remain committed to an open, liberalized, and fairly consistent view of civil rights. He has advocated this view consistently in the media and applied it in court across a variety of key issue areas. As part of his plan to grow the Liberty Counsel into a premier conservative Christian litigating firm, Staver has pursued media- and reputation-oriented goals as a supplement to the twin goals of education and policy influence.

The analysis also provides a basis for understanding the position of the Liberty Counsel and various firms on such hot-button issues as gay rights and religious expression. The commitment of the Liberty Counsel to a liberalized religious expression argument clearly ends when openness precludes religious conviction. While the internal culture of the Liberty Counsel promotes dedication to liberal principles of tolerance and judicial principles supporting incremental policy change, several issues threaten the internal consistency of this position. The threat of this inconsistency is in large part the story of the broad American culture at the dawn of the twenty-first century. As we struggle with the conflict between liberal virtues of tolerance and religious conviction, New Christian Right firms like the Liberty Counsel will continue to exert influence on the course of policy. And, as the Liberty Counsel grows into its future as a movement leader, it will have to face and meet these cultural tensions.

Table 3.1. Liberty Counsel Litigation by Year and Jurisdiction

Year	USSC	SSC	USCA	USDC	SCA	SCO	Other	Total
1989	0	0	0	1	0	0	0	1
1990	0	0	0	0	0	0	0	0
1991	1	0	0	0	0	0	0	1
1992	1	0	0	0	0	0	0	1
1993	0	1	1	4	1	1	0	8
1994	1	0	1	7	0	0	0	9
1995	2	0	7	9	1	0	0	19
1996	0	0	3	2	0	0	0	5
1997	1	0	1	2	1	0	0	5
1998	1	1	2	1	0	0	0	5
1999	3	0	4	0	0	0	0	7
2000	1	0	3	2	1	1	0	8
2001	0	0	2	4	1	0	0	7
2002	1	0	2	10	0	0	0	13
2003	3	1	3	5	0	0	0	12
2004	0	0	2	1	2	0	0	5
Total	15	3	31	48	7	2	0	106

Source: Lexis/Nexis Legal Database

Note(s) : USSC =United States Supreme Court; SSC =State Supreme Court;
USCA =United States Court of Appeal; USDC =United States District Court
SCA =State Court of Appeal; SCO = State Court of Origin

Table 3.2. Liberty Counsel Litigation by Year and Type

Year	Sponsorship	On Brief	Amicus	Total
1989	1	0	0	1
1990	0	0	0	0
1991	0	0	0	0
1992	0	0	1	1
1993	8	0	0	8
1994	9	0	0	9
1995	17	0	2	19
1996	4	0	1	5
1997	3	1	1	5
1998	3	2	0	5
1999	3	0	5	8
2000	5	0	3	8
2001	7	0	0	7
2002	10	0	3	13
2003	8	0	4	12
2004	3	0	2	5
Total	81	3	22	106

Source: Lexis/Nexis Legal Database

Table 3.3. Liberty Counsel Participation by Year and Issue Area

Year	Church/State Schools	Church/State Public Places	Abortion Protestation	Abortion Rights	Sexual Orientation	Family Policy	Other	Total
1989	0	1	0	0	0	0	0	1
1990	0	0	0	0	0	0	0	0
1991	0	0	0	0	0	0	0	0
1992	1	0	0	0	0	0	0	1
1993	1	2	5	0	0	0	0	8
1994	3	1	3	1	0	0	0	8
1995	2	7	7	1	0	0	2	19
1996	2	2	0	1	0	0	0	5
1997	4	0	0	0	0	1	0	5
1998	2	4	0	0	0	0	0	6
1999	5	2	0	1	0	0	0	8
2000	5	2	0	0	0	0	1	8
2001	2	3	2	0	0	0	0	7
2002	2	7	3	0	0	1	0	13
2003	4	5	0	1	1	1	0	12
2004	0	2	1	1	1	0	0	5
Total	33	38	21	6	2	3	3	106

Source: Lexis/Nexis Legal Database

Table 3.4. Liberty Counsel Participation, 1989–2004, by Type and Issue Area

Type	Church/State Schools	Church/State Public Places	Abortion Protest	Abortion Rights	Sexual Orientation	Family Policy	Other	Total
Sponsorship	19	34	19	3	0	2	3	80
Counsel on Brief	2	1	0	0	0	0	0	3
Amicus curiae	12	3	2	3	2	1	0	23
Other	0	0	0	0	0	0	0	0
Total	33	38	21	6	2	3	3	106

Source: Lexis/Nexis Legal Database

Table 3.5. Liberty Counsel Federal Court Participation by Type and Issue Area

Type	Church/State Schools	Church/State Public Places	Abortion Protest	Abortion Rights	Sexual Orientation	Family Policy	Other	Total
Supreme Court Participation								
Sponsorship	0	0	1	0	0	0	0	1
Counsel on Brief	0	1	0	0	0	0	0	1
Amicus curiae	6	1	2	1	1	1	0	12
Total	6	2	3	1	1	1	0	14
U.S. Court of Appeals Participation								
Sponsorship	9	9	4	1	0	1	0	24
Counsel on Brief	0	0	0	0	0	0	0	0
Amicus curiae	5	1	0	0	0	0	0	6
Total	14	10	4	1	0	1	0	30

Continued on next page

Note(s): Sponsorship is determined by the name of Liberty Counsel or attorney employed by Liberty Counsel listed as Attorney of Record within the published court opinion. Similarly, Counsel on Brief is determined by the nam of Liberty Counsel or attorney employed by Liberty Counsel listed as On Brief within the published court opinion, and *amicus curiae* by the same listed as *amicus*, or preparer of an amicus brief (e.g., for another organization) within the published court opinion.

Table 3.5—Continued

Type	Church/State Schools	Church/State Public Places	Abortion Protest	Abortion Rights	Sexual Orientation	Family Policy	Other	Total
U.S. District Court Participation								
Sponsorship	10	21	11	1	0	1	3	47
Counsel on Brief	0	0	0	0	0	0	0	0
Amicus curiae	0	1	0	0	0	0	0	1
Total	10	22	11	1	0	1	3	48

Source: Lexis/Nexis Legal Database

Table 3.6. Liberty Counsel Litigation across Jurisdictions by Type, Issue Area, and Appearances

Participation	Jurisdiction	Issue Area	Appearances in Court
Case Sponsorship:			
	Trial to CLR[a]		
	1) Madsen v. Women's Health Center [b]	Abortion: Protest	6
	Intermediate Appellate to CLR		
	No cases fall into this category		
	Trial to Intermediate Appellate (petition for higher review[c] denied)		
	2) Adler v. Duval County School District (I & II)	Church/State: Schools	7
	3) Christ's Bride Ministries v. SEPTA	Church/State: Public Places	2
	4) ACLU v. McCreary County	Church/State: Public Places	2
	Trial to Intermediate Appellate (no petition for higher review)		
	5) Morris v. City of West Palm Beach	Church/State: Public Places	2
	6) Muller v. Jefferson Lighthouse School	Church/State: Schools	2
	7) Hoover v. Wagner	Abortion: Protest	2

Continued on next page

[a]CLR = Court of Last Resort

[b]The Supreme Court combined the federal and Florida cases Cheffer v. McGregor and Operation Rescue v. Women's Health Center, respectively. Both cases were sponsored by the Liberty Counsel and argued by Mathew Staver.

[c]Petition for higher review: Includes requests for rehearing en banc and petition for certiorari.

Table 3.6—Continued

Participation	Jurisdiction	Issue Area	Appearances in Court
	8) *Jews for Jesus v. Hillsborough Cnty Aviation Auth.*	Church/State: Public Places	2
	9) *Libertad v. Welch*	Abortion: Protest	2
	10) *Johnson-Loehner v. O'Brien*	Church/State: Schools	3
	11) *Cheffer v. Reno*	Abortion: Protest	2
	12) *Martin v. City of Gainesville*	Church/State: Public Places	2
Amicus curiae Participation:			
	Intermediate Appellate to CLR		
	13) *Campbell v. St. Tammany Parish Sch. Bd.*	Church/State: Schools	2
	14) *Santa Fe v. Jane Doe (2000)*	Church/State: Schools	2
	Trial to Intermediate Appellate (no petition for higher review)		
	15) *Van Orden v. Perry*	Church/State: Public Places	2
	16) *Campbell v. St. Tammany Parish Sch. Bd.*	Church/State: Schools	2
		Total Appearances:	**42**

Source: Lexis/Nexis Legal Database

Chapter Four

Wise as a Serpent and Innocent as a Lamb

The American Family Association's Center for Law and Policy

The American Family Association—Center for Law and Policy is very much as one would imagine a conservative Christian litigating interest group. It is a small group of closely allied attorneys who fight a war to thwart social bias against Christians and the American family. The firm is the project of a crusader against pornography, obscenity, and gay rights. He has won the animosity of powerful corporate and liberal interests through persistent and carefully orchestrated boycotts. His organization has the ear of Congressmen and local community leaders. Since 1990, he has invested millions of dollars into supporting one of the leading New Christian Right law firms. No conservative Christian law firm could have better credentials.

Members of the firm speak articulately about the role of the church in civic life, the threat to the faithful from a corrupt and perverse society, and a political and social return to values upon which the nation was founded—ethics of Judeo-Christian origin. These are themes with which many characterize the Religious Right in the United States. In fact, most of what the American Family Association—Center for Law and Policy (CLP) does (and how it explains why it does it) is considered in the mainstream of the New Christian Right. However, the law firm is unique in many respects. The CLP combines the litigation methods pioneered by firms like the ACLJ with an agenda comprised of traditional conservative Christian issues. Further, it couples traditional methods of organizing religious law firms (under the auspices of a powerful, non-legal parent organization) with an aggressive and punishing approach to litigation. Perhaps most importantly, the CLP is primarily a grassroots trial-oriented law firm dedicated to representing those members of the New Christian Right caught in the toils of the law—street preachers, abortion protesters, and school children or parents who experience religious intolerance in schools or the workplace.

Throughout its history, the firm has undergone extensive changes in structure and personnel while scoring significant victories in court. What has remained constant over the years is its record of engaging in the most aggressive trial-level litigation. The firm has consistently moved to challenge social policies that do not square with conservative Christian beliefs. On its agenda are core issues that resonate with its membership: defending abortion protesters, challenging public school book selections and state educational systems, opposing gay-rights legislation, and defending zoning ordinances aimed at stopping

91

pornography. This chapter is dedicated to exploring the ever-broadening influence of the CLP through litigation and policy making.

God's Hammer, Wildmon's Stinger: Founding the CLP

Marines in the Trenches

The CLP is a highly aggressive, trial-oriented conservative public interest law firm composed of six attorneys. It is led by its general counsel, Steve Crampton, the third attorney to guide the firm since its inception in 1990. Previous leaders include Benjamin Bull[1] and Bruce Green,[2] who built the organization from the ground up after it survived a false start. Green's primary reason for building a small law center was to keep it highly mobile, agile, and prepared. When interviewed in 1998, he stated that the CLP is capable of sending its attorneys to any part of the country in a matter of hours and appearing in court on behalf of its clients within a day. According to Green, an aggressive approach to trial-level litigation has shaped the CLP into a lean outfit, geared toward defending the First Amendment rights of Christians at a moment's notice: "We've tried to build a small very aggressive elite group of trial attorneys, not necessary motion attorneys, but trial attorneys. So we've engaged in a great deal of very aggressive litigation. That's our approach."[3]

The CLP specializes in doing whatever is needed in defending believers. It has gone to what other organizations would consider extreme lengths to provide what Bruce Green called "adequate representation." In a case occurring in Connecticut Federal District Court (a case that all CLP attorneys refer to as defining the role and mission of the organization), the CLP leased a house in which to live and direct strategy throughout the trial. CLP attorneys rotated between Tupelo and Connecticut for a period of six months. While this case was certainly special to the organization, such efforts by the CLP are not so unusual. In part, this is because the organization defines its mission differently than other New Christian Right firms. As Steven Crampton points out, this difference is reflected in the kinds of cases the CLP takes.

> Other organizations look at the CLP, and not unfairly so, as the Marines. We are the first in, the trenches kind of guys—we are a grassroots organization and that is our strength. The law center reflects that identity. Our cases almost without exception originate in the trenches. And, so we might spend longer because we take cases that won't be completed in six months or a year—protracted litigation. And since the other side has so much invested in the trial, that also increases the settlement rate for us and limits our appellate agenda.

Thus, the jurisdictional emphasis of the CLP is on the trial level, reflecting its desire to work for the average Christian caught in the toils of the law.

Rev. Don Wildmon and the American Family Association

Twenty-eight years ago, in Tupelo, Mississippi, a Methodist minister named Donald Wildmon founded an organization called the National Federation for Decency (NFD). Initially running it out of his home, he used the NFD to launch campaigns against pornography, the programming choices of major media groups, and "an erosion of the civil and Constitutional rights of people of religious faith, particularly Christian groups." After a number of years of campaigning and boycotting companies including American Airlines, the 7-11 Corporation, Kmart (owner of Waldenbooks), and Disney, the NFD changed its name to the American Family Association (AFA) in 1987[4] and started what has become a nationwide network of 160 radio affiliates. The radio stations provide an array of programming including contemporary religious music, preaching, Bible and life lessons, and other forms of religious education. They also serve as a network to communicate with AFA membership and create support for AFA campaigns against offending corporations or governments.

The AFA maintains a network of "Faithful and True" support groups, which function as "AA for the pornographically addicted."[5] Additionally, the AFA claims over five hundred local chapters scattered throughout the country.[6] Individuals are steered to local chapters and area support groups when they call the national office in Tupelo. Local chapters mount campaigns against local businesses and national chains that advertise during what it defines as objectionable programming, and picket local stores that sell pornographic video and printed materials. The national headquarters often prompts local campaigns, and these campaigns are in line with the official AFA view that our society is prey to the "destructive and corrosive effect of pornography."[7]

In coordinating nationwide campaigns, a part of AFA strategy is to tape local programming at the Tupelo headquarters and distribute information on programming content and advertising to its chapters nationwide. Examples include campaigns against CBS affiliates that aired condom advertisements during the *Howard Stern Show*, and against Pepsi, which started a nationwide ad campaign involving pop artist Madonna. National campaigns have extended to include lobbying Congress over funding for the National Endowment for the Arts.[8] Wildmon and the AFA have won some impressive victories, including a halt to the Pepsi/Madonna ads and an agreement from 7-11 not to sell pornographic magazines in its stores. In 1998, the national AFA scored its greatest victory, convincing the Texas State Board of Education to divest $44 million in Disney stock. The decision came after the board considered information provided by the AFA in its thirty-minute film "How Texas is Bankrolling the Disney Empire."[9] The campaign against Disney did not stop there—the AFA continues to boycott Disney as of this writing. "I have just one motivation," said Wildmon in a 1995 interview, "to protect the family."

> This country was built on the family. In the past 30 years, the family has been under attack. During that time crime has risen, illegitimacy has risen; drug use

is all but out of control. That's what happens when the family is weakened. The family is God's way of establishing order in the universe.[10]

Wildmon is confident that he can consistently marshal the AFA's two million members and take on any business that he believes undermines family values. Business and media enterprises have found it difficult to ignore Wildmon and the AFA. In addition to a membership base of 2,000,000, the AFA is affiliated with sixty-seven religious denominations[11] and has considerable clout in Congress. However, for much of its existence, the AFA was vulnerable in the courts. In the 1980s, that is exactly where its opponents chose to attack it.

Need for a Stinger

The law center was founded as part of both the AFA's business and ministry components; a CLP lawyer also works to support AFA business interests, such as its radio network. As the parent of the CLP, the AFA oversees the law center's budget, provides staff support, and houses it in its Tupelo, Mississippi, headquarters. Because of its strong connection to the causes of its membership, the AFA encouraged the development of a "grassroots law firm" capable of defending the rank-and-file at the initial stages litigation. Consequently, the CLP has become one of the core enterprises of the AFA's vast media and grassroots network. The integration of the CLP into the AFA's daily activities did not happen by chance. It grew out of the parent organization's experiences during the late 1980s and two fairly publicized suits brought against it from one of its primary targets.

As a result of its boycotting strategy, the Wildmon organization has been threatened with legal action for reasons including libel. A prime example is the 1988 AFA-sponsored boycott directed at Penthouse Magazine, Playboy Corporation, the American Booksellers Association, and others. This campaign developed into one of the AFA's largest efforts to counter the sale of pornography by merchant stores and booksellers. In response, both the Playboy Corporaton and Penthouse Magazine filed suit against the AFA in Florida Federal District Court under the Racketeer Influenced and Corrupt Organizations (RICO) statute. One commentator, describing the alleged illegal activities, noted that "[a]mong the [alleged] 'patterns of racketeering' employed by the defendants have been letter-writing, boycotts and threats of boycotts. (Cesar Chavez is lucky the good guys approve of his letter writing, boycotts and threats of boycotts.)"

In the complaint filed in federal court in Florida, the American Family Association is charged with acts of "extortion" in trying to get magazine and book retailers, wholesalers, distributors and publishers to stop "selling certain materials protected by the First Amendment." These acts consisted of sending "numerous" letters and postcards, picketing the home of an officer of a wholesale distribution company, and threatening to hold a press conference to tribution company, and threatening to hold a press conference to expose . . . some stores for acting "illegally" under Florida law by selling magazines that carry ads for obscene videos.[12]

The suit, filed on the basis of the success of the AFA boycott (the corporations alleged that more than 1,400 convenience stores had refused to sell their goods), prompted the founding of the AFA Law Center under the leadership of Benjamin Bull. Bull successfully challenged both suits, which were dismissed.[13] However, the legal efforts of Penthouse brought a flood of media exposure to the AFA, not all of it sympathetic. The press revealed (and the AFA admitted publicly) that the AFA's claim of illegal activity by booksellers was an incorrect interpretation of Florida statute. However, using RICO to prevent boycotting struck a chord of illegitimacy with the press and of fear within the AFA.[14]

An artist receiving funding from the National Endowment for the Arts brought the second lawsuit against the AFA. The suit, requesting $5 million in damages, alleged that the AFA had violated copyright laws by using cropped portions of the artist's work in its membership newsletter and that the AFA had libeled the artist in public letters to members of Congress. Bull won dismissal on most counts, but the AFA became subject to a restraining order enjoining it from using or distributing the artist's work. Damages awarded to the artist amounted to one dollar.

During the early 1980s, Wildmon had considered establishing a public interest law firm focused on defending the religious liberties of Christians. *Penthouse v. American Family Association* (1989) spurred him to proceed, and add protecting his organization in court to its job description. The availability of in-house legal counsel would act as a deterrent to those corporations that attempt to stop AFA-led campaigns through legal means. According to Green, "the Penthouse case was, for lack of better terms, the last straw."

> There was both a concern for the exercise of our Constitutional rights as an entity, and at the same time the general push of the public out there. So he came up with the idea of founding a law center that would be involved in the defense of Christian civil liberties generally without charge. And at the same time would be Don Wildmon's "stinger" to defend the American Family Association.

Although the AFA has had in-house legal counsel since the mid-1980s (to assist in corporate work, FCC applications, and some *amicus* activity in Supreme Court cases), the creation of the law center represented a fundamentally new direction for the AFA in making use of the courts. It was designed to pursue religious liberties litigation and protect the AFA when its activities outside the court involved it in litigation. Early forays into the courts by AFA attorneys did not attempt either of these two primary functions.

Commenting on the founding of the CLP, Wildmon stated that he had learned about the courts by example—the ACLU's example. He defined the CLP's new strategy as putting foes of Christianity on notice. The CLP would

"initiate actions that will put the pornographers, militant homosexuals and hu-
manists on the defensive."

> Just as we have established over five hundred local chapters of the AFA to fight
> for our rights in the public arena, we will establish a network of Christian law-
> yers across the country who will fight our battles in the courts.

The AFA moved swiftly from simply affecting the democratic process to an all-
out assault on its enemies in the court system.

Goals and Religious Ideology

In my examination of the CLP's organizational culture, two important characteristics stand out—the important place of religious principle within the organization and the influence of its relationship with its parent organization (the AFA).
Recognizing the circumstances that led to the creation of the CLP is important
for understanding its mission and place within the New Christian Right. The
CLP was born out of a conflict involving the AFA in which that organization
felt threatened and vulnerable. As the CLP developed, the parent organization
provided significant resources and general guidance. Although the AFA does
not exercise direct control over the CLP's litigation agenda, its influence has
shaped the organization, its goals and emphases. In particular the variety of resources the AFA provides has significantly impacted the CLP's litigation
agenda, limiting the kinds of behavior in which it will engage. Furthermore, an
examination of the CLP points up the significant influence of both religious
ideological motivations and goals on group litigation behavior. The importance
of religious principle within the CLP has significantly influenced the group's
approach to litigation and, in particular, the arguments it makes in court.

At first blush, the goals of the CLP appear to be very much like those of
other New Christian Right litigating firms. The organization seeks to defend the
rights of believers in the public sphere and to engage the culture in an effort to
transform its values. Its former general counsel, Bruce Green, stated that the
CLP has two primary aims: "One [purpose] would be to defend the existing constitutional rights of believers when they are being infringed. The second would
be to advance a particular cause." Delving deeper into the CLP reveals that religious ideological concerns are very closely entwined with these goals in ways
that contrast with other movement law firms. Other organizations approach religion in terms of the law. The CLP approaches law in terms of religion. The
contrast is important. Many New Christian Right firms discuss religion in public
life in terms of successful legal arguments (i.e., equal access and free expression
arguments). In contrast, the CLP discusses law in terms of religious principle.
The distinction may seem cryptic but has tremendous impact on organizational
emphases and approach to litigation. The CLP defends the rights of believers not
simply so that religion may become one voice among many in a plural society,

but also to present arguments for retaining principles it defines as central to the moral core of the nation. Thus, the CLP's view of religious doctrine and law explains in part why it selects certain litigation emphases over others. I turn first to an examination of the CLP's doctrinal motivations and then to an examination of the CLP's goals and its relationship with its parent organization.

The Lamb's Innocence: Doctrinal Motivations

The centrality of religious principle to the organizational life of the CLP cannot be overstated. When queried about specific methods of engaging the courts, each of its attorneys articulates a comprehensive worldview that is based primarily on a religious interpretation of law and politics. Religious principle informs every aspect of the CLP's work, from the cases on its litigation agenda and the arguments presented in court to the structure of the firm itself. As Brian Fahling notes, "We don't leapfrog our faith when we go to court."

> That means, in our interaction with the culture, we cannot give up the ultimate justification for our approach, which is rooted theologically in our faith. The courts, the policy makers, or just the average person listening on a talk show does not make the same assumptions as us.

Fahling, Crampton, and their compatriots are clearly skilled attorneys. But, they engage in the practice of law as a tool for achieving the overall spiritual mission of the CLP. The CLP exists as a lean and aggressive firm not simply so it can take the best advantage of the courts or to protect and defend the rights of believers. The firm takes its present form so that it can best encounter the legal culture and make arguments that if accepted will align the law with religious principle.

Below, I explore the religious motivations of the organization to gain a clearer understanding of how the CLP makes use of the courts. Perhaps more than any other New Christian Right firm, the CLP is concerned about justifying its motivations for litigation. The underlying motives of the organization are distinctly less secular and inform its work to a larger extent than other organizations included in this study. Moreover, a discussion of the role of religious principle will provide an understanding of ways in which principle shapes the organization's agenda, enabling or constraining aspects of its litigation behavior. I find that under the rhetoric, the CLP takes a much different approach to encountering the culture than the typical and knee-jerk reactions of New Christian Right legislative lobbyists.

The hallmark of the CLP is a complex system of thought that melds reformist religious doctrines (e.g., an emphasis on mankind's fallibility and the efficacy of biblical teachings as a guide for constructing social policy) with conservative jurisprudential themes (natural law, principled decision making, and an intentionalist approach to constitutional interpretation). For the CLP attorneys, these juridical themes fold logically into a Christian worldview that specifies the individual's place before God, within society, and before the law that society creates. Thus, the CLP's jurisprudence is part of its broader Christian perspective on law that provides the overriding principles for engaging in litigation or any other effort to affect and critique public policy.

The CLP's Christian perspective on law has been labeled dogmatic, unbendingly doctrinaire, and strident. Judges have even accused them of being homophobic and racist. To many onlookers the CLP is an old guard law firm that lives on principle, and often dies on it, too. Certainly, it appears that way on the surface. For example, Brian Fahling, in giving a general description of the CLP's way of thinking, states, "our jurisprudence is based on the principles of the Declaration of Independence that undergird the Constitution and are Judeo-Christian in origin."

> We do not believe the Constitution is a living and breathing document. It did not mean something two hundred years ago, and something else today. But, it is not the Constitution that we look for foundational principles. We go back to the starting place that is enunciated in the Declaration of Independence: "All men are created equal and have been endowed by their creator with certain unalienable rights. Among these life, liberty and pursuit of happiness." These then were embodied in the Bill of Rights. You have to go back and prove what rights are for the individual.

A more careful examination reveals a much more nuanced approach to law and the society that is not so unyielding and finds a common ground between faith and secular policy. "We describe ourselves as Augustinian in our approach to the culture," says Fahling.

> There is a City of God and a City of Man, and we recognize that the City of Man will never be perfect. We know that governments were not created exclusively for Christians. So, governments have a legitimate function—they are charged with creating an environment in which man can pursue happiness and where evil is punished. The common ground that we share with the rest of mankind deals with those areas.

While it is true that the CLP strives to embed the rationale behind religious principle into law, its general counsel articulates a position based much more on the common ground existing between the faith and culture, rather than the typical New Christian Right notion that America is a Christian nation. "We are very opinionated and we talk in strident terms sometimes," says Steve Crampton.

> But, the means through which we seek to implement principles is not a sledgehammer. We want to import what we understand the Constitution to mean in nineteenth-century America, but we recognize that we cannot simply drop the whole package in. We attempt to preserve the principles within the context of a culture that is 180 degrees different today. So [our view of religion and politics] informs the argument and the way we approach cases, but does not overwhelm

and dictate every little particular. We are not so naïve as to think that it can be imported wholesale.

This remark is significant, for it demonstrates just how blended religious and legal principles are within the CLP. Crampton and Fahling view certain interpretations of the Constitution as compatible with religious principle, as a means for dropping in a package of secular interpretations that comport with the goals of religious doctrine. Furthermore, both Fahling and Crampton find common ground among religious and secular goals, although the assumptions behind those goals may differ. "To state it in secular terms," says Fahling, "it is the idea that government's function is limited in some respects. The respects in which it is limited are germane to all of us—you don't need to be a believer."

> When we engage the law or policy, we don't thunder in the language of the Bible. The point of contact is common practical notions. We don't insist that the unbeliever agree with us on the ultimate justification—that is a matter of hearts and minds. But, to the degree that God's law remains written in our hearts we can agree on common practical notions. What we do then is take what drives us and then find the common ground. In law and policy, these issues are germane to all of us. They have no business being lifted out and held up as though they are exclusively Christian arguments. And that is where the Religious Right has shot itself in the foot. We keep wanting to thunder the Bible. We create the impression that, for example, the issue of homosexuality is a distinctly and unique Christian issue. Of course not—it is common to mankind.

A "common practical notions" approach has had its problems, because (as Fahling is quick to point out) the basis for consensus has eroded. The CLP believes that courts have contributed in part to this society-wide erosion. But, in an effort that is central to the identify of the organization, the CLP struggles to stem the tide of erosion by making arguments in court that have their genesis in Christian principle.

This does not mean that the CLP wholly rejects an incrementalist approach to change in law and policy, but it does mean that the CLP places limits on what it will do to achieve change and align law with religious principle. Such an approach requires considerable creativity on the part of its attorneys to make arguments that courts find palatable. When Fahling was questioned about how the principled approach works when litigating, he responded that "pragmatism is not simply bad."

> We practice principled pragmatism, a pragmatism that recognizes the realities of the day, and the culture and the environment. Practical realities of life do not suggest a principle one way or the other. We are not talking about absolute truth with regard to a piece of legislation. But, for example with abortion, I think it is best to chip away, rather than swooping in and dying on the hill of principle. You don't accomplish anything there. The end sought through incrementalism there is to save the unborn. You don't save any of the unborn by trying to do the impossible. So, we do what we can.

But, for the CLP principled pragmatism in law is hard to come by when interacting with a culture it perceives to be "180 degrees opposite" from religious principle. The CLP lays the blame for the cultural erosion they perceive at the feet of the modern pragmatism of the federal courts. In continuing their explanation of the CLP's view of religion and law, Crampton and Fahling try to outline what is the jurisprudential philosophy that they oppose and with which they maintain a constant battle. Much of their concern lies with the power that courts have assumed to regulate. "There is an internal logic [to present-day court decisions]," says Fahling, "in a sense that they set up these tests."

> But, the big lie is that these tests constrain the Court. They do have tests, but they are drawn in such a fashion as to allow the Court to come to any conclusion it wishes. So, there is logic, but it is not one that follows the dictates of the rule of law, which is at a minimum predictability of outcome.

> **Crampton**: Which goes back to the problem with pragmatic approach to constitutional law. It's not pragmatism when the Supremes or other courts construct a basis for justifying any decision. For example, one of the cardinal rules of courts in the permit application process is that you may not delegate to a public official *unbridled discretion* to decide who may have a license and who may not. Courts use [this rule] in the sexually oriented business arena as well. But, they refuse to apply that standard to themselves. What they have is unbridled discretion.

> **Fahling**: They have stolen from us the right to govern ourselves. There is no self-government anymore; only on the unimportant issues do they allow the legislatures to make decisions.

Later, the two referred to a particular case litigated by the CLP as an example of their frustration with this level of pragmatism. The case involved a ministerial association that made a gift to its local high school for a Ten Commandments monument. The district turned this into a historical display and sought money from other sources to erect other monuments along with it, whereupon the families of several students sued the school district. At trial, the federal district court ruled that the religious nature of the original gift was so compelling that the high school could not break the association regardless of what it did. On appeal, Fahling argued that "the district court's ruling sends a message to public officials—beware of Christians bearing gifts."

> Because if you are a Christian, your religious purpose is imputed and you are penalized. In this case we have a group of small-town people who just want to make a gift to a high school, be involved in the community, and they were vilified by the lower court for this. Having a religious faith that motivates you to give to public institutions is tantamount to being a leper. So, I was able to get back to constitutional principles and common practical notions.

Crampton: In these kinds of cases there are no fixed principles—with that kind of jurisprudence, they can do whatever they want. There is an enormous inefficiency built into that kind of approach because no one can ever know until a particular court has looked at it, and a particular judge has opinioned whether it is okay. It is like getting your blessing from the local religious official.

Fahling: This isn't constitutional law, this is interior decorating and landscape architecture. If you want to be a technocrat that is an expert in landscape architecture, create a program at law schools.

The CLP's critique of pragmatism goes far beyond arbitrariness on the part of courts to capture its concern over the equal protection arguments made by the Supreme Court in cases like *Romer v. Evans* and *Lawrence v. Texas*, and to the manner in which other New Christian Right firms have used pragmatism to achieve immediate ends. In contrast with other firms, Crampton points out, "The biggest distinction between us and other New Christian Right litigators is that we are the only group that refuses to litigate in Title Seven cases (of the Civil Rights Act of 1964) against a private employer."

We refuse on the view that it is inappropriate for government to dictate to private employers who they can hire. The reason is that the arm of the government has no place telling private businesses, which really are no different than private individuals, what they can and can't think and do in hiring practices. We do not condone racism and those prejudices that those acts are meant to reach. But, there is a problem when we look to government for the solution to all of our problems. And, we are feeding that government monster by agreeing to litigate those cases. When presented with this argument, most of our compatriots in litigation would agree with that general proposition. But, consider the Employment non-Discrimination Act that the homosexual lobby has had introduced in Congress and comes closer to passing with each session. All the Christian employers who have been arguing Title Seven for years are going to have to hire homosexuals, and they are not going to be happy.

Thus, in some ways, the CLP views the pragmatism of its sister firms as losing sight of the religious principle to be mapped onto law, with the ultimate result that the arguments made in support of tolerance for Christians come back to haunt those same Christians later.

According to the CLP, the courts themselves created the context in which New Christian Right firms could collude to advance unprincipled reasoning. They have fundamentally misinterpreted the Constitution by attaching meaning to clauses where no such meaning existed in the past. Most ominously for the CLP, this misinterpretation has led to a rejection of principled arguments by the courts and provided a license to regulate speech and thought based on content. Fahling cites *Romer v. Evans* as an example of a case impacting the CLP's mission in which the Christian principles are subverted by the reasoning of the Court.

Romer v. Evans tells us that the only reason you could ever seek to limit homosexual rights is because of animus in your heart. So now all Christians who subscribe to an orthodox worldview with respect to that issue can have nothing but animus with respect to their views on homosexuals. Is that not now a compelling interest for the government to eradicate [that viewpoint]? If you are preaching up in your pulpit [against homosexuality] can the government demonstrate a compelling interest? Absolutely.

The tangible manifestation of these views is a firm that, while poised to take advantage of new methods for engaging the courts, approaches litigation with a very different emphasis compared to the other groups examined in this research. It is not fair to say that the CLP avoids the pragmatic approach of the new Christian litigators in favor of arguments based on strict principle. Clearly, the CLP's principled approach is more sophisticated than a simple principle versus pragmatism contrast. However, it is fair to say that the CLP attempts to meld principle with pragmatism in a way that differs significantly from other New Christian Right firms. Furthermore, the CLP's interest in advancing legal arguments based on principled jurisprudence has created some tension between it and other Christian litigating groups. The centrality of religious principle to the CLP's identity provides a contrast between it and its fellow New Christian Right litigators. When asked to make that contrast, Crampton stated that the CLP tends to "take the broader historical view with an understanding of structural and recognizing the long-term policy implications."

But, we do not buy into changes [courts make] in a blind sort of way. What other organizations have done is bought into the Supreme Court's rules of today. The Court has made up the new rules, and they [other New Christian Right litigators] never get beyond it.

The CLP sees the behavior of other groups (behavior identified in this study as embodying a new level of sophistication in the courts) as ultimately unsound in theory and frequently unprincipled in practice. Fahling states that the CLP's jurisprudence sets it apart from its sister organizations, including the ACLJ. According to Fahling, these organizations have confused the role of law with their goals for influencing policy. They no longer ask if the means they use to a particular end are justifiable. They simply pursue the policy goal, even when it means losing their principled position.

On the other hand, these contrasts are differences of degree rather than kind. It would be a mistake to assume that the CLP is isolated from its compatriots by a disagreement over the role of religious principle. There is no such dogmatic assertion of principle within the CLP. The organization maintains strong ties to other New Christian Right litigating firms. Furthermore, its position on ideological difference extends even into an assessment of its opponents. "It is not written in Holy Scripture that only this much government is allowed," says Fahling. "We can disagree, find some equilibrium."

I assume that for the opposition—the Clintons, the Bidens of the world—the end for them is justice. Their goal is to do what is right. I am willing to take the charitable view and say they have the same goal I do which is to do what is best for mankind, to pursue the well-being of the citizens of this country. So, we can engage in civil dialogue if we don't impute evil motives to others. Both sides, are guilty of this—if you disagree with me you are immoral. Reasonable minds can differ. On each side, we have this mentality that we have to have all or nothing, or we've failed. So, I can say that affirmative action has a moral dimension, and those who support it seek justice.

In later analysis, I consider how differences among the groups create differences among their litigation agendas, and I consider what role religious ideology has to play in explaining those differences. It remains to be seen how the CLP's stance may influence the kinds of cases it litigates, the potential that those cases will be accepted for appellate review, or if judges interpret its efforts to make principle-based arguments as a sign of stridency and inflexibility. There is some evidence that federal appeals court judges have rejected CLP logic with considerable vigor and venom.[15]

Goals for Litigating

The second characteristic of the CLP's organizational culture implicates its relationship with its parent organization, the AFA. When questioned about the CLP's specific strategic focus, the general counsels' responses reflected the parent organization's involvement in the life of the CLP. For example, Bruce Green stated that he cares very much about influencing public attitudes and perceptions, but is unlikely to use the courts for that purpose, because the parent organization is so involved in changing public perceptions through boycotts and public campaigns.

> We are truly a litigation group. [Others have] an educational component. We exist fully for litigation, and in that context primarily trial work. So we are purely a litigation group. But, the parent organization is very interested in [changing public perceptions and education]. Because of the bifurcation of responsibilities [between the parent AFA and the CLP] we would be less likely to use the legal system to solve the public perceptions and public views of an issue. Not that we would be opposed to that. It's just we would be less likely to do it because it's not an area that we work in regularly. The parent organization does that. We seldom think of using the legal system that way.

The statement is particularly important for understanding how the CLP has traditionally engaged the courts and what it hopes to change about the present situation. First, it suggests that because of the parent organization's involvement, the CLP's mission is somewhat attenuated. There are some things that it has not considered as goals for resorting to litigation. For example, using the courts to address public opinion or bringing the attention of the public to their cause are not regular options. Secondly, the limitations placed on the organization's goals affect its litigation agenda. The CLP is predisposed to certain litigation behaviors as a result of its default pursuit of certain goals. The discussion of goals, below, takes up this consideration in more detail. However, from this discussion, one can conclude that the overall influence of the parent organization is felt throughout the CLP. The mission and agenda of the AFA influences the life of the CLP from the potential reasons for engaging in litigation to the types of litigation behavior it will emphasize.

The CLP participates in litigation in pursuit of two goals it identifies as equally important. First, it is concerned about setting precedent or obtaining a favorable interpretation of existing legal doctrine. However, the CLP places a decided spin on this goal, pursuing an agenda largely dominated by trial-level litigation over involvement in appellate litigation. Crampton quickly points out that trial-level litigation has its place in effecting court-crafted policy and that the CLP emphasizes it for two reasons. He believes that a trial-level concentration will put the organization in a better position upon appeal because it has been able to maintain complete control over issues and arguments throughout the trial. Further, it can maximize its impact on policy because relatively few cases are accepted for appeal beyond the intermediate level.

The consequence of a trial-level orientation is that the CLP's appellate agenda is much less comprehensive than other New Christian Right litigating firms. It may appear that the CLP limits its appellate agenda purposefully, perhaps preferring to take cases it knows it can win and avoiding cases in which they know that judges will respond negatively to their principle-oriented arguments. While some of this may be true, it is an oversimplification of the CLP's strategy in the courts. Regardless of the motive (explored more fully below), the CLP's involvement in precedent-building cases is generally confined to participation in intermediate appellate courts (not courts of last resort). The CLP is prepared to take select cases to the Supreme Court, appealing for *certiorari* review three times in the last five years.[16] Thus, an organizational concern for influencing policy by winning on appeal exists with the CLP but has taken a significantly different form than that of the other primarily appellate court New Christian Right litigators.

It is in an evaluation of the CLP's trial-level emphases that we see the parent organization's influence most strongly, as well as an effort within the CLP to develop beyond this influence. Because of the AFA's grassroots orientation, the CLP has a mandate to act primarily on behalf of Christians who find themselves (or place themselves) within the toils of the law. It moves to defend the First Amendment rights of believers at their point of entry into legal conflict. This sometimes provides opportunities to establish the firm's credentials as much as an appellate-level victory might. Crampton provides an example when discussing the plethora of cases and conflicts over gay rights during 2003 and 2004. "Perhaps because of our more principled jurisprudence and a worldview that is more comprehensive," he says, "we saw the danger of this issue early on."

With our "mother ship" [the AFA] seeing some of the developments out there and being out front of the issue, we became the go-to organization when the media had a legal debate they wanted to pitch, or whenever a new set of cases came up. Because the gay rights issue was on our radar perhaps more quickly than others.[17] It is an enormous issue that most New Christian Right groups have not acknowledged yet.

This emphasis, developed out of the parent organization's influence, allows the CLP to provide a service to rank-and-file Christians but also allows it to be selective in what cases it chooses to appeal. According to Crampton, the organization finds a balance between defending the rights of believers and looking for imminently appealable cases—a balance that other New Christian Right litigators do not pursue. "Other organizations often get involved at the appellate level," says Crampton, "or at a time when the trial is almost concluded."

> These organizations mine cases and come in at mid-level. So, they will take [cases] right into the appellate courts, and they look for that over trial-level involvement. We don't appeal everything, and try to be judicious in what we do appeal. We also have a high settlement rate—we inevitably settle during the course of litigation. In much of our work there is no opportunity to appeal— when we win we don't get appealed very much. So, often we don't have an opportunity to participate on appeal.

This arrangement presents a trade-off for the organization between a high level of policy influence (and all the trappings of that influence, including notoriety) and serving the legal needs of those AFA constituents whose need is greatest. "Every good law firm wants to take a precedent-setting case," notes CLP Staff Attorney, Michael DePrimo.

> There are some Christian legal groups out there that will only take cases that they think will set a good precedent. We are not like that. If we have clients who are godly, law-abiding citizens whose rights are violated and we have the resources, we'll take the case regardless of whether it is a precedent-setting case, or your run-of-the-mill street preacher case. The fact is what we are looking to do is vindicate the rights of Christians.

The CLP's second goal is establishing its reputation with the courts and its sister organizations. This goal, as with its interest in policy influence, is cast in terms of trial-level litigation. According to Crampton, this means developing a reputation for zealously defending its clients and a perception with judges that the CLP is a professional outfit. This has been a theme for the CLP over the years. "You have to be honest and say that [reputation and perceptions] always are a concern to you, I suppose to varying degrees," Bruce Green stated when asked about the importance of reputation to the CLP.

> We are concerned that the courts will see us as a professional and civil law firm
> that takes its role and responsibilities in court seriously. At the same time be-
> cause we litigate in various context and jurisdictions we get no favorite courts
> and if we are going to represent our clients zealously and do a good job we
> have to be willing not to be intimidated in various jurisdictions. So we're con-
> cerned that the courts will see us as very professional and civil and concerned
> with our role as officers of the court. At the same time we must very zealously
> represent our clients.

Thus, the CLP has cast its interest in developing a reputation in terms of those
norms that are characteristic of trial-level courts—concern for providing adequate and full representation, and a perception among trial-level judges that the
firm is competent. But, these concerns for reputation are subject to the CLP's
primary interest in achieving favorable legal rulings. The CLP's interest in reputation may also be viewed as a consequence of limitations placed on it by the
parent organization. Given the emphasis in the AFA on grassroots lobbying
methods, and given its interests in defending its members when attacked in the
courts, it is not surprising that the CLP would cast its goals in terms that are
consistent with its parent organization's vision for litigation involvement.
Plainly, developing a reputation for zealously representing clients furthers a perception of the CLP as a legal defender of the faith among those who are threatened with a trial-level determination as to the legality of their religiously motivated actions.

Finally, the CLP is also concerned about elevating its image as a movement
leader. It has largely pursued this goal by developing alliances with other New
Christian Right litigating firms. Bruce Green noted that conservative Christian
firms "need to work together, be supportive of the other groups that are committed to the same causes.

> We want to be known as ready, willing and able to assist our colleagues, with
> the ability to work together for a common cause of course. We don't like the
> idea of being out there by ourselves alone and trying to do this work by our-
> selves.

Cooperation has always been a strategy that the CLP has been willing to pursue.
For example, the CLP participated in an early attempt to coordinate litigation as
one of the founding members of the Alliance Defense Fund (ADF). Crampton
sat on the ADF grants committee, and the AFA provided thousands of dollars in
yearly contributions to the ADF. When it became clear that this kind of clearinghouse approach to coordinating litigation would not work and Wildmon
withdrew his sponsorship, the CLP began pursuing more direct alliances with
certain firms. In early 2003, the CLP formed an alliance with the Liberty Counsel and several other firms specifically to coordinate gay rights litigation. As the
issue caught fire, the CLP was at the forefront of New Christian Right litigation
and often served as the movement's voice on gay rights in the media.

The CLP's Organizational Structure and Resources

The CLP enjoys many benefits from its relationship with the AFA. It has a large and stable monetary resource base, it never lacks for monetary or physical resources, and it also enjoys a good deal of independence in setting its own goals and managing its own litigation agenda. However, the use to which it puts these resources and benefits is a reflection of its ties to Donald Wildmon and his desire for frugality and fiscal responsibility. Following several leadership changes, the CLP entered a brief period of growth in the early 1990s. The CLP went about developing and acquiring the resources and expertise that have allowed it to mature and grow. In this section I underscore the unique character of the CLP by exploring the development of its internal organizational structure and use of resources. I uncover its efforts to acquire and use monetary and staff resources, to recruit legal talent, and to develop support among sister organizations.

Organizational Structure

The CLP's "no-frills" approach to law is also reflected in its physical organization. Staff Counsel Michael DePrimo notes the aggressive nature of the firm, which seeks out cases through its network of supporters, balancing its mission against its resource limitations.

> We are involved in cases where protest activities have come under attack from federal, state, or local governments. We regularly go into the cases to defend street preachers, abortion protestors. Any time we see this happening, government using its muscle to deny rights, we take a good look at it. If we have the resources we take the case.

This aggressive attitude has had significant influence on the internal structure of the firm and relationships among staff. Since the CLP represents clients all over the country, it often encounters indifferent attitudes from judges who have no sense of the CLP's reputation as a trial-oriented law center and who may have low expectations for the level of professionalism exhibited by Christian attorneys. The indifferent (and occasionally hostile) legal environment has encouraged close relationships among the six attorneys comprising the law center. "Every lawyer genuinely loves the other members of the firm," notes Patrick Bond, the assistant general counsel who handles the AFA's corporate work.

> There are often disagreements, but there is such respect from one to another. The relationship of the lawyers extends beyond the law center. We socialize one with another, with each other's families. So, there is a genuine oneness among the lawyers and the families that may be unique in a law firm. The camaraderie is high, and I've never been in a law firm that has what we have in the sense of camaraderie.

The CLP's physical surroundings are also a reflection of the internal structure. The law center's offices contrast highly with those of the other firms included in this research. At best, the facilities can be described as austere. Nothing expensive adorns the offices. The attorneys work in small, undistinguished offices situated around a common work area. Nothing of note distinguishes the general counsel's office from that of his least-senior associates. The office arrangements of the CLP are an external representation of the firm's internal organizational structure—no frills, equal treatment among attorneys and staff, and a lean organization focused on litigation. Working relationships between attorneys and staff are structured around the parent organization's requirements for frugal use of resources. CLP attorneys work with staff on aspects of litigation, but there is no duplication of effort. For example, CLP attorneys are responsible for generating their own letters, briefs, and pleadings, rather than dictating these to support staff. Staff members participate at a much higher level than is generally expected of legal assistants, assisting attorneys during the discovery stage of trial and working with little supervision from staff attorneys.

Thus, the firm uses its internal structure and the mandates of its parent organization to maximize the use of its resources. Ultimately, the character of the organization has been formed by the two influences of the parent organization and the uncertain legal environment in which it often works. These two influences have shaped the CLP into a firm with an aggressive approach to seeking out litigation, a functional approach to applying resources to its task, and a strong sense of community among its members.

The CLP does not maintain any regional offices, although it works closely with a nationwide network of volunteer attorneys. Thus, decisions about what cases to place on the organization's agenda are quite centralized and under the authority of the general counsel. The CLP's entire litigation agenda is handled by its six attorneys with the resources and assistance of the parent organization. CLP attorneys can and have managed a caseload of national scope and can appear in court quite quickly when required.[18]

Resources in Abundance

The resources so vital to the life and growth of a litigating interest group are provided fully and completely to the CLP by its parent organization. The CLP looks to the AFA for monetary and physical resources, authorization to hire new staff, technical support, and overall sponsorship. In return, the CLP handles all of the parent organization's corporate work and defends it when its activities create the threat of legal action. There are certain consequences for this arrangement, and questions arise over the autonomy of a legal firm funded completely by a non-legal entity. This section will address the level of resources available to the CLP, how those resources have developed over time, and the benefits and consequences of the firm's funding arrangement with the AFA.

The money directed by the AFA to the CLP derives from the individual contributions of AFA members. Like many other Christian grassroots organizations, the AFA is a donor-supported organization funded by direct mail and radio solicitations for funding. The average contribution to the AFA is $17, with little or no monetary support coming from foundations or large private donations. The AFA has a huge donor base including individuals who have been active members for decades. Staff often note the loyalty of their membership, stating that this faithful support is maintained by Don Wildmon's insistence on frugality and financial accountability. Members are not asked to donate more than a set number of times per year, and the AFA is not known as an organization that makes inordinate demands from its members. Members are encouraged to direct their donations to one or another of the organization's core programs. The CLP is listed as one of the key programs to which members can contribute. Additionally, a portion of general donations (those donations not directed to any one program) is set aside for the CLP's budget. In return for their contributions, members receive regular organizational newsletters and updates, as well as other materials designed to elevate their interest in social issues. The CLP contributes legal updates to these organizational newsletters an average of one month out of the year. It also publishes *The Christian Lawyer,* its own monthly newsletter sent out to supporters and volunteers nationwide.

There is little direct evidence of the amount of money spent by the AFA on the CLP. One scholar states that the budget of the CLP amounted to $750,000, or 15 percent of the AFA's annual budget in 1990.[19] In 1995, indications were that the CLP's budget had increased to over $1 million annually.[20] More recent estimates are unavailable. The AFA, citing reasons of confidentiality, is unable to release specific financial information. However, staff members indicate that the amount of financial resources available to the CLP has increased steadily over the course of its life. The steady increase in funding has occurred without expanding the number of attorneys within the firm, and without current staff expending organizational resources in an effort to acquire that funding.

Both Crampton and Green have commented on the beneficial relationship that exists between the parent organization and its law firm, noting that the costs borne by the parent are considerably greater than the portion of its budget dedicated to the firm's use. In addition, the parent also bears the institutional costs of soliciting and acquiring monetary resources. "Because we are a division of the American Family Association," says Green, "we do not have a lot of the fundraising responsibilities that some interest groups have."

We have a very streamlined organization. We do not have the type of overhead expenses that a law firm normally has, and so that money is put back into litigation itself. And we have been very fortunate to be funded largely by the AFA, with the necessary funding to litigate our cases. Our [parent] organization is frugal. They do not invest in frills, they don't spend a lot of money on fundraising, and we don't have fancy accommodations, and all that goes into litigation.

The importance of the AFA here cannot be overstated. The CLP finds itself in a unique situation relative to other New Christian Right litigating firms. It is able to maximize the use of its resources mainly because the costs of procuring resources is borne elsewhere, and it does not need to invest its time and finances into acquiring more. Additionally, the monetary resources provided by the AFA appear to be boundless. Crampton notes that the resources of the CLP have grown steadily over time, and continue to do so. Green noted that the center has never experienced a financial squeeze from the Wildmon organization.

> I have absolutely no recollection of ever having a shortage of funds to litigate any case as far as is necessary to do that. In fact it has strengthened us tremendously to know that financially we can take a case as far as necessary. I cannot think of a situation right now in which we could not take a case all the way to the United States Supreme Court and ever have any concern about finances. I am not aware of any time that there's ever been a concern for finances in our organization. And I attribute that to very fiscally responsible policies in our organization.

While this kind of arrangement might be beneficial in certain respects, there have been indications that it has caused internal friction. Ben Bull, the founding general counsel, left for the ACLJ in part because of a concern over running a law firm that is overseen by non-lawyers. Additionally, Jay Sekulow related the general impression among Christian litigators that the ACLJ model (litigators running the daily and strategic responsibilities of a firm) was attractive to many. The shift of top legal talent to the ACLJ during the 1990s, and away from firms like the AFA, indicates that this might have been the case.

Thus, the financial relationship between the AFA and the CLP might include a potential negative aspect. But, when questioned about the specifics of the center's relationship with its parent, Crampton emphasized its positive nature (funding availability, etc.) and emphatically stated that he has almost complete discretion over the firm's agenda. In particular, Green, Fahling, and Crampton noted separately that Wildmon and the AFA board of directors have little or no knowledge of the specifics of cases the firm is litigating. This provides the CLP with a significant level of autonomy. "We serve a useful function if we are ever needed for the corporate entity," says Green.

> [Wildmon has] no direct knowledge of a single case unless it is unusual and was brought to his attention. [Otherwise] he is not the kind of person to get involved in that. The board has been very supportive in that [as well]. On a quarterly basis I do come to a board meeting, and I make a presentation to the board about our cases.

AFA Vice-President Tim Wildmon confirms the notion that the CLP is given significant autonomy by the parent organization.

If they have something they really believe in we leave it to them. To be honest with you, 98 to 99 percent is at the discretion of [the general counsel] on the cases they take. And he knows there are financial ramifications and restrictions, and he uses good judgment about that.

Interestingly, there is considerable flux in resources available to the CLP, but only in the sense that there is even more money available to the firm if it requires extra resources for a particularly important case.

According to the wishes of the parent organization, the number of attorneys employed by the CLP has remained constant. However, Wildmon indicated that there is money to acquire new legal talent, and the number of attorneys was set by Green, not the parent organization, as the maximum needed to efficiently pursue the center's agenda. Generally, there are two methods by which the CLP goes about acquiring legal talent. The primary method is based on an attorney profile developed internally. Secondarily, the organization may select from its corps of more than 400 volunteer attorneys. The present team of AFA attorneys has been together for about ten years. Of the six attorneys presently on staff, three were members of Regent Law School's first graduating class. However, there is no developed pipeline from Regent Law School to the CLP, as is the case with other organizations. There is some overlap between the two methods of acquisition. Benjamin Bull hired Bruce Green as an associate counsel based on his match with the organization's profile and also because of his participation as a volunteer attorney. Upon Bull's departure, Green quickly hired Brian Fahling out of a firm in Seattle. Although Fahling and Green were acquainted in law school, Fahling's experience as a trial attorney made him an immediate asset to a group deprived of the general counsel who also acted as its trial specialist.

The CLP uses its network of volunteer attorneys in much the same way as the American Center for Law and Justice—it identifies cases in various jurisdictions in part through its volunteers and then manages those cases while volunteers act as second chair local counsel. Green noted several reasons why he did not rely on volunteer attorneys to pursue local actions in the manner of the Rutherford Institute.

Our volunteer attorneys are normally used not to litigate under the name of the CLP by themselves, but to assist as local counsel. We do that for a number of reasons. One is, there are so many willing to assist, so it is not difficult to find lawyers. But they specialize in estates or personal injury or insurance defense. We don't want to be put in a situation where you deal with rather technical constitutional issues and they would not think that they were prepared. So very fine lawyers, our experience has been. Ours are very good lawyers, but they are used as local counsel as a general rule.

Within this network of volunteers is a core group that participates more consistently than other volunteers. Yet, the CLP would not consider allowing even these more experienced and skilled attorneys to operate under the name of the

AFA or litigate cases without the oversight of a CLP attorney. Crampton states that he continues to use volunteers but will never turn a case over to local counsel. Any arguments made in court or on brief are generated by the CLP and not by local counsel. The CLP has broken off relationships with local attorneys who are unwilling to work under the CLP's guidance.

Strategizing Like a Serpent: The CLP's Litigation Agenda

In this section, I turn to a discussion of the CLP's litigation agenda, or the things it does to pursue its objectives for policy influence, particularly through litigation. Below, I provide a general overview of the CLP's litigation agenda, paying particular attention to internal and external limitations placed on litigation activities. This overview includes a general summary of both litigation and litigation-related activities such as negotiation, mediation, and public policy initiatives undertaken by the organization. Next, I consider various issue areas that make up the CLP's litigation agenda, exploring these areas in light of the CLP's involvement in significant cases. Finally, I turn to an in-depth analysis of trends in CLP litigation participation including its strategic and issue-area emphases.

Internal and External Limitations on Litigation

A notable characteristic of the CLP's litigation agenda is the limitations placed on it both internally and externally. These limitations take three forms—the organization limits its agenda to cases involving governmental action, it engages in very little *amicus curiae* activity, and a large portion of its work is not reflected in the public record of litigation. First, the CLP limits litigation against private employers. It will consider pursuing a Title Seven case, involving religious discrimination by a private entity, but only under unusual circumstances. The organization often takes action against municipalities, and defends them less frequently (for example, when sexually oriented business zoning ordinances are challenged in court). Thus, the mission of the CLP to defend the rights of believers in the public sphere is reflected directly in limitations it places on its own litigation agenda.

Second, the group rarely uses its resources for *amicus* work. The center is dedicated to trial-oriented litigation and pursues cases providing the best opportunity to use developed expertise in a defined set of issue areas. Largely, these areas include First Amendment issues of free expression (usually taking the form of abortion protestation cases) and free exercise, as well as litigation in the area of family values—an amalgam of issues including pornography, textbook disputes, religion in school, and other related sub-areas. However, participation as *amicus* does not figure prominently in the CLP's strategy for litigating in these areas. In 1998, when asked if the center would participate as *amicus* in a case where a municipality preferred to use its own counsel, Green reiterated the group's commitment to litigation sponsorship and its policy to refuse any requests for *amicus* participation.

> Typically because of the difficulty of those kinds of cases we believe we can be of best assistance if we come in and direct the litigation. Actually litigate a very aggressive manner to defend the rights of those municipalities and that we are much more help that way than in the *amicus* work itself. Normally we would seek lead counsel.

This policy remains largely unchanged. In fact, the CLP has done less *amicus* work since Green's departure in 1998 than it did beforehand. Thus, the CLP limits its policy impact to those cases in which circumstances allow it to participate fully in litigation. As the CLP has begun cooperating more formally with other New Christian Right firms, its insistence on participating as case sponsor has remained consistent. It believes that, as the lead trial-oriented firm among New Christian Right Litigators, it is best placed to handle trial-level litigation, particularly in the recent series of gay marriage and gay rights cases. In these cases, the CLP, Liberty Counsel, and other firms have formalized an agreement to cooperate at all stages and to share resources, coordinate arguments, and offer general support across jurisdictions.

Finally, the CLP's litigation agenda is not completely or accurately reflected in the record of its trial and appellate participation because of the high rate of settlement it incurs. While this is true of the Liberty Counsel and ACLJ, it is particularly noteworthy for the CLP. Various aspects of the center's agenda are absent from the public record of litigation, including many conflicts it has successfully mediated and the occasions in which it has assisted local governments with public policy initiatives. CLP attorneys note that the vast majority of the conflicts in which they become involved are dispensed through negotiation, transmittal of a demand letter, or settled out of court after a lawsuit is filed. Since these suits do not appear among the list of cases the CLP has litigated, a large part of the firm's litigation behavior is excluded from direct consideration. However, Fahling stated that the center becomes involved in more than 100 cases each year that are concluded before going to trial. These cases are referred to the center by the parent organization[21] or other conservative litigating groups.

Both Crampton and Fahling note the significant addition to the workload because of these cases, and Bruce Green provided an example of such a situation that arose immediately before our interview.

> I got a call before I came to meet you and a woman said that she was not allowed to have a Christian activity in a local public park. She has what we consider a drop-dead date where the activity is scheduled and she has been told she can't do that. Those are the kinds of things that we seek injunctive relief for— we're not seeking financial damages, we deal with Constitutional rights. . . . [Writing a demand letter is] a very common practice. I don't know any group that would want to litigate against municipalities or the states, or anyone. All of

them that I know are interested in the rights of their clients and if they can discuss it, if they can send in a demand letter to generate some discussion, if they can even use the telephone to resolve a matter prior to litigation, it's less expensive, less troublesome, much more civil.

Mediation and Negotiation

The CLP's general policy is to stay out of court and avoid litigation where possible. Fahling also notes that in many cases where the CLP does file suit, the conflict is negotiated to a resolution in a matter of days, and certainly before any scheduled hearings. However, Green notes that writing demand letters has a second important purpose.

> We use the demand letter approach in order to resolve matters and to avoid litigation. But, we also use it to identify those government entities that are set in concrete, that need litigation to keep them from infringing on rights. It serves a dual purpose.

The policy of approaching conflicts with the intent not to litigate assists the CLP to identify those parties that require more aggressive treatment in the courts.

Other cases do involve the initial stages of a lawsuit but are settled after litigation has commenced. While the CLP has become involved in literally hundreds of such cases, they also fail to be reflected in their trial and appellate record. Most receive little notice from the news media. However, in 1999, Fahling's suit against the City of Fountain Valley, California, on behalf of an immigrant church generated considerable press. This case is an excellent example of the kind of governmental action that prompts an aggressive response from the CLP. It is also an example of an important event for the organization that fails to find its way into case law books.

In July 1999, the City of Fountain Valley cited the Shalom Alliance Church, consisting of largely Chinese immigrant and urban membership, for violation of a city commercial zoning ordinance prohibiting worship by groups of fifty persons or fewer within city limits. The inspector issuing the citation was quoted as saying, "If it were any other type of meeting of less than 50 people, there would be no problem. It's that the church is actually conducting worship there that is the problem. City code expressly prohibits worship from being conducted outside the areas defined as residential in our city."[22] The ordinance, among four other zoning ordinances to generate legal challenges in Southern California over the last several years, prohibited churches while allowing lodges and fraternal organizations to meet within commercial limits. The citation issued by the city included provisions for imprisonment and a $1,000 fine per day if the church did not "immediately cease to operate church services or bible study sessions at this facility."[23]

The pastor's efforts to dissuade the city from enforcing the citation did not result in a change in policy, so he called the American Family Association. Fahling reflected that the "statement [by the city inspector] was so palpable, it warranted our investigation." He filed suit against the city alleging the zoning ordinance involved content-based discrimination against religious speech, and he requested a restraining order, compensation for litigation expenses, and damages in the amount of $10 for injury to parishioners' constitutional rights.[24] The response from the city was immediate. City attorneys quickly drafted a new land use policy that did not include prohibitions against religious speech and assembly. City officials were quoted as noting the important role churches play in the community and the unintended and unconsidered consequence for speech that the ordinance created. Ultimately, the case was settled out of court after the new ordinance was instituted.

This situation involved a significant outlay of resources by the CLP. The center committed its chief litigator to clients on the other side of the country and bore the costs of using local counsel, filing the suit, and negotiating an outcome with the city. Both Fahling and DePrimo state that situations such as this one are characteristic of what the CLP does on a daily basis. Its litigation agenda is national, often involving the actions of municipalities, and in most cases these conflicts are resolved outside of the courtroom.

Public Policy Initiatives

A second aspect of CLP behavior related to its litigation agenda is its involvement in public policy initiatives. The center's involvement in public policy initiatives has been substantial. "We've helped draft the language for a referendum on partial birth abortion in Washington State and in Arizona," says Fahling.

> In West Virginia we worked on legislation that allows the state legislature to stop public institutions from supporting certain kinds of advocacy—in this case an advocacy program developed for homosexuality based on a social justice policy at West Virginia University. Here in Tupelo County, I drafted a county provision that kept homosexuals from obtaining special rights, or being categorized as gender or race. Not just homosexuality either, any other sub-group claiming special rights. I've also participated in drafting guidelines for curriculum to allow school districts if they want to teach competing theories to evolution, and also scientific theories challenging evolution.

Public policy initiatives are a component of what the CLP does but also remain largely excluded from the record of its involvement. In particular, the CLP's involvement with municipalities is notable. "One of the things we've done historically," Green acknowledged, "is to assist municipalities with the enactment of ordinances designed to defend against possible secondary effects of sexually oriented business."

> So we assist with drafting and the enactment process itself, the fact-finding, the

entire process of enacting ordinances in that area—[developing] model ordinances, site plans, etc. But, we go beyond that to give the municipality that is
pretty unseasoned at this some help. We have even sent lawyers out and walked
them through the process of how you accumulate your data. How you go about
your fact-finding, and exactly how to see that process through the enactment itself.

The CLP is deeply involved in various other public policy areas. It assists
local officials and AFA members with ordinances that ban benefits for governmental employees involved in same-sex relationships. Additionally, the center
has been consulted on ordinances that limit legal penalties for those who choose
not to do business with gays, relying on religious convictions. Where able, the
CLP works directly with municipal governments to draft such policies. However, where it has met with resistance from local governments, it has worked to
support local groups sponsoring ballot initiatives. Green notes that same-sex
marriage ordinances are a growing segment of the center's work. As noted
above, the CLP is also available to litigate on behalf of cities when these ordinances are challenged. Such services are offered free of charge to municipalities,
as to all CLP clients. However, Fahling states that the instances are very low in
which the CLP has assisted in the drafting of a model ordinance and then defended that ordinance in court.

Another public policy area in which the CLP has invested significant resources is partial birth abortion. Its most intense involvement came during the
1998 election season when the CLP assisted in drafting a referendum that appeared on the ballot in Washington State. Although the issue failed, the CLP
was largely responsible for developing the legal rationale for such initiatives—
the Inevitable Delivery Theory.

Inevitable Delivery Theory suggests that the partial birth procedure can be
distinguished from those procedures protected under current abortion policy.
Advocates maintain that, while the Court has abandoned much of *Roe*'s logic,
the definition of abortion has remained relatively constant, applying to procedures to abort a fetus in utero. "It occurred to us that something different is happening here," says Fahling.

[The partial birth procedure] is not abortion. Everybody kept calling it abortion,
keeping it in a realm in which we couldn't win. We can't win in the abortion
debate, we lose every time. But, what they were trying to prescribe was not
abortion because something distinct was happening. Using *Roe* and *Casey*, we
argue that it is not abortion because all the jurisprudence and all the medicine
and science says abortion occurs *in utero*. As soon as the amniotic sack is rup-
tured, there is the onset of birth. Live or dead we don't know, but it will be a
birth. It occurred to us that we moved from an *in utero* termination of a pregnancy to a monumental medical, and now legal, event. All the Supreme Court
jurisprudence up to this date beginning with *Roe* had only contemplated one
thing. The language is unmistakable and that is *in utero* destruction of the fetus.

The CLP and like-minded organizations appear to be gaining ground in this area after a series of early defeats. The ballot initiative that failed in Washington State went on the ballot as a "Partial Birth Infanticide" ban. Fahling acknowledge that the name itself may have had something to do with the narrow defeat of the measure. However, the AFA and organizations including the Family Research Council have had success in convincing legislatures to pass similar bans and getting initiatives on the ballot in states that fail to do so. In September 1999, Missouri and Virginia passed partial birth bans after intense lobbying from conservative groups, with Missouri's Democrat-controlled House and Senate overriding the veto of its Democratic governor. Despite these victories, partial birth bans do not appear to withstand judicial scrutiny when challenged in court. To date, ten state laws have been challenged, and all have lost in the initial stages of litigation. [25] Debates in the U.S. Congress have proceeded on the assumption that what is being banned is a type of abortion. Fahling holds the National Right to Life (NRL) responsible. "Unfortunately, others in the Religious Right in Congress have adopted the National Right to Life's position that partial birth abortion is abortion."

> Our theory is inevitable birth theory—it's not abortion. You could have constructed a legislative record on that. But, the NRL has screwed it up in my estimation, so profoundly as to exceed the capacity of words to describe. But, that is an example of how we examine things creatively, blending law, history, science, and medicine.

Abortion Protestation

A hallmark of the CLP's litigation agenda is defending abortion protesters. Its commitment to them is longstanding and is part of the reason the CLP exists. The vast majority of cases in which the CLP has participated as case sponsor at trial and on appeal are abortion protestation cases. It is one of only two New Christian Right litigating firms to directly challenge the constitutionality of the Freedom of Access to Clinic Entrances (FACE) act.[26] Furthermore, although it eventually broke ties with Randall Terry, the CLP was the counsel of record in cases brought against Operation Rescue, at one time the most prominent anti-abortion protest organization in the country.

The CLP represented several abortion counselors accused of violating the FACE act. The CLP's participation in *U.S. v. Vasquez* marked the beginning of its reputation among conservative Christian litigators as one of the premier trial firms in the movement. The CLP represented two of the defendants in a trilogy of cases filed in Connecticut Federal District Court.[27] The suit was brought jointly by the Connecticut attorney general's office and the U.S. Department of Justice—the first time national and state governments joined together to prosecute persons alleged to have violated the FACE act. Video of the defendants, Carmen Vasquez and Bobby Riley, showed them speaking to several individuals. These conversations took place outside a court-imposed buffer zone around a Hartford abortion clinic. The defendants argued that their speech, leafleting, and other activities (including providing food, money, and diapers to a women's shelter) were protected speech under the First Amendment. The cases were in litigation for two years, with a trial lasting six months. During that time, the CLP expended vast resources in defense of their clients, overseeing depositions and the trial from rented property in Connecticut, and flying their attorneys between Tupelo, Mississippi, and Hartford, Connecticut.

According to Green, the Justice Department cooperated with the Connecticut attorney general in an effort to expand the reach of the FACE act to cover behavior that had been previously protected—leafleting and counseling of patrons prior to entering an abortion clinic.

> We thought that case was very important because of its test case scenario. Also [it represented] the most outrageous abuse of prosecutorial power we ever seen. Not only for that reason, but it was a defining case for us as far as developing the skills and abilities to litigate in the biggest cases, in most hostile context with a small group of attorneys . So it was very important for us we think—in the future we can litigate that kind of context.

Brian Fahling describes the activities of the government and the CLP's strategy in litigating against the national and Connecticut governments. "Bruce identified the case right away. We all saw immediately that it would be a huge case, a defining case for us."

> So we mapped out our strategy, and our strategy was to crush the government. Which was a little odd, but having gone up there and discovered the outrageous nature of the lawsuits we needed only know the truth was on our side. Certainly reasonable minds couldn't disagree. Even people on opposite sides of the issue when the truth came out couldn't be on the opposite sides of a miscarriage of justice. And so our goal was to crush the government. That was our goal, and that's what we did through the litigation process by the grace of God.

Amid a high level of media exposure and an initially unsympathetic judge, the CLP defended its clients by arguing a First Amendment claim against a battery of state and Justice Department attorneys. It faced these formidable forces alone, only turning to its sister organizations for assistance on the state's motion to seal video evidence. Fahling ultimately convinced the judge and jury that his clients had committed no FACE violations and that FACE should not be extended to include counseling activities outside permanent buffer zones as the governments argued. The CLP's performance in this case signaled its emergence as a major player among conservative Christian litigating firms.

Following its performance in this case, the CLP has taken a series of abortion protestation cases that have resulted in favorable appellate rulings. These include *Bischoff v. Osceola County*,[28] *Lytle v. Doyle*,[29] and *Faustin v. City and County of Denver*[30] in which the CLP successfully defended protesters against state interference. In all three cases, the CLP prevailed on appeal. In *Bischoff*, the CLP defended protesters who alleged that they had been arrested by police despite following orders not to impede traffic. The CLP asked the court on appeal to determine whether other protesters who perceive the threat of legal action as a result of police conduct against these individuals involved in the protest have standing to sue where the trial court dismissed their complaint without an evidentiary hearing. Both *Lyle* and *Faustin* dealt with general protest in public places. In *Lyle*, police prevented protesters from displaying signage on a highway overpass. The Fourth Circuit struck down Virginia Code § 46.2-930 as applied to those holding such demonstrations. Similarly in *Faustin*, Denver County sheriffs prevented abortion protesters from displaying signage. The city and county alleged that the protesters violated the Denver Municipal Posting Ordinance, as well as the Colorado Outdoor Advertising Act. The CLP prevailed in both cases and continues to make defending abortion protest an integral part of its litigation agenda.

Equal Access in Schools and Public Places

While the CLP deals with many disputes over religion in schools and in public places, it finds that most of the disputes brought to it are settled before litigation commences, as the conflict with the City of Fountain Valley demonstrates. Consequently, the CLP has a less developed agenda for influencing policy in both the Church/State: Schools and Church/State: Public Places issue areas, nor does it attract high profile cases. Two cases present exceptions to the current state of the CLP's litigation agenda. The first, *Brown v. Polk County*,[31] represented one of the few instances in which a major conservative litigating organization prevailed in the 1990s by relying solely on the free exercise clause and not making an argument for protection of religiously motivated behavior as free speech. The second, *Saxe v. State College Area School District*,[32] overlapped with the gay rights issue area and dealt with the advocacy of religiously based viewpoints on homosexuality by public school students.

The CLP became involved in the Isaiah Brown case on appeal and argued it before the Eighth Circuit sitting *en banc*. Brown was fired by Polk County, Iowa, administrators for a variety of factors including "religious activities" that included beginning staff meetings with prayer and referencing his religious beliefs in statements to his subordinates. When asked to stop such activities he complied. While Brown was also disciplined (and ultimately fired) for a range of concerns including budgetary and managerial policies, Polk County officials testified at trial that the conflict over religion in the workplace played a role in the decision to fire Brown. Ultimately, the court determined that the county failed to accommodate Brown's religious beliefs in violation of federal law.

Green was particularly proud of the CLP's role in obtaining a favorable precedent, even in a limited jurisdiction, and hoped that free exercise cases might make up a greater percentage of the CLP's work.

[W]e're concerned that there have not been enough precedent-setting free exercise decisions recently. We think that is something that needs to be addressed. We think that the Ike Brown case was an important case, a precedent setting case. And it has been referred to as that and used in other jurisdictions. Now that's just the beginning. We think a lot of work needs to be done in the area of free exercise and that's an important area, and difficult area. It's one where there are not a lot of cases. But, that's one of our interests.

Although free exercise cases remain only a small part of the firm's litigation agenda, it remains committed to litigating in the area; the CLP has litigated eleven cases involving religion in public places and schools since *Brown v. Polk County*.

The *Saxe* case presented the CLP with the opportunity to pursue its goals across multiple issue areas including equal access in schools, family values, and, tangentially, gay rights. The case involved a conflict over a school district's anti-discrimination policy that prohibited speech that might be interpreted as denigrating or offensive to the hearer's sexual orientation. The plaintiffs, all professing Christians and either employees, administrators, or students, claimed that the policy had a chilling effect on their right to free speech, particularly regarding moral objections to homosexuality they might voice. Fearing punishment under the policy, they filed suit alleging that the policy was unconstitutional.

The school district prevailed at trial, and the trial court's opinion outlined a "harassment exception" to the free speech right. On appeal the CLP prevailed on the merits. The Third Circuit was unwilling to limit the speech of students or employees who raised moral objections to homosexuality, or to expand the definition of harassment to include any speech that others might find objectionable. The case was a tremendous victory for the CLP at the appellate level in a case where a school district attempted to expand the reach of speech codes far beyond both state and federal laws. The equal access component was, of course, central to this case—the CLP acted to protect the capacity of Christians to advocate a particular idea and belief publicly. But, this case is also significant because of its implications within the sexual orientation issue area. The case was finally concluded in 2000. Both Fahling and Crampton note that gay rights showed up on the CLP's radar very much earlier than on that of other New Christian Right litigators. Because of cases like this, the CLP was poised to take on the gay rights issue when conflicts over gay marriage erupted in 2003.

Gay Rights and Family Values

In the minds of CLP attorneys, the sexual orientation and family values policy sub-areas are very closely linked. Gay rights are said to threaten the institution of marriage, gay adoption to threaten the traditional family, and gay rights in education to legitimize a homosexual lifestyle in the minds of children. Fahling refers to recent actions by the Supreme Court and state courts on the issue of gay rights as "tampering with our cultural DNA."[33] However, the family values policy area contains several themes with which the CLP has become deeply involved. In effect, family values is the bread and butter of the entire AFA organization, and the CLP is deeply engaged in protecting the interests of traditional American families in a variety of contexts.

Litigation in the area of family values does not have the same broad policy content as the abortion and church/state policy areas. It does not have any particular coherent line of cases to boast, and litigating in the interests of the American family generally means pursuing actions against practices said to undermine the traditional family unit. The CLP has litigated cases involving pornography, portrayal of violence in the media, and textbook content. Of the three groups included in this study, the AFA-CLP is most active in this area. It has participated in several significant cases including a series of zoning cases and television programming disputes. However, until the recent trend in gay rights issues coming before courts, the majority of its work in the family values issue area was done outside of court, or with the threat of litigation.

The sexual orientation issue area includes a number of policy concerns relating to the legal status of gay couples. These include same-sex partner and health benefits ordinances, same-sex adoption laws, civil unions, and laws criminalizing homosexual conduct. In recent years, New Christian Right litigators have become swept up in litigation surrounding gay rights and sexual orientation. While the CLP was involved in various conflicts over gay rights as far back as 1990, these conflicts focused largely on same-sex health benefit requirements and city ordinances, or adoption laws. However, as noted earlier, with the Supreme Court's decision in *Boy Scouts of America v. Dale*,[34] gay rights began to assume an increasingly important position on the New Christian Rights litigation agenda. This was particularly true for the CLP. Beginning in mid-2003, Crampton notes that the CLP began spending between one-fourth and one-third of its time on the gay rights issue. The issue has become so central that the CLP and Liberty Counsel have recently teamed up to coordinate litigation strategy and confront gay rights issues on both coasts. Below I describe some of the events that prompted the creation of the first New Christian Right coalition to manage litigation in a particular policy area on a national scale.

Furthermore, the Supreme Court's decision in *Lawrence v. Texas*, coupled with conflicts on both coasts, brought the CLP to the front of the fray. In November 2003 and February 2004, the Massachusetts Supreme Judicial Court ruled that the state violated the Massachusetts constitution by denying civil marriage licenses to gay couples.[35] On February 12, 2004, San Francisco Mayor Gavin Newsom ordered the county to begin issuing marriage licenses to gay couples. Furthermore, the mayor of New Paltz, New York, began the same practice, as did the cities of Ashbury Park, New Jersey, and Seattle, Washington.[36] At around this time, the CLP and Liberty Counsel entered into their mutually supportive agreement to coordinate litigation on gay rights. These two organizations filed suit to halt issuance of marriage licenses to gay couples in San Francisco, are participating in the cross-complaint filed by the city against the State of California, and filed suit against the mayor of New Paltz. While they were unsuccessful in their efforts to restrain Newsom, they did achieve some measure of victory when a judge halted issuance of marriage licenses to gay couples in the New Paltz case.

The slew of litigation after the *Lawrence* and *Goodridge* decisions resulted because neither resolved the issue of gay marriage or of the national legal status of gay couples. In fact, the *Lawrence* decision came under immediate attack in the Kansas Court of Appeals,[37] revealing that there is considerable conflict within the courts over how to resolve the issue legally. An amendment, proposed by President Bush, would ban gay marriage but allow states to recognize the legal status of gays through the creation of civil unions and partnerships.[38]

The CLP's response to these events included a flurry of policy statements, press releases, and letters written to the governor of California and the California Department of Justice,[39] and many statements to the media. In fact, it is difficult to find reporting on the California and New York cases that do not include statements from the CLP condemning government actions that are often supported by judicial decisions. Furthermore, the CLP issued a statement, authored by Fahling, in support of the Federal Marriage Amendment. That policy statement asserts in part that heterosexual marriage is antecedent to law and is something that law must recognize as biologically part of a natural order. "Marriage, like life itself, was not created by government," Fahling writes.

> Our Constitution, through the Fifth and Fourteenth Amendments, affirmatively protects life because the Founders were painfully aware that governments in every age and culture have demonstrated a willingness to deny the right to life. The definition of marriage, however, has never been questioned—until now. There *was* no need or thought about affirmatively protecting the definition of marriage in the Constitution because no government in any age or culture had tampered with the essence of marriage—the indispensable necessity of male-female union.[40]

Because such statements raise the ire of gay rights activists and have led to a flurry of accusations, both Crampton and Fahling felt compelled to defend themselves. "I hope that as often as we have noted before—our obligatory disclaimer—it isn't personal with us," Crampton stated. "We really don't have ill will against those engaging homosexuality," says Fahling.

> But, this is an important issue, and there is such a total identification and almost a desperate way that homosexual activists are caught up in the lifestyle and it does define them in a way that any other issue does not. There is a level of debate and the level of violent response to a position that is principled. When you challenge homosexuality as a legitimate lifestyle choice, or make any challenge to the legitimacy of it, those remarks are treated as animus on the level with racism. There is an effort to place homosexuality on the level of race or any other cultural attachment. And it is not. It is not something indelibly imprinted, like race. It is a matter of choice of conduct. Like choosing to cheat on your wife.

Although it has developed crucial ties to other New Christian Right firms in

the process of litigating gay rights cases, the CLP's has experienced mixed re-
sults in court. The organization met with some success in California and New
York. However, along with the Liberty Counsel and Thomas More Law Center,
it was unable to halt the legalization of gay marriage in Massachusetts after the
Goodridge decision. In the *Largess* case (discussed in detail in chapter 1), the
CLP and Liberty Counsel filed suit in federal district court, arguing that the
Massachusetts Supreme Court's decision denied the people of Massachusetts a
republican form of government under Article IV, section 4 of the U.S. Constitution. Mat Staver of the Liberty Counsel was quoted as saying, "We will argue
that the Massachusetts Supreme Judicial Court exceeded its power when it redefined marriage from the 'union of one man and one woman' to the 'union of two
persons.'"[41] Crampton stated in a CLP press release, "The people of Massachusetts have been deprived of their constitutional right to a republican form of
government." The press release went on to state the goal for bringing such an
unusual argument to the courts.

> The federal lawsuit alleges that the Massachusetts Supreme Judicial Court,
> when it purported to redefine the institution of marriage in Massachusetts to in-
> clude same-sex partners, usurped the authority of the legislative branch in such
> a drastic way as to deprive the people of Massachusetts a republican form of
> government—the form of government that is guaranteed to all states by Article
> IV, section 4 of the United States Constitution. Brian Fahling, CLP senior trial
> attorney, said, "when the court legislated same-sex 'marriage' last year in the
> Goodridge case, it removed all pretense that Massachusetts is a government of
> the people, by the people, and for the people; now, it is government by oligar-
> chy." "Unelected judges legislating social policy" said Fahling, "is not a repub-
> lican form of government, it is tyranny by another name.[42]

Although the federal district court forcefully rejected the arguments presented
by the coalition of New Christian Right litigators, the value of such a coalition
was made apparent to Crampton. "This case," he stated "is illustrative of how
closely our groups are working together:"

> [The] CLP provided the legal theory and argument for the Art. IV, sec. 4 claim,
> Thomas More provided the client, Liberty Counsel prepared the pleadings and
> will argue the case, and the American Center for Law & Justice and their cli-
> ents will be joining our lawsuit today or tomorrow.[43]

The CLP's Litigation Participation

In this section, I examine trends within the CLP's litigation agenda. I begin with
a general examination of litigation participation over time, jurisdiction, preferred
litigation method, and issue area. Next, I examine CLP litigation in federal
court. Finally, I examine its use of case sponsorship and the test case strategy, or
sponsoring the same case across jurisdictions until its final adjudication, some-

times before a court of last resort. The analysis of trends in CLP litigation demonstrates that the organization remains true to its mission to defend believers' rights in society and to litigate issues affecting the American family. However, the CLP's goal of effecting policy change occurs within a limited jurisdictional scope.

Participation by Year, Jurisdiction, and Strategy Type

Table 4.1 reveals the frequency of the CLP's litigation involvement over time and by jurisdiction. Row totals show the raw amount of CLP litigation (i.e., the number of times it has participated in litigation for each year of its existence). No clear trend emerges in the frequency of the CLP's litigation efforts, and its litigation participation in each year remains relatively low. There are various explanations for this. First, the CLP claims to litigate primarily in trial courts. Decisions rendered by trial-level courts tend to be published and reported to case law databases with less regularity than decisions rendered by appellate courts. It is possible that data for CLP participation at lower court levels is missing and its participation is under-reported. However, while the CLP appears not to have compiled a list of all its litigation participation, it offers an explanation of its own for the low number of reported instances that it has participated in litigation. This explanation, developed above, regards the vastly greater number of instances that it resolves matters out of court as opposed to participating in an adjudicated resolution through a full trial. Although the number of litigated cases remains low for the CLP, it resorts to litigation quite frequently as a means toward resolving disputes outside the judicial process.

Table 4.1 also shows instances of CLP litigation by jurisdiction. Several interesting trends emerge. While the AFA is organized as a trial-oriented law firm, it litigates before U.S. Courts of Appeal frequently. Excluding those Supreme Court cases in which the AFA participated as *amicus* during its early history, more than 47 percent of all cases litigated by the CLP were filed in appellate courts. The CLP's claims to litigate primarily in federal courts are sustained by the data, with almost 80 percent of all cases falling in either federal district courts of federal courts of appeal.

In table 4.2 I explore CLP litigation by year and type of participation. Table 4.2 shows that the primary and preferred method of participation by the CLP is case sponsorship. In 72 percent of all recorded instances, the center participated as case sponsor. Moreover, as will be shown later, the bulk of instances in which the CLP participated as sponsor occurred in federal court cases—twenty in U.S. Courts of Appeal and twenty-three in U.S. District Courts. The CLP engages in one other type of participation. Table 4.2 reveals that the center has participated as *amicus*, particularly in early stages of its existence. However, while the center has consistently engaged in case sponsorship since 1992, instances of *amicus curiae* participation have declined since 1998, and the organization did not participate as *amicus* at all from 2001 to present. This is consistent with Crampton and Fahling's account of CLP preferences in carrying its message to the courts. Furthermore, as noted above, the CLP most often declines to participate as *amicus* even where it is invited and where that is its only option for participating. Finally, the CLP has never participated as Counsel on Brief. Given its emphases, it is not strange that this form of participation has little appeal for the CLP. It clearly prefers to maintain control of the case itself and rarely works with other organizations. As we have seen, this may be changing in the near future as the CLP begins coordinating litigation with other New Christian Right litigating firms.

Trends in Participation Rates across Issue Areas

Tables 4.3 and 4.4 examine AFA participation in various issue categories. More than other firms, the CLP has been called upon to represent its parent organization in court. Thus, inclusion of cases in which the AFA was a party posed a problem for categorization. Since these cases involved important policy questions (and each case fit clearly into one category), I have included them in the analysis. These cases boost the number of instances where the CLP acted as case sponsor and add to the family policy category. However, since defending the parent organization in court is a significant component of the CLP's mission, to exclude these cases would limit the analysis significantly.

In this discussion of tables 4.3 and 4.4, I examine category (column) totals, trends in issue participation across type of participation and over time, and other characteristics of CLP issue involvement. Table 4.3 shows CLP issue participation over time. Column totals demonstrate where the AFA invests its energy and resources, and which issue areas are most crucial to fulfilling the mission of the organization. Clearly, Abortion: Protest, and Family Policy issue areas are most significant, followed by both church/state issues. Until 2000, the CLP did not participate in an abortion rights case after filing *amicus* briefs in three Supreme Court cases during the early 1990s.[44] Finally, while both Green and Fahling list legal conflicts over sexual orientation among the issues that most concern their supporters, the AFA has just begun establishing a record of participation in bringing those concerns to the courts, and it is currently participating in a slew of cases on the gay marriage issue.

An examination of row entries yields a richer sense of issue-area importance, that is, what issues have been most significant to the CLP over time. Although Family Policy provides the second highest category total, the AFA appears to be litigating less and less in this issue area. Early years of the organization's existence show it litigating a significant number of family policy cases each year. Yet, in 1994 and 1995 emphasis begins to shift to the church/state issue areas and to Abortion: Protestation. The most current years show that the AFA has all but ceased to litigate directly on behalf of the American family.

When interviewed, CLP attorneys indicated that family policy is an important component of the CLP's work and that they prefer to take a role in formulating policies such as the anti-pornography, zoning, and partial birth Infanticide provisions described above. However, that the CLP is currently involved in little family policy litigation is a most surprising finding, given the emphasis on pro-family policies within the parent organization and the stated goal of the CLP to protect the parent organization in court. When the AFA has been threatened with litigation, its efforts to influence policy in the area of family values have provoked those conflicts. Obviously, the AFA is no longer threatened regularly with suits that end in a trial. The center, having served its initial purpose of discouraging lawsuits against the Wildmon organization, has now moved on to other issues.

Table 4.4 reveals that the CLP is most consistently in court to represent the interests of abortion protesters and less consistently there over church/state issues. This table also reveals an interesting contrast between Family Policy and Abortion: Protestation issue areas. While both make up a significant portion of the CLP's agenda, the CLP pursues the goal of defending abortion protesters almost exclusively through case sponsorship, while the bulk of CLP involvement in the Family Policy issue area has come in the form of *amicus* participation. While table 4.3 revealed a rather irregular use of the courts by the CLP in the Church/State: Schools and Church/State: Public Places issue areas, table 4.4 shows that this participation has come in the highest form of involvement—case sponsorship.

The CLP's participation in litigating the Isaiah Brown case, and Green's comments that the organization would continue to seek precedent setting free exercise cases, suggests that it would litigate more regularly in the issue area. However, while it continues to find cases in which to participate, the center is not as consistent in making its policy goals known in court. It should also be noted that many cases in all of the most central CLP issue areas are settled outside of a courtroom. One example of the CLP's commitment to resolving disputes is that used above to illustrate exactly this point. The California local church-zoning ordinance challenged by the CLP did not end with a judicial decision on the merits of the immigrant church's claim. However, the CLP was particularly active in effecting a changed policy in that community—behavior that does not appear as an instance of litigation participation on the part of the CLP.

Table 4.5 examines only the sixty instances in which the CLP participated in federal court cases. These instances represent 88 percent of all recorded CLP litigation participation. The table divides these instances by jurisdiction, and each jurisdiction is examined according to participation type and issue area. Comparison of row totals (participation type) across jurisdictions confirms that (excluding the early Supreme Court *amicus* work) case sponsorship is the CLP's preferred method for litigating, particularly in federal court. Furthermore, the overwhelming majority of all sponsored cases (forty-three of forty-seven total) occurred in federal court. Notably, for a firm that professes a trial orientation, the CLP sponsored almost as many cases at the appellate level as it did in federal district courts. The fact that almost 41 percent of all CLP-sponsored cases occur at the federal appellate level, and that these cases make up almost 30 percent of all instances of CLP litigation participation, is significant. The CLP is more involved in appellate work than even its chief counsel conceived. Thus, a multi-faceted examination of the CLP's litigation agenda suggests the possibility that the goal of effecting precedent may carry almost the same weight within the CLP as defending believers' rights through trial-level litigation.

The CLP's Continuing Litigation

Table 4.6 outlines the CLP's appellate-level litigation agenda more closely by examining continuing litigation, defined here as participation in a case through the trial and appeals process. Very little of the CLP's litigation agenda represents a continuing commitment to litigate across jurisdictions. Of the sixty-eight instances of CLP litigation examined, only fifteen (or just over 22 percent) were part of a process of litigation across jurisdictional levels. The bulk of these involved litigation from trial to appellate courts with no further attempt at higher review.

Two aspects of CLP continuing litigation are not present in table 4.6. First, the CLP has made several appearances in appellate court in which they have contested specific aspects of a trial case or trial court ruling. Most notably, this occurred in the Connecticut FACE Act trilogy cases. However, upon appellate review these decisions were remanded back to district court for further action, and no appeal on the merits emerged out of any of these cases. Second, the CLP made several "multiple appearances" at the appellate level which are not reflected in table 4.6. This occurs when an organization returns to argue a case before the same court on several different issues, which a court deals with in separate opinions. Since these multiple appearances do not involve litigation across jurisdictions, they do not appear in table 4.6.

While case sponsorship accounts for almost 55 percent of the CLP's federal appellate participation,[45] in only six out of thirty-six total instances of appellate participation did the CLP appear in a case in which it had participated at trial. So, for example, it is worth noting that in its most profound appellate victory (*Brown v. Woodland Joint ISD*) the CLP did not participate at trial. Thus, the case does not count as part of a strategy of continuing litigation, did not provide the AFA with the opportunity to control or contribute to the court record at trial, and does not appear in table 4.6.

What does appear in table 4.6 are six cases that have been crucially important to the CLP in pursuit of its goal to defend believers. Three cases involve the Abortion: Protestation issue area. In two of these three cases the CLP successfully defended protest activities from government regulation.[46] In a fourth case, the CLP defended a group of individuals who protested the Walt Disney Company's alleged support of homosexuality through an unofficial "gay days" celebration at Walt Disney World in Florida. The CLP litigated the *Saxe* case, which overlapped the Church/State: Schools and Sexual Orientation issue areas. Finally, the CLP litigated against the city council of San Francisco and, after losing on appellate, requested Supreme Court review. The case involved a resolution and two ordinances passed by the city condemning a public ad campaign encouraging homosexuals to renounce homosexuality. While unsuccessful at trial and on appeal, the CLP made free expression the centerpiece of this case. Among all the cases listed, the CLP actions exhibited the most depth of involvement and also account for its one loss among the list. Thus, while the CLP's agenda of continuing litigation is limited, where it has sponsored cases across jurisdictions it has been extraordinarily successful.

Conclusion: Organizational Life and Culture

This chapter has surveyed the internal organizational characteristics and external actions of the CLP that will be used in later analyses to compare it to other New Christian Right law firms. In analyzing the CLP, I have investigated internal organizational culture, goals, structure and resources, litigation emphases, and behavior. The CLP identifies policy influence as its primary aim and acknowledges the importance of other goals for achieving its aims in court. The organization is also deeply involved in the formulation of policy—crafting zoning ordinances for municipalities that wish to regulate sex-related business and partial birth abortion initiatives. Furthermore, the analysis reveals an organization that at first blush appears to advocate ideas comporting more closely with a traditional understanding of New Christian Right ideologies, issue positions, and guiding principles than with those of its fellow litigators. CLP attorneys have adopted patterns of viewing social conflict that place significantly less emphasis on the open, tolerant, and liberal view of civil rights and equal access adopted by other New Christian Right litigators.

The litigation agenda of the CLP differs significantly from that of other movement litigators, including the other two incorporated into this study. Despite almost unlimited resources, a steadily growing monetary base, and increased staff support, the CLP does not pursue a case sponsorship strategy that would indicate deep involvement in litigation. Nor is it increasing its levels of involvement over time. The differences in internal culture and litigation agendas among the three groups suggests that perhaps the CLP's internal culture limits its ability to engage the courts. Perhaps it litigates only those issues on which it can prevail, or refuses to take cases in which it knows judges will not show sympathy to its arguments. As with the Liberty Counsel and the ACLJ, the story of the CLP mirrors the central social conflicts of present-day American culture. The struggle between liberal tolerance and religious conviction is at the heart of those issues most closely associated with the CLP's mission. But, for example, while other New Christian Right firms face a challenge to the internal consistency of their logic on openness, tolerance, and equal access (a challenge largely brought about by the gay rights issue), the CLP faces little internal turmoil. The difficulties it faces have much more to do with the kind of influence it can hope to assert on policy in the future.

Table 4.1. CLP Litigation by Year and Jurisdiction

Year	USSC	SSC	USCA	USDC	SCA	SCO	Other	Total
1989	2	0	0	0	0	0	0	2
1990	4	0	0	0	0	0	0	4
1991	1	0	1	1	0	0	0	3
1992	0	0	1	4	0	0	0	5
1993	0	0	4	0	0	0	0	4
1994	1	2	0	2	0	0	0	5
1995	0	0	3	3	0	0	0	6
1996	0	0	6	0	1	0	0	7
1997	0	0	1	1	0	0	0	2
1998	0	1	3	1	0	0	0	5
1999	0	0	1	4	0	0	0	5
2000	1	0	4	3	0	0	0	8
2001	0	0	1	5	0	0	0	6
2002	0	0	1	1	0	0	0	2
2003	0	0	2	2	0	0	0	4
2004	0	0	0	0	0	0	0	0
Total	9	3	28	27	1	0	0	68

Source: Lexis/Nexis Legal Database

Note(s) : USSC =United States Supreme Court; SSC =State Supreme Court;

USCA =United States Court of Appeal; USDC =United States District Court

SCA =State Court of Appeal; SCO= State Court of Origin

Table 4.2. CLP Litigation by Year and Type

Year	Sponsorship	On Brief	Amicus	Total
1989	0	0	2	2
1990	0	0	4	4
1991	1	0	2	3
1992	4	0	1	5
1993	2	0	2	4
1994	3	0	2	5
1995	5	0	1	6
1996	5	0	2	7
1997	2	0	0	2
1998	3	0	2	5
1999	5	0	0	5
2000	7	0	1	8
2001	6	0	0	6
2002	2	0	0	2
2003	4	0	0	4
2004	0	0	0	0
Total	49	0	19	68

Source: Lexis/Nexis Legal Database

Table 4.3. CLP Participation by Year and Issue Area

Year	Church/State Schools	Church/State Public Places	Abortion Protestation	Abortion Rights	Sexual Orientation	Family Policy	Other	Total
1989	0	0	0	1	0	1	0	2
1990	0	0	0	2	0	2	0	4
1991	0	0	0	0	0	3	0	3
1992	0	0	0	0	0	5	0	5
1993	2	0	0	0	0	2	0	4
1994	1	0	2	0	1	1	0	5
1995	0	3	2	0	1	0	0	6
1996	1	1	3	0	0	2	0	7
1997	0	0	1	0	0	0	1	2
1998	1	1	2	0	1	0	0	5
1999	1	0	4	0	0	0	0	5
2000	2	0	3	1	1	1	0	8
2001	1	0	2	0	2	1	0	6
2002	0	0	1	0	1	0	0	2
2003	0	0	2	1	0	1	0	4
2004	0	0	0	0	0	0	0	0
Total	9	5	22	5	7	19	1	68

Source: Lexis/Nexis Legal Database

Table 4.4. CLP Participation, 1989–2004, by Type and Issue Area

Type	Church/State Schools	Church/State Public Places	Abortion Protest	Abortion Rights	Sexual Orientation	Family Policy	Other	Total
Sponsorship	8	4	20	1	5	6	1	45
Counsel on Brief	0	0	0	0	0	0	0	0
Amicus curiae	1	1	2	4	2	9	0	19
Other	0	0	0	0	0	4	0	4
Total	9	5	22	5	7	19	1	68

Source: Lexis/Nexis Legal Database

Table 4.5. CLP Federal Court Participation by Type and Issue Area

Type	Church/State Schools	Church/State Public Places	Abortion Protest	Abortion Rights	Sexual Orientation	Family Policy	Other	Total
Supreme Court Participation								
Sponsorship	0	0	0	0	0	0	0	0
Counsel on Brief	0	0	0	0	0	0	0	0
Amicus curiae	0	0	1	4	0	4	0	9
Total	0	0	1	4	0	4	0	9
U.S. Court of Appeals Participation								
Sponsorship	4	2	9	0	2	2	1	20
Counsel on Brief	0	0	0	0	0	0	0	0
Amicus curiae	1	0	0	0	2	4	0	7
Total	5	2	9	0	4	6	1	27

Continued on next page

Note(s): Sponsorship is determined by the name of the CLP or attorney employed by the CLP listed as Attorney of Record within the published court opinion. Similarly, Counsel on Brief is determined by the Liberty Counsel or employed attorney listed as On Brief within the published court opinion, and *amicus curiae* by the same listed as *amicus*, or preparer of an *amicus* brief (e.g., for another organization) within the published court opinion.

Table 4.5—Continued

Type	Church/State Schools	Church/State Public Places	Abortion Protest	Abortion Rights	Sexual Orientation	Family Policy	Other	Total
U.S. District Court Participation								
Sponsorship	4	2	10	1	2	4	0	23
Counsel on Brief	0	0	0	0	0	0	0	0
Amicus curiae	0	0	0	0	0	1	0	1
Total	4	2	10	1	2	5	0	24

Source: Lexis/Nexis Legal Database

Table 4.6. CLP Litigation across Jurisdictions by Type, Issue Area, and Appearances

Participation	Jurisdiction	Issue Area	Appearances in Court
Case Sponsorship:			
	Trial to CLR[a] (*No cases fall into this category*)		0
	Intermediate Appellate to CLR (*No cases fall into this category*)		0
	Trial to Intermediate Appellate (petition for higher review[b] denied)		
	1) *American Family Association v. San Francisco (2002)*	Sexual Orientation	2
	Trial to Intermediate Appellate (no petition for higher review)		
	5) *Lytle v. Doyle (2003)*	Abortion: Protestation	2
	4) *Faustin v. City and County of Denver (2001)*	Abortion: Protestation	2
	2) *Bischoff v. Osceola County (2000)*	Sexual Orientation	3
	3) *Saxe v. State College Area School District (2000)*	Church/State: Schools	2
	6) *Riley v. Jackson (1996)*	Abortion: Protestation	2
Amicus curiae Participation:			
	Trial to Intermediate Appellate (petition for higher review[b] denied)		
	7) *Equality Foundation v. City of Cincinnati (1995)*	Sexual Orientation	2
		Total Appearances:	15

Source: Lexis/Nexis Legal Database

[a]CLR = Court of Last Resort; [b]Petition for higher review: Includes requests for rehearing *en banc* and petition for *certiorari*

Chapter Five

Good Lawyers, Good Christians, or Good Christian Lawyers?

Analyses of interest group legislative lobbying or grassroots mobilization activities have proposed an array of influences on interest group behavior.[1] However, they have predominantly emphasized external institutional influences on the choices groups make—the political environment, available resources, legal and policy environment, and institutional rules that limit behavior. Those who study interest group litigation have paid significantly more attention to internal motivations.[2] However, motivations are difficult to uncover, requiring significant interaction with the subjects of study and careful integration into any analysis. In this study, I seek to expand our conception of internal motivations to include consideration of belief systems as a component of research into interest group litigation. In short, I hope to demonstrate that it is worthwhile for scholars to pay attention to internal culture and belief systems in an organizational context. I propose that beliefs can help explain in part how groups develop goals and then select some behavioral options over others when attempting to accomplish their goals through litigation. This study is meant to be a tentative first step in that direction.

In this chapter, I make general comparisons among the American Center for Law and Justice (ACLJ), the Liberty Counsel, and the American Family Association's Center for Law and Policy (CLP). These comparisons are based on variables developed in previous chapters, including differences in goals, organizational structure, resources, ideology, and litigation behavior. Furthermore, since external environment is held constant in this analysis, I explore variation in the groups' internal characteristics as an explanation for differences in their litigation behavior. All three groups encounter the same politico-legal environment and demonstrate little variation in what goals they identify as primary. Yet, these three groups have taken divergent approaches to litigation. Significant differences exist in their use of the courts while pursuing long-term policy influence. How then do we sort out the various internal influences that shape what a group attempts to do in court?

I begin this chapter with a general comparison of the three groups on variables traditionally used in the study of interest groups. These include goals, organizational structure, and resources. On many of these variables, the groups exhibit little or no important differences. This would lead to a general conclusion that the groups exhibit no important differences in the behavioral choices they make. I then compare the group's litigation behavior. A close comparison of the three groups' litigation agendas reveals important differences where we would expect none. I move to a general analysis of the role religious ideology plays within each organization, its importance relative to other characteristics, and its general influence on litigation behavior. In the next section I use religious ideology to explain why the CLP behaves so differently from the ACLJ and Liberty Counsel. I explore whether the CLP's religious ideology limits its commitment to pursuing policy influence through appellate litigation. If so, in what ways does it shape the litigation agenda?

In considering a range of internal characteristics and circumstances that influence behavior, I find that religious ideology shapes the CLP's agenda, but in ways we might not understand if we did not explore the complexities of its internal environment. Religious ideology influences the organization in three important ways. First, religious ideology limits the CLP's appellate agenda, but rather than keeping the CLP out of court, it limits the arguments the CLP presents to courts when it does engage in appellate litigation. Members of the CLP must engage in a creative process that balances principles with its common practical notions approach to litigation. This process takes considerable time and energy, thus limiting the number of cases it can manage as part of an appellate agenda.

Second, the CLP's understanding of its role as Christian litigator makes it less afraid to lose cases than the other two organizations. The CLP's commitment to religious principle is vindicated when it presents courts with particular arguments and not simply when it wins cases or sets precedent. Thus, the CLP is more likely than other groups to litigate cases it will probably lose. Third, the importance of religious ideology actually enlarges the CLP's litigation agenda, but at the expense of an appellate focus. The CLP believes that all Christians caught in the toils of the law deserve its full attention and resources, not simply those whose cases raise unique policy questions. The CLP is more likely than the other two groups to engage in protracted litigation that has no real chance of exerting a broad influence on policy. These findings suggest that religious ideology reduces the proportion of appellate litigation making up the CLP's litigation agenda, but not because the CLP takes reactionary legal positions. Rather, its desire to construct creative arguments that do not compromise its principles and to serve a particular constituency as a matter of principle reduces its appellate agenda.

I conclude the chapter by considering how goal setting influences the CLP's litigation agenda. Here, the CLP's relationship with its parent organization limits what goals it can legitimately pursue. Because the parent organization handles media exposure and fundraising activities, the CLP has had difficulty building a reputation and achieving movement leadership. These two aspects of organizational life are important for attracting quality cases necessary for exerting broader policy influence. The CLP is currently developing its own program for increasing media exposure and reputation-building activities. It seeks in the future to balance its interests in broad policy influence with its desire to provide representation to its constituency.

Group Comparisons

Comparing Group Goals

A comparison of the three groups included for analysis reveals that all give primary emphasis to policy influence over any other goal, including reputation-oriented goals and media-oriented goals. However, they also note the significance of a multi-faceted approach to policy influence that involves pursuing goals across the spectrum in support of the central mission of policy influence. The American Center for Law and Justice emphasizes policy-oriented goals, while noting that increased reputation is a byproduct of policy influence. It does not emphasize litigation for purposes of developing a reputation as a specialist in First Amendment litigation. However, the ACLJ does enjoy a good reputation as a result of its policy orientation and its success before the Supreme Court. Sekulow notes the importance of media-oriented goals as necessary for attracting cases with characteristics suited for broad influence on policy.

In the past, the Liberty Counsel has emphasized education as part of its policy orientation. However, it has recently moved toward a position more congruent with the ACLJ's approach, pulling the trigger on litigation more quickly. The educational aspect of policy influence still remains, but the Liberty Counsel has begun to recognize its potential as a movement leader and to recognize that litigation is its primary avenue to a much broader influence on policy. In fact, Staver now discusses education in terms of litigation—those recalcitrant institutions that offend even settled policy are now treated to the threat of litigation almost at once. Like the ACLJ, the Liberty Counsel enjoys a solid reputation as a premier litigator for the New Christian Right and a public persona in the media. Staver recognizes the importance of reputation- and media-oriented goals. Reputation and a media focus play important supportive roles to the primary goal of the organization—litigation for policy influence. As Staver notes, both provide the context for identifying cases with the potential for broad policy influence. "If our constituents don't know, or are unaware that there is a resource and a tool for them to resolve a religious liberty issue," he says, "they aren't going to contact us. [A media presence] naturally does bring you higher quality cases."

The CLP emphasizes policy-oriented goals, but also notes an interest in maintaining its reputation as a zealous representative of its clients' interests. This concern for reputation dovetails with the CLP's desire to represent any Christian experiencing an abuse of law, and not just those in conflicts that raise interesting or unique claims. Thus, reputation is not simply a byproduct of the CLP's litigation efforts, but a real asset in approaching courts and working with sister organizations. It strives to improve its standing in the courts and within the movement. However, lately the CLP has begun to consider rebalancing its interests in policy influence with the goal of representing its constituency fully. It has recognized that a multi-faceted approach is necessary for attracting quality cases. The CLP is developing plans to elevate its reputation movement-wide by expanding its media presence.

Comparing Resources

A comparison of group resources reveals few real differences among the groups in the development of resources over time. Clearly, the ACLJ is the best-funded organization of the three. However, none is cash-starved or starved for resources in any other way. All have significant external support in the form of monetary donations. In addition, each has a relationship with a prominent leader within the New Christian Right. As a result, each receives support from that leader's other organizations in the form of offices, support staff, and intangibles such as credibility within the movement and an instant reputation by association.

An exploration of monetary resource levels reveals some differences among the groups. The ACLJ boasts a $12 million budget. Over its life, its budget has grown significantly, doubling after seven years. Beginning in 1993, the ACLJ's annual budget of $6 million grew by $2 million each year until reaching a stable $12 million per year in 1997. The organization has begun an active program to recruit large donors and instituted an endowment to secure and stabilize its financial position. The CLP has a smaller budget, but has always enjoyed stable monetary resources provided by its parent organization, as well as relief from costs normally associated with interest group maintenance such as costs for fundraising activities. In this respect, the CLP has a long history of financial stability, while other New Christian Right firms have only begun to solidify their financial position. The CLP's budget has remained constant at a generous 15 percent of its parent organization's own budget. The little direct evidence that documents the CLP's budget suggests that it has been growing steadily in proportion to the parent organization's own financial resource acquisitions, and the CLP expends little effort to acquire that money. In contrast, both the ACLJ and Liberty Counsel, despite the notion that they have Rev. Pat Robertson and Rev. Jerry Falwell respectively to fall back on, raise their money completely independent of other enterprises. Thus, the ACLJ must expend its own energy to acquire the $12 million each year that makes up its operating budget.

Several implications for the study of conservative Christian litigators emerge from this comparative analysis. First, financial stability, perhaps even more than the growth of financial resources, is a concern for these litigating firms. Each has made efforts to stabilize their financial and budgetary forecasts by developing a stable funding base. Second, each has gone about acquiring resources in very different ways. The ACLJ has used its association with Rev. Robertson to leverage its reputation as a top-flight litigation firm into a huge annual budget and stable financial situation. The Liberty Counsel has taken a similar approach to acquiring financial resources, but had also focused on acquiring legal talent and an expanded reputation through its association with Rev. Jerry Falwell. The AFA relies on the fortunes of the Wildmon organization.

Comparing Group Behavior

I move now to a direct comparison of group litigation behavior. To facilitate comparisons among the groups I examine categories of litigation behavior defined within the interest group litigation literature as commonly employed strategies for pursuing goals within the courts. This comparison centers on an examination of what strategies the three groups emphasize and how those strategies match with their stated desire for broad policy influence. Thus, in table 5.1 I have categorized various kinds of litigation participation and attempted to refine our treatment of case sponsorship in particular.

In distinguishing options for litigation behavior, I employ three decision rules. *First, where similar behaviors are distinguished only by differences in jurisdiction of the court, I order them based on judicial hierarchy.* For example, instances of case sponsorship occurring at the appellate level are distinguished from those instances occurring before trial courts. Thus, the jurisdiction of the court assists in my effort to clarify subtle differences in how groups employ litigation strategies. The use of jurisdiction as a decision rule for categorizing litigation behavior does not necessarily correspond with the level of commitment required. It is entirely possible that a group might find some litigation before a trial court more demanding than litigating the same case on appeal. However, generally speaking, the stakes become higher as a case moves through the court system, higher court decisions have greater potential impact on policy, and arguments obtain a greater degree of abstraction. It is sensible to establish separate categories of litigation involvement based on jurisdiction when seeking to clarify a group's commitment to policy influence.

Second, I distinguish participation as case sponsor based on how far the case proceeds through the court system. Epstein defines case sponsorship as initiation and management of a case by a group in an effort to guide courts toward consideration of specific legal questions.[3] Under this definition, a group will sponsor a case for the purpose of receiving a decision favorable to its position. To sponsor a case a group must invest considerable time and resources. It must commit to managing many aspects of the case, preparing and submitting pleadings, responding to the submissions of opposing counsel, researching points of law, developing legal arguments, and appearing in court to present those arguments. If a group wishes to pursue a test case strategy, it must commit to doing all of the things noted above throughout an appeals process.

The present analysis distinguishes between two types of case sponsorship. These two types are "one-shot" case sponsorship (instances where a group sponsors a case, either at trial or before an appellate court, but does not pursue the case any further or participate at other stages) and the test case strategy (instances where groups participate in the same case across jurisdictions). For the purposes of this study, I expand the traditional definitions of sponsorship and the test case strategy to reflect this difference in commitment of organizational resources. The further a case proceeds on appeal, the greater the commitment of time, energies, and other resources required from the sponsoring group. However, there are many possible levels of involvement associated with this strategy, and table 5.1 distinguishes the range of options associated with case sponsorship. These options run from "one-shot" case sponsorship before a trial or appellate court to the full test case strategy (sponsoring a case from trial to final disposition before a court of last resort). Epstein and others classify case sponsorship that is initiated after a trial court decision as an intermediate behavior. This kind of case sponsorship generally receives less weight because it reflects a lack of control over the trial court record. Control of the trial court record is necessary for a group to achieve the aim of influencing policy by obtaining a favorable ruling. Lack of such control is a threat to the group's ability to present arguments that achieve that aim.[4]

Third, I take into account petitions for higher review. Clearly, for two behavioral options (full test case strategy and case sponsorship from an intermediate appellate court to a court of last resort), an appeal for higher review was granted. However, I also distinguish cases in which a party's appeal for higher review has been denied from those in which no appeal for higher review was made. I do not consider whether the appeal for higher review came from the group under analysis or from its adversary in court. In such cases, even where the opposing party has filed the petition, a group must invest resources to present the court with an argument supporting it position to deny review.

Table 5.1 identifies two other behavioral options. A group that participates as Counsel on Brief generally works in collaboration with the group sponsoring litigation. The organization lends its expertise to that of the sponsoring group, assisting that group in framing legal questions and arguments, and perhaps even taking over certain aspects of a case. However, it does so without bearing other costs associated with litigation or appearing in court. A group may also participate as *amicus curiae*. Reasons for pursuing an *amicus curiae* strategy vary along with the amount of institutional resources committed when participating. At times, *amicus* participation requires little involvement from a group. At other times, it signals that a group is involved as deeply as circumstances allow, given that it does not represent any party in a case. An *amicus curiae* brief may be prepared and submitted for only a small proportion of what it costs to participate as case sponsor, but the outlay of time and resources varies as well. Some groups participate as *amicus* and spend very little time crafting new arguments not presented in party briefs. Other groups spend considerable time and energy crafting new arguments and coordinating arguments with other like-minded organizations.

Traditionally, scholars have equated the goal of policy influence with case sponsorship and use of the test case strategy in particular because these strategies allow a group to exert much influence on the policy output of courts. As noted above, the three groups included in this analysis define similar goals for litigation—each has noted that it has established policy-oriented goals. Thus, one would expect that the litigation behavior of these groups will not vary significantly and that they will prefer the test case strategy to other behavioral options. However, distinguishing various options within the case sponsorship category provides the opportunity to examine the nuances of group litigation behavior. The probability that a case will move from trial court to the U.S. Supreme Court is extremely low. A group that is deeply committed to achieving policy influence through litigation can reveal that commitment through other forms of case sponsorship. These forms include sponsoring a case after trial to its final adjudication before a court of last resort, sponsoring a case from trial to its final adjudication by an intermediate appellate court, or through one-shot litigation. Thus, distinguishing behavior within the case sponsorship strategy provides conceptual clarity and an opportunity to closely examine relationships between internal group characteristics and external manifestations of group behavior.

Table 5.2 displays group behavioral emphases according to type of litigation participation. The table reveals the number of recorded instances each group engaged in litigation as *amicus curiae*, Counsel on Brief, and case sponsor. Additionally, case sponsorship is broken out into two categories. The first, "one-shot" case sponsorship, is divided into sub-categories that include single instances of sponsorship occurring at the appellate ("Appellate Only") and trial ("Trial Only") levels. The second, entitled "Test Case," represents all those instances where each group has participated across any jurisdictional level in the same case. By definition, this category includes appellate participation, but may or may not include trial court participation in the same case.[5] The table also includes the percentage of total litigation participation that each number represents. From this table we see that all three groups are fairly committed to sponsorship as their preferred method for litigating. Combining all the categories of case sponsorship together, we see that the Liberty Counsel litigates the greatest percentage of cases as sponsor (76 percent), followed by the CLP (72 percent), and the ACLJ (64 percent). The ACLJ participates most as Counsel on Brief. However, as noted in chapter 2, it has not developed a pattern of participation using this behavioral option. Notably, the CLP, which emphasizes increased reputation as a secondary goal, does not use this intermediate behavioral option at all. This is unusual, given its desire to increase its reputation among sister organizations. Participation as Counsel on Brief would be one logical way to gain that reputation among its peers, yet it has avoided doing so altogether. There are indications that the CLP is developing ways of collaborating with other groups. For example, it has formed an alliance with the Liberty Counsel to coordinate litigation across the nation in gay rights cases. Furthermore, the CLP devotes more resources to *amicus* participation than its members realize. Perhaps the CLP has substituted *amicus* participation for a defined Counsel on Brief strategy as a means to gain credibility.

Table 5.2 does display something unusual about the behavioral emphases of the three groups, revealed in a comparison of the "Test Case" and "One-Shot" categories. All three groups state that their primary goal is to influence policy. Thus, we should expect that all would emphasize a test case strategy over "one-shot" case sponsorship since a test case strategy provides the greatest opportunity to exert that influence. Table 5.2 reveals that both the ACLJ and the Liberty Counsel exhibit a commitment to using the test case strategy as a significant part of their overall litigation agenda, but the CLP emphasizes the test case strategy much less than the other two groups. It uses the test case strategy 19 percent of the time as a means for effecting policy through the appellate process, a little more than one-half of the proportion that the Liberty Counsel and ACLJ devote to such participation. This difference in litigation strategies among the groups is somewhat confounding, as all the groups emphasize policy influence.

To put a finer point on this finding, in table 5.3 I extract only those instances of litigation participation falling within the "Test Case" category of table 5.2. Here, the test case category is broken out into categories representing the most involvement in an appellate process to the least. Thus, the categories include the full test case strategy (case sponsor at the trial level through to a ruling by a court of last resort), an attenuated test case strategy in which a group becomes involved in litigation after trial (intermediate appellate to court of last resort), and sponsorship at the trial level including an appeal to an intermediate court, but no further. This last category is divided into two sub-categories—those involving a petition for review by a higher court that was denied, and those where no petition for higher review was made. The first number in each cell displays the number of actual cases associated with each category, while the number in parentheses displays the number of recorded instances in which a group appeared before a court as sponsor in those cases.[6] I address each group in turn, below.

Table 5.2 reveals that for the ACLJ, the test case strategy is a significant part of its overall litigation agenda. Table 5.3 shows that it has participated deeply in cases on appeal. For example, the ACLJ has participated in twelve cases before the Supreme Court as sponsor.[7] In nine of those cases the ACLJ participated as sponsor at the trial and/or appellate levels.[8] Furthermore, in fully one-third (sixty-five) of all instances of participation, the ACLJ shepherded a case through an appeals process. These instances reflect participation in twenty-four separate court cases. Of those twenty-four, the ACLJ participated in six that moved from a U.S. District Court to the U.S. Supreme Court,[9] two in which its participation began upon appeal and then moved to the Supreme Court,[10] one that moved from state trial court to the Supreme Court,[11] and one that moved from state trial court to state court of last resort.[12] In another fourteen cases, ACLJ participation began at the trial level and ended in a U.S. Court of Appeal. The ACLJ petitioned for *certiorari* review in four of these cases (which petition was denied).[13]

An examination of the Liberty Counsel's participation reveals an organization that has employed the test case strategy but not been as fortunate in pushing cases up to the U.S. Supreme Court. The thirty-two instances of Liberty Counsel participation noted in table 5.3 represent use of the test case strategy in twelve separate cases. Thus, approximately 30 percent of all Liberty Counsel litigation involved participation across jurisdictions through an appeals process. The Liberty Counsel participated in two that moved from a state or federal trial court to the Supreme Court. However, both of these cases arrived at the Supreme Court together, were consolidated, and were heard by the Court as *Madsen v. Women's Reproductive Health Services*. They are represented in table 5.3 as one case. Eleven cases ended in an intermediate appellate court after Liberty Counsel participation at both the trial and appellate level.[14] These data suggest that the Liberty Counsel has moved beyond the formative stages of policy influence, made a strong commitment to influencing policy, and is developing its use of the test case strategy in pursuit of that goal.

For the CLP, use of the test case strategy is almost nonexistent. The CLP petitioned for *certiorari* review in one case in which it was also involved at trial. In five other cases the CLP prevailed on appeal. However, it is notable that the CLP became involved in fourteen cases after trial (these cases fall into the "One Shot" appellate litigation category of table 5.2), but despite losing a large proportion it did not apply for higher review even once.[15] While case sponsorship accounts for 72 percent of the CLP's total litigation participation, pursuit of a test case strategy accounts for only 19 percent. Furthermore, that participation falls in the two most attenuated test case categories. While previous analyses revealed that the CLP prefers case sponsorship to other forms of litigation involvement and that the CLP is before appellate courts quite often, this organization does little to engage the courts through an appeals process. Consequently, the CLP is not able to control many aspects of its litigation agenda, even where it has been successful.[16] Despite almost unlimited resources, the CLP has not developed aspects of a test case strategy that would provide the greatest opportunity to influence policy.

Culture and Religious Ideology: "In the World, but Not of It"

The surprising finding that emerges from this research is that three organizations with similar goals pursue such diverse litigation agendas. Of particular significance, the CLP does not regularly employ a test case strategy as part of its litigation agenda. Analysis of the CLP's jurisdictional emphases in chapter 4 revealed that it appears before appellate courts approximately 48 percent of the time. However, the amount of time it spends before appellate courts as part of a test case strategy is substantially less than its two compatriots. It prefers case sponsorship to other kinds of participation, but it does not continue that sponsorship through an appeals process where it has the opportunity, appealing beyond the intermediate stage only once in its history. Furthermore, the variation in litigation behavior among the groups exists where we would expect little and is not explained by appeal to external group characteristics such as funding or legal environment. Each group identifies policy influence as its primary goal, but each has taken different approaches to litigation that cannot be fully explained by variation in resources or a traditional conception of goal setting.

In his work comparing Evangelical and Catholic litigating firms, Kevin den Dulk notes that an examination of religious litigators must consider normative influences, such as religious ideology. These concerns impact the capacity of groups to engage the legal system for policy influence. Thus, when conservative Christian litigators have "[d]ifferent understandings of how to be 'in the world but not of it' . . ." conflicts can emerge in " . . . approaches to engaging the 'world' through legal advocacy."[17] In this section, I seek to explore different understandings of what it means to be a conservative Christian litigator. These different understandings ultimately influence how groups perceive their capacity to influence policy and what they define as appropriate behavior for exerting influence on court policy decisions. Below, I explore the influence of religious ideology and complexity in goal setting on groups' commitment to litigation as a tool for policy change. I explore evidence that differences in religious ideology may explain differences in litigation strategies for which traditional research cannot account. Furthermore, I explore how goal setting affects litigation behavior. I suggest that goal setting is a complex process in which groups must determine how to allocate resources among a set of goals rather than simply channeling resources to one primary objective. Some goals are primary to a group's mission, while others are secondary yet important in achieving a group's aims. A successful group is one that implements a full range of activities in furtherance of its primary goal.

Religious Ideology among the Groups

The ACLJ and Religious Ideology

I turn now to a discussion of religious ideology among the groups. In an earlier chapter, I defined religious ideology as a particular "worldview" or normative code based on religious principle that helps individuals or groups establish interpretations of social reality. Generally, religious ideology is part of an ethical belief system that guides behavioral choices for those who adhere to it. Thus, religious ideology may limit the sphere of possible alternatives for behavior and help determine what actions are appropriate in various contexts. Here, I explore the importance of religious ideology for each groups' approach to policy influence. Plainly, all three groups share common religious and ethical belief systems to which they hold fast and which are critically related to the policy goals they hope to achieve through litigation. However, differences exist in the relationship of religious principle to organizational behavior for each of the groups. I explore how each group understands the role of religious ideology in how it interacts with its legal environment.

The American Center for Law and Justice is strongly committed to further-
ing the role of the church in society. However, Jay Sekulow does not work to
overrun secular society or direct policy to a place where choices are guided on
the whole by considerations of Judeo-Christian ethics. Instead, Sekulow has a
distinct vision for his work as a litigator for the New Christian Right. He hopes
to secure a role for the church in social life. Consider Sekulow's statement concerning the interaction between religious conviction and social policy. "Abra-
ham Kaifer, and a couple of others [write] that politics is very important," he
says.

> But as important as politics is, politics never raised anyone from the dead.
> We're not going to carry the day on the culture with politics alone. It's got to
> be salt and light [a reference to the New Testament]. Our job is to keep [the]
> avenues open, make sure the church can be the church. . . . We're there to make
> sure the church's voice can be heard. Somebody said once we're Jesus' law-
> yers. Jesus doesn't need a lawyer. Jesus doesn't need Jay Sekulow, [or] the
> ACLJ. But the church does. I believe the church needs organizations that will
> defend the integrity of Christians in the public square.

The ACLJ approaches litigation with the notion that religious convictions are
entirely appropriate for social discourse and that religion should be welcomed as
one perspective among many within a pluralistic society. But, more important is
what does not appear in this statement. Sekulow jettisons the idea (commonly
advocated by New Christian Right leaders in other arenas) that the culture will
return to a state of moral purity only if our political leaders create policy based
strictly on values derived from religious principles. While these same religious
principles clearly guide the ACLJ's internal culture (they are, as Sekulow has
stated many times, principles to live by), Sekulow does not identify victory in
the culture wars as his primary concern.

Joel Thornton, Sekulow's chief lieutenant, reinforced this notion when reflecting on the status of religious freedoms in the United States. Specifically, he
addressed a case in which the ACLJ had become involved several years before—the arrest of a group of high school students during the National Day of
Prayer in 1994. This case did not result in litigation (only the threat of an ACLJ
lawsuit) and ended with a formal apology issued by the school district to the
young people involved. "The arrests at the flagpole are not indicative of what is
generally done in America, but it happened," Thornton stated. "We are not asking that the state make people come to Bible studies, or to pray on campus. All
we are asking is that the opportunity exist for people to do so, that we can be
heard." Thornton provided another more general example of the role religious
ideology plays at the ACLJ. When queried about traditional conservative
themes, such as a break down in the moral fabric of the nation, he responded
with something far from the usual New Christian Right mantra on God, politics
and moral values. "We don't live in a Christian nation. We are not a Christian

nation, and never have been one. It is not what was intended for us. I don't think God is too upset about that, and I differ with other Christians on this."

Clearly, religious ideology plays a role in the ACLJ's approach to litigation for policy influence—Sekulow hopes to use the courts to advance the role of the church in society. But, the perspective of ACLJ leaders on religion in public life supports a pragmatic orientation centered mainly on how the ACLJ defines success for itself. The ACLJ defines victory in the courts by a measure different than complete validation of its core religious and ideological beliefs. Sekulow's organization has adopted another standard, defined by its "place at the table" organizational philosophy that makes it easy to enter courts and present arguments with which judges are familiar. For the ACLJ to realize its goals for policy influence, courts do not have to adopt its particular religious and ideological views. They simply must endorse an interpretation of civil rights that tolerates religious expression in public forums and allows the church to pursue its goals of evangelism, protest, and social criticism. This twist on religion in public life supports the role of courts as protectors of civil freedoms and policy developers. To support conservative Christian legal claims, courts are not required to endorse Judeo-Christian principles as important for making judicial determinations. But, they can support an idea that is congruent with mainstream constitutional rights doctrine. By striking down policies that Sekulow brands as viewpoint discriminatory, courts endorse the constitutional values of liberty, individuality, and democratic participation—they fulfill their role as instruments for preserving an atmosphere of expressive freedom.

The Liberty Counsel and Religious Ideology

Much like the ACLJ, the Liberty Counsel is committed to finding a role for the church in a plural society. While Staver sometimes frames his interests in a slightly different manner than Sekulow (emphasizing education over litigation), these emphases are consistent with the Liberty Counsel's primary litigation interests of religion in public schools and public places. However, while leaning strongly toward the ACLJ's perspective on religion in society, Staver is neither as exuberant about the state of religious liberties in this country, nor as suspicious of secularism and the law.

As noted earlier, Staver was part of the group of young attorneys that pioneered the free expression argument in establishment clause cases, and is among those who adopt civil rights–era rhetoric to rationalize the role of the church in a plural society. However, his views on the potential for acceptance of religious views in society are slightly less optimistic than Sekulow's. When asked how he felt about being Protestant in the United States today, he was less than jubilant.

> It depends on where you put yourselves historically. If I compare this country to the rest of the world, it's a great place to be. If I compare where we are [now] to the rest of the century, we've lost ground. If I look at, for example, the

religious liberty aspects of situations now in 1998 versus thirty years ago there are huge changes. In 1968, you are not going to have students who are told "you cannot bring your Bible to school." [These problems] just seem to be proliferating around the country. In 1968 you wouldn't have equal access issues where students are told you can't have a Bible club on campus, or if you do it has to be after hours that the other clubs meet during the day. So, in comparison to that there has been a tremendous shift in America, and that trend is something that I resist as I attempt to maintain liberty.

This may be the response of a tired Christian warrior dealing with a large litigation agenda and fighting the same equal access battles over and over again. But, it seems more typical of the Liberty Counsel's general approach to litigation in recent years. Lately, Staver has taken a more aggressive stance toward public schools that deny Christian students equal access. Setting aside his goal of education for a time, he declared war on public school districts in the Southeast that refused to comply with court decisions on religion in public schools or abused his efforts to bring educational information to their attention. This reflects a general feeling that there are those who resist his efforts to ensure that a Christian perspective on social issues is at least tolerated and not thrust to the fringes.

The CLP and Religious Ideology

Like the ACLJ and Liberty Counsel, the CLP is strongly committed to securing a role for the church in public life. Its members discuss that role using the same language as other New Christian Right litigators. When asked what the primary goal of the CLP is in court, Brian Fahling echoed both Jay Sekulow and Mat Staver.

Obviously we have organizational goals, and one of those is to ensure that the highways and byways remain open for the preaching of the Gospel. Which is not earth shattering, but in today's culture we are finding more and more that Christianity is being squeezed out of the public square. So we want to make sure that Christians who simply want to exercise constitutional rights are not prevented from doing that. And, we [use the law to] protect our clients.

This kind of rhetoric is typical of New Christian Right litigators. Taken on face value, it is congruent with the free expression argument that is at the heart of Sekulow's place at the table approach. It also appeals to the constitutional values of expressive freedom and equal treatment. However, when we dig beyond this general statement, we find that the CLP has a very different understanding of the connections between religious ideology and its role as a litigator for the movement. The CLP is distinguished from firms like the ACLJ and Liberty Counsel in the connection it makes between religious principle and the goal of policy influence through litigation. One can sense within the CLP a strong desire that the law and social policy comport with principle derived from faith in God and from the Bible. This preference is generated internally and flows directly from its religious ideological position.

However, to infer that the CLP approaches the courts with a culture war in mind is grossly mistaken. Rather, the organization's primary concern is for fostering social and cultural cohesion around a set of values that originate in religious principle. The erosion of common social goals is a primary concern for the CLP, one that has coincided with an erosion of religious belief in the United States. It has developed an approach to litigation that emphasizes commonalities among perspectives in a plural society. "It always has been, and continues to be my view that law and policy must be conducted on the common ground that exists between believer and unbeliever," says Fahling.

> That means I do not argue from the Bible as such, rather, I argue based upon what is common to all men. The whole of my life and thinking is formed according to my ultimate justification, but I do not require that others first accept my ultimate justification before we can agree. In law and policy I am not seeking religious converts—that is not the business of government. Rather, I seek order and justice for all. When I speak of the Bible and the Constitution, I do not mean that the secular world must look to the Bible for a proper construction of the Constitution.

Instead Fahling seeks out those areas of life in which biblical principle overlaps with what is commonly practical in society. In this sense, the CLP resists the very social fragmentation that the ACLJ and Liberty Counsel seek to use to the church's advantage. Through litigation, the CLP encourages courts to cultivate social consensus and support collective social goals. It pursues this objective in court under the heading "common practical notions," and it defines its role in part as holding courts to standards based on those principles of the Western legal tradition that it identifies as religious in origin but also justifiable using secular reason. Where courts arrive at decisions that contradict both, the CLP has a harsh critique. Consider this statement from Brian Fahling on the source of legal rulings that squeeze Christianity out of the public square:

> It is basically political atheism, a distinctly modern notion. In the past, even pre-modern atheists would recognize the idea that a common understanding of God or a god was necessary to a civil body politic. Today we have Jacques Chirac's French secularism as the soul of our modern state. To me that [event] was chilling,[18] but it was also an indication of how our courts think. It puts secularism on a religious plane.

What then does the CLP envision as the proper basis for judicial decision making? Once again, we see clear links to the group's religious ideological position. Consider this statement from Brian Fahling on the proper basis for determining what civil rights the Constitution can (or should) support.

You have to go back and prove what rights are for the individual. What has happened of late is that that has been taken out of the picture. Now, the fundamental rights have been endowed by man, so to speak, or by government. That is skewed. That is why we can now have fundamental rights that are different from, or contrary to, those rights that are endowed by God. We've replaced the creator with government.

If this is the legal philosophy that underlies all the arguments that the CLP offers to courts, then one must wonder whether the CLP's approach to litigation is congruent with institutional norms of courts. According to Fahling, the CLP does not define victory as courts adopting its view of the proper justification for law and policy. But, what does the CLP do when confronted with precedent that goes directly against its religious ideology and that appellate courts are unwilling to jettison? Does a fundamental disagreement reflected in law limit the influence of the CLP in the courts? These questions are the topic for consideration below.

Religious Ideology and the Institutional Norms of Courts

Here, I consider the influence of religious ideology on the litigation behavior of the three groups, contrasting the behavior of the CLP to the ACLJ and Liberty Counsel. I find that the ACLJ and Liberty Counsel's religious ideology promotes participation before appellate courts, easing their way into appellate litigation by allowing the groups to conform to appellate court norms. However, religious ideology influences the appellate agendas of all three groups by subtly shaping the arguments they believe they can legitimately make. Because of its emphasis on principle, the CLP must work harder than the other groups to craft arguments that meet the expectations of appellate courts without violating the internal values of the organization. Furthermore, religious ideology helps define success for the CLP in important ways that differ significantly from other New Christian Right litigators. Finally, religious ideology promotes a particular emphasis on trial-level litigation within its overall litigation agenda.

Principled Pragmatism and Legal Argument

Religious ideology structures litigation behavior because it determines in part organizational compatibility with the institutional norms of courts, which is in turn reflected in the arguments a group presents to courts. In particular, appellate courts exhibit a decided preference for legal arguments advocating limited or incremental policy adjustments. Various studies point to the importance of providing appellate courts with reasoned arguments supporting this kind of institutional approach to policy development.[19] This norm requires that groups accept previous policy developments and argue for limited policy change. Groups that differ in the importance of religious ideology also exhibit differences in their capacity to present courts with this kind of legal argument.

In earlier chapters, discussion of the three groups led to the conclusion that all practice principled pragmatism when approaching the courts. However, the ACLJ and Liberty Counsel place a decided emphasis on pragmatism rather than principle. This was revealed in part by the language they use to describe religion and law. Sekulow and Staver speak of religion in legal terms, employing the language of legal right rather than emphasizing the religious principles they seek to elevate. This pragmatic stance is reflected in their litigation behavior, which is characterized by a willingness to depart from the strict principles dictated by religious ideological beliefs. In other words, they are willing to "play by the rules," that is, by the norms of policy makers in the courts. This is accomplished with little internal dissonance—there is no indication that members of the ACLJ and Liberty Counsel believe they have compromised their faith. Quite the opposite is true. New Christian Right litigators emphasizing pragmatism over principle do not see religion as the sole source of structure for policy making. Thus, they are relatively unconstrained in the arguments available to them to present in court.

The ACLJ's litigation record provides an important illustration of its pragmatic emphases. The example comes from Sekulow's participation in the abortion protestation case *Schenck v. Pro-Choice Network of Western New York*. Sekulow argued this case before the Supreme Court, challenging an injunction against protesters who came within fifteen feet of a person entering an abortion clinic. On brief, Sekulow argued that health risks associated with abortion procedures are not cause for limiting speech. However, during oral argument, Sekulow was forced to clarify this position when talk turned to violence at abortion clinic protests. While arguing against a "medical exception to the First Amendment,"[20] he did stipulate that both the state and abortion clinics have an interest in protecting the well-being of those about to undergo an abortion procedure. Making this stipulation presumes the validity of a right to abortion. In effect, Sekulow accepted that courts have recognized the abortion right and that he accepts court precedent as binding. While abortion is a violation of his religious principles dictating the sanctity of human life, Sekulow was willing to play by the rules of the court to achieve his purpose,[21] which was to influence policy such that the church remains free to engage in protest of social policies and evangelism taking the form of sidewalk counseling.

In contrast, the CLP practices a principled pragmatism with accent on the principle. As a result, one might easily (and erroneously) conclude the CLP takes a polar opposite position to the other groups. Perhaps the influence of its religious ideology is such that as an article of its faith it cannot depart from internalized religious principles. It might be easy to conclude this from various statements made by CLP members, perhaps most clearly articulated by Brian Fahling's assertion that the CLP "will not compromise principles just to win a case." Furthermore, the CLP offers an alternative to the "place at the table" approach of the ACLJ and others. Like some in the litigating arm of the New

Christian Right, the CLP has concerns about an approach that conflates religious freedom with "pornography, commercial advertising, racial invectives, flag burning, and other forms of 'protected' speech."[22] For some New Christian Right lawyers such an approach may harm their cause as much as it helps. Fahling and Crampton would say that this is because, in taking the pragmatic approach, their fellow litigators lose sight of the principles that distinguish them from the legal environment in which they litigate. Addressing the current trend toward playing the litigation game according to the norms of the courts, Fahling said, "Christians need to recapture the high ground, you've got to behave in a principled fashion."

> I heard one [Christian] lawyer make an argument for stopping a particular activity based on the commerce clause, and he justified this with the argument that "the other side has been doing it for years." That kind of thinking will lead us straight to hell. You've got to have some principled opposition. Just because the end sounds good, you've got to ask the questions "is it appropriate, is it proper, is it a legitimate means to an end?" [If we don't] we cease to be lawyers. We need to ask these questions, and not go along with it because it seems like a good idea.

But, does the CLP's emphasis on principle mean that it would be unable to participate in a case like *Schenck* because it would be unable to stipulate to the abortion right? Would the CLP be able to make Sekulow's argument, or does its principled position place it outside the policy making mainstream? "We would litigate a case like that," says Steve Crampton. "But we would never make that kind of stipulation."

> One of the things we bring to the table is more creativity in fashioning new arguments and ways around obstacles in the average constitutional case for our kind of practitioners. The way we achieve that is by discussing it in roundtable. We constantly do this—trying to sharpen our arguments and ways around the seemingly insurmountable.

> **Fahling**: This could be articulated in a way that would not intrude on our conscience. It didn't intrude on Jay's conscience, but we wouldn't be able to make that stipulation because it would suggest something that I find repugnant. But, I could satisfy the court in how I articulated it. We are not against incrementalism properly defined. Sometimes the context suggests using tools available, because you will accomplish something good. The means [employed] must be according to authority in aid of a legitimate end.

Crampton recognizes that balancing principles with the common practical notions approach takes much of the CLP's time and energy. But, despite the extra commitment, the CLP is not excluded from appellate court litigation. Rather, it takes more work for the CLP to craft arguments that conform to the institutional norms of courts. The CLP must balance its principles with the need to make arguments that hold some attraction to appellate courts. It may be harder for the CLP to take strategic advantage of the institutional norms of courts, but this does not indicate that it is left out of the policy-making process altogether. In point of fact, the CLP has been successful in crafting these arguments, as its appellate record of cases won demonstrates. The tangible result of this internal dynamic is that the CLP must restrict its appellate agenda. It has limited time to undertake the extended and creative process of crafting arguments that work under its common practical notions approach to litigation. Thus, the number of appellate cases that can occupy space on its litigation agenda is more constrained than for organizations that take the approach of an ACLJ or Liberty Counsel.

Religious Ideology and Successful Arguments

One alternative interpretation of the problem the CLP presents for the study of interest group litigation involves the potential for success before appellate courts. Perhaps because religious ideology so dominates the organization's response to its legal environment, it is only willing to become involved in cases it is sure to win. Conceivably, the CLP only takes cases that allow a trial court to apply settled legal doctrines corresponding with the group's own principled position. Such cases clearly offer limited chance for appeal because appellate courts are unlikely to revisit such established doctrines. This is particularly true regarding run-of-the-mill religious equal access cases, which make up a large segment of the CLP's litigation agenda. The CLP may pursue this strategy to maintain a presence in court, serve the needs of its constituency, and avoid approaching appellate courts—courts that it knows are less than willing to consider principled arguments unless those principles overlap with longstanding precedent. On this view, the CLP will generally take cases it considers a legal slam–dunk or in which it has a good chance to prevail on the merits because the constitutional doctrine is clear. There is no incentive for the CLP to take cases it is likely to lose. In such cases, it will be unable to make arguments that courts will accept, its failure will be almost assured, and it will waste valuable organizational time and resources.

When asked what incentive he could identify for taking a case that he knows the CLP will lose, Crampton responded, "Other groups would make that argument even more strongly—why take a case that they know they will lose?" He went on to indicate that selection bias exists on the part of other New Christian Right litigators. According to Crampton these groups become involved in trial-level cases either because they are easy cases in which they have a clear chance of success or because the case raises unique policy questions. However, they will refuse those cases that are either a sure loss at trial or that have no chance for setting precedent. "We want to win as much or more than anybody," he said.

We will take cases we think we may lose, but nevertheless there is a strong policy statement to be made. We may be different in that respect. And, we don't
mind taking cases that we should win on, but know we won't because of the
disposition of the court. We don't mind losing. It is phenomenal what happens,
but you just can't let some things go. We will make the arguments that are not
calculated to fit within the little crevices that the courts in their oversight have
left us, but make a broader argument that a lot of the judges have never heard.
And who knows but that seed planted in their minds may bear fruit in later
years. Sometimes the opportunity, and maybe necessity, arises in court. I think
there is still a positive effect in taking cases that we will lose.

On the other hand, while maintaining a principled position is always uppermost
in the minds of CLP attorneys, this does not mean that it will make the extreme
legal argument without any regard for legal propriety or success. The common
practical notions approach does not require the CLP to live and die in court on
its principles. Rather, it requires that the CLP find a common ground between
religious principle and legal policy. This cannot happen if the CLP were to insist
on dressing its own religious ideological arguments in legal clothing. Brian
Fahling provides an example that illustrates how the principles that guide the
CLP's internal organizational culture relate with the legal arguments the CLP
makes in court. "I am not going to make an argument to the court like Brevard
Hand did in Alabama—a whole argument against the incorporation doctrine,"[23]
says Fahling.

I may think he is right historically, but I am not going to go in there and argue
to the court that you have no jurisdiction because the incorporation doctrine is
illegitimate. Well, I think it is illegitimate, but that is not a winning argument,
and not one I should be making in court. I can make it in law reviews and public policy pieces.

While the CLP has won some important victories at the appellate level,
courts have also exhibited skepticism when considering the arguments it offers.
Chances are good they will continue to do so.[24] For example, it is highly
unlikely that courts (not to mention the society) will accept the idea that limiting
gay rights is simply endorsing a collective social good. Thus, one might assume
that the CLP's common practical notions approach seriously limits its policy
influence. But, this misconstrues the CLP's own definition of success. The CLP
understands the proper role of the Christian not as cultural conqueror, but as the
light of religious reason in a world that constantly strays from the proper path.
Similarly, the Christian lawyer is not one that conquers the courts, but one that
makes the principled legal argument. The important role that the CLP plays is to
present courts with legal argument based on principles having their genesis in
religious belief and some connection to broad social goals. When it does so, it
fulfills its mission within the legal system successfully.

Thus, the CLP differs in some important ways from its parent organization
and from the broader New Christian Right movement. It is much less willing to

frame policy matters in terms of cultural purity or to claim a direct connection between religious doctrine and proper policy. This is particularly true of its role in the gay rights debate. In the many recent gay rights and marriage disputes, the CLP has demonstrated that it does not employ the fiery rhetoric of a Conservative Coalition when approaching the issue. Rather, the CLP emphasizes a broader historical understanding of human relations. "We've got three millennia and more of human testimony," says Fahling, "pagan, secular, and religious."

> If that is the case, why do we make these things that are part of creation into matters of redemption. We have a point of contact there. We are not as successful in our larger organization [the AFA], but they are coming along.

What that means precisely is that the CLP's common practical notions approach to litigation offers an alternative to perhaps the basic philosophical position of the New Christian Right (including its own parent organization) on religiously motivated political behavior. This position was reflected in the idea of a culture war in the first place—that salient policy questions such as gay rights and abortion must be framed in biblical terms for Christians to successfully engage the culture. Common practical notions alter the rationale for Christian participation and urges them not to cast issue positions as exclusively religious claims. To some this might seem like a semantic game that rationalizes the imposition of Christian values on society anyway, while allowing the CLP to assuage its more liberal-minded conscience. For the CLP this is a valid and time-honored method of approaching a culture that has strayed from an order conforming to the natural world. That the CLP is present to make arguments that advance this worldview is sufficient—it never declared a culture war in the courts, and thus cannot perceive its participation in the courts as winning or losing a contest for control of the culture.

Religious Ideology in Action: Serving the Rank and File

A related facet of the CLP's understanding of its role as Christian litigator is its service to rank-and-file members of the New Christian Right. The organization describes itself as a trial-oriented law firm in part because it believes average and ordinary Christians should be given full and free legal support when they are prevented from exercising religious freedom or from participating in the public square. Clearly, other firms (particularly the Liberty Counsel) are engaged in exactly this kind of work. But, with the CLP it's almost a genetic component of its organizational mission and culture. The idea of creating a law firm dedicated to serving the Christian rank and file was part of the CLP's mission from the moment Donald Wildmon envisioned the organization. Other New Christian Right litigators view the CLP as the defenders of basic religious freedoms for any Christian who experiences oppression in the United States. In reality, the CLP also fulfills a gate-keeping function. It does not agree to represent anyone in any dispute regardless of the claim. "We are selective," says Crampton.

> Someone walks in with a dead-bang loser of a case, no policy overtones. Obviously, being a public interest law firm, we can and will refuse a case. On the other side—once we accept a case, we will take it as far as is necessary. We don't have to take every case that walks through the door, but once we do we are committed to them.

Perhaps more than any other New Christian Right litigating firm, the CLP emphasizes dispute resolution and early trial litigation. In that respect, the Liberty Counsel is a rival. The Liberty Counsel is currently litigating the largest number of cases among all New Christian Right firms. Its litigation agenda boasts the largest number of sexual orientation cases, and it is particularly active at trial. Table 5.2 reveals that the Liberty Counsel's "One-Shot" trial-only litigation makes up a greater percentage of its litigation agenda than for the CLP. However, the CLP is constantly involved in trial-level disputes that are not reflected in its overall litigation agenda. As noted in chapter 4, the CLP resolves a large number of cases through mediation before and immediately after initial filings. In a vast majority of cases making up its trial-level litigation agenda, the CLP is present from initial filing to settlement or the end of trial. When asked to elaborate on the CLP trial-level orientation and its commitment to broad policy influence, Crampton responded, "Yes, we do a lot of trial level work and work in the trenches."

> But, we believe that this enables us to better present arguments at the appellate level. And, we look to take them up. I guess I call it taking the long view and bring our perspective in on the context and the current cases and issues on a daily basis.

This orientation toward providing ordinary Christians with legal services has influence on the configuration of the CLP's litigation agenda. Because of its desire to represent all Christians, and because Christians bring all manner of disputes to the CLP (including those that are both easily resolved and unfit for adjudication), the organization boasts a large litigation agenda. However, because the CLP employs a large segment of its limited resources on an area of interest largely unrelated to policy influence, the CLP experiences an even greater reduction in its ability to focus on appellate litigation. Not only does the CLP invest more resources than other organizations into crafting appellate arguments, but also its own mission prevents it from making up for this imbalance by channeling more resources into appellate litigation.

Goal Setting and Policy Influence

This analysis also points to the influence of goal setting on organizational behavior. Political scientists have thought of groups in terms of discrete categories of goals (one group being committed to policy influence while another emphasizes reputation or media influence). Furthermore, they have examined groups emphasizing a particular category of goals. Initial studies assumed that the primary goal of any litigating interest was to see its policy aims become law. Beginning with Clement Vose's *Caucasians Only* (1959), scholars focused on successful and coordinated group litigation efforts to shape public policy.[25] Largely, scholars focused on groups like the ACLU or the NAACP and their successful efforts at policy influence.[26] However, they soon turned their attention to a broader range of groups to explore the full scope of activities and influence. Studies have focused on the supplementation of successful test case strategies with other tactics including acquiring necessary resources,[27] pursuing an extended test case strategy through which groups acquire "repeat player" status,[28] and coalitional behavior.[29] Furthermore, social scientists focused on organizational resources as an explanation for litigation participation. Some linked resources with environmental factors to explain why groups seek policy influence.[30] Others focused on organizational capacities such as financial resources and their sources, professional staff, and internal structure.[31]

Scholars have also examined litigation behavior within the context of goal setting, internal motivations, and legal environment. Epstein notes that differences in goals across groups are revealed in behavioral differences, and she identifies a range of goals that include policy-influence, reputation-oriented and media-oriented goals. In *Women's Organizations' Use of the Courts*, Karen O'Connor also identifies a range of possible goals into which groups may fit. Significantly, she notes (perhaps the only scholar to do so) that the process of goal setting involves complexity. Groups can pursue multiple or overlapping strategies that reinforce a group's main objectives. Thus, a group seeking policy influence must also develop organizational competencies in other areas in support of that primary goal.

The groups provide examples of how necessary pursuing multiple goals has become in the world of public interest litigation. Both the ACLJ and Liberty Counsel recognize the importance of a multi-layered strategy. A dominant feature of the ACLJ's goal setting is the integration of various goals in pursuit of the centerpiece of ACLJ organizational life—policy influence on a national level. Other goals (such as reputation and media influence) are crucial to the ACLJ as well. But, they appear to be important only insofar as they support the central aim of influencing policy formulation. Sekulow is not only the face of the ACLJ, but also of New Christian Right litigators. In fulfilling this function he has often been in front of the media.[32] Furthermore, he uses media outlets directed at conservative Christians. Sekulow's radio program, *Jay Sekulow Live!*, is designed to influence public perceptions about the place of religion in

society. It does this by addressing specific situations encountered by its listener-
ship and educating Christians about religious rights in their communities, work-
places, and schools. However, the primary goal of all of Sekulow's media presence is to provide a pool of high quality potential cases from which the ACLJ
draws those with the best chance at appellate review. Sekulow notes the differences between his radio call-in show and his litigation efforts while recognizing
that the program works to further the central goals of the organization. For example, he states that "the radio program is completely separate [from the litiga-
tion]. It's caller-driven; it's 'Jay-driven.' We've had great success with it and it
also gives us a good sense of what's going on out in the market." Once again,
the overall goal of policy influence peeks through—the ACLJ will pursue only
those opportunities and aspects of organizational life that support its primary
goal. Perhaps the clearest statement linking various organizational goals to the
ACLJ's dominant goal came when asked if his organization was concerned
about influencing public attitudes and perceptions. Sekulow responded, "Absolutely. Because public attitudes and perceptions impact judges, and judges make
law. They're supposed to interpret laws, but they make them."

While policy influence is the Liberty Counsel's primary goal, Staver describes an approach that integrates the three predominant strategies in a common
enterprise. For Staver and the Liberty Counsel, reputation is absolutely crucial,
as is getting the Liberty Counsel's name in front of potential clients. The Liberty
Counsel has traditionally used religious media outlets to publicize its name.
However, Staver has recently begun advertising in secular media outlets because
"we think it is a media to which Christians have migrated." He also notes the
primacy of media in attracting more clients with better cases. "It is very important that there are people out there who have information about the existence of
the Liberty Counsel, so that things can be addressed."

> We have created on our web site comment forms where people can tell us
> where they heard about us. There is not any one source. They have found us
> from searches on the web, from a media source, from somewhere else. We are
> targeting our radio program to both Christian and secular talk radio programs.

The CLP also hopes to achieve a level of policy influence within the
movement typified by the ACLJ. But, its members understand that the goal cannot be fulfilled without a reputation for leadership established through a media
presence. "[The ACLJ] is more successful at locating the precedent setting
cases," notes Crampton. "They established themselves early as the preeminent
Christian law firm and as a result of that they tend to get the best cases. And, we
certainly over time hope to raise our presence and do something similar." Yet,
the CLP's experience with goal setting has been distinctly different from the
other two organizations. This is true mainly because of its relationship with its
parent organization, the AFA. The AFA is a media-driven creature. It's primary
product is radio programming directed at grassroots political involvement, education, and worship. Because of this, the CLP's legal agenda has not achieved a

prominent position within the AFA's media stream. Recently, the CLP has begun reevaluating its position relative to the parent organization. This is in part a product of an internal evaluation of the organization and its limitations. CLP attorneys realize that while the AFA has provided massive support, its emphases have also limited the CLP's organizational viability and effectiveness. Like the Liberty Counsel, the CLP has begun to understand that goals are not mutually exclusive categories—an organization that hopes to influence policy cannot neglect its reputation or fail to advertise its position as a movement leader within the media. If it is to have a chance to influence policy, the CLP must cultivate a reputation that attracts high-profile cases with solid facts and clients involving appropriate policy areas. Without channeling resources into activities that build reputation and increase movement leadership, the CLP faces an attenuated pool of cases from which to draw. "Media influences everything," Crampton notes.

> Communications today is the end all for everyone—non-profit or business. To the degree that your communication is sound is the degree to which you ensure that you won't suffer an untimely demise. If you use communications appropriately then you get awareness, brand name. But, to the extent that you do not have brand awareness it doesn't matter how much substance you have. You simply won't get the cases; you won't draw clients and cases.

The CLP has become so self-conscious about not taking advantage of the AFA's media resources that it has hired an attorney with a media background and plans to tap into his abilities to raise awareness of the CLP. Thus, the organization has come to the conclusion that it cannot leave such activities to its parent organization and expect to thrive.

In recent years the CLP has increased its presence within the AFA's media stream. CLP attorneys have developed daily radio spots for use on the AFA's network in which they inform listeners about recent cases and conflicts, address salient issues, and encourage listeners to call the CLP if they encounter religious discrimination. "We are in a transition phase," says Fahling.

> We are looking for higher quality cases. In the past, we kind of reveled in our anonymity. The good side is that we got to do what we want to do. The reality of this, though, is that to engage the culture, the culture has to know that we exist. So, a low profile can hurt you. We have never utilized the media capacity of the AFA, and we are starting to tap into that now—starting to do TV interviews and create a media presence. If we raise our profile we'll get better cases. Part of the reason that the ACLJ and Liberty Counsel get better cases is because of the media profile, people know about them. There are still people who are AFA supporters and don't know about the law center. So, we have got to raise our profile.

Crampton recognizes that the previous organizational configuration has limited the CLP's ability to influence policy. But, he is also cautious about what a high-profile media presence can do to the organization. "Part of what you have seen in the past is a result of what comes in the door," he states.

What comes in the door is in turn affected by your media presence. One aspect of our existence that perhaps impacts our ability to attract good cases and clients in a negative way is that Don Wildmon is an iconoclast. He has had the reputation [as a political outsider] and it has served him and us very well. Currently, the AFA has no D.C. presence, no legal or legislative lobbyists in D.C. now, for about two years. Some important things are breaking and we end up being the last ones to know about it. We are taking strides to increase our profile. But, part of our jurisprudence, and perhaps our nature too, gives us pause in overdoing that. Obviously it enhances our own stature, but we do it not so that we can be legends in our own minds, but it allows us to participate more fully in engaging the culture in ways we haven't thought about. So we do a lot of the trench work. There is a real danger in our work. If you start believing your own press you've got problems. Your media image overshadows the substance of your product, and we would rather it be the other way around—more substance than smoke and mirrors.

The upshot of the CLP's experience with goal setting is that the limitations imposed on the organization by its parent have also limited its appellate agenda. Cases that are desirable from the standpoint of policy influence come to organizations because they develop a reputation as effective litigators and movement leaders, and because they are known among their constituency. These are precisely the organizational attributes that are downplayed within the CLP because of its parent organization's media emphases. However, once the CLP is able to implement a media strategy, it should have a resource at its disposal that few organizations can boast. The AFA's radio network is extensive, and its membership base stable. If the CLP can position itself to take advantage of its parent organization's strengths, it will begin to increase the resources it devotes to appellate litigation and develop a long-term strategy for policy influence.

Conclusion

In this analysis of conservative Christian litigators, I have focused on explanations for the litigation emphases and strategic preferences of three leading New Christian Right litigators. The explanations I offer flow from internal group characteristics that have received relatively little emphasis from interest group scholars. I employ qualitative data developed in previous chapters to characterize the three groups and compare them on a range of variables including litigation behavior, and those variables I use to explain differences in behavior— religious ideology and group goals.

I find that religious ideology explains a good deal of what is different about the litigation emphases and practices of the three groups. While the place of religious ideology within the ACLJ and Liberty Counsel encourages participation in an incremental policy process, religious ideology within the CLP limits the range of legitimate responses that the organization can make to policy concerns. Rather than excluding the CLP from the policy process undertaken by courts, the organization must undertake a creative process to develop arguments that courts will accept and which do not violate its religious ideological principles. The need to engage in this creative process saps the resources of the organization, demanding that the CLP invest more institutional resources than other organizations when approaching appellate courts. Furthermore, religious ideology influences how the groups envision their role as litigators. The ACLJ and Liberty Counsel understand their role as litigators in largely legal terms, employing a range of arguments and strategies to shape policy and limit the impact of losses. The CLP is less concerned about losing and more interested in presenting courts with legal arguments derived from broad principles that have their genesis in religious ideals. In a final and related area, religious ideology influences how groups define the constituency they serve and how they serve them. While all three groups seek to provide basic legal services to Christians caught in legal conflicts over religious rights, the CLP emphasizes this kind of service far more. The need to serve the rank-and file New Christian Right membership limits the resources that the CLP can invest in appellate litigation. The CLP devotes more of its time and energy to trial-level litigation than do the other two groups as a result of its religious commitment to protect the interests of the church at its most basic level.

I also determine that the process of goal setting has implications for the litigation behavior of groups. While the ACLJ and Liberty Counsel bear the burden of fundraising and managing their media presence, the CLP has been relieved of these burdens by its parent organization—a media giant with significant financial resources. While this can be viewed as a significantly positive influence on the organization, it has also placed restraints on the CLP's development. Compared to the ACLJ and Liberty Counsel, it has not pursued a multi-faceted strategy to develop a recognizable image or to enhance its reputation among its constituency. In part, this is because the CLP is overshadowed by the activities of its parent organization. Thus, both the number and quality of disputes coming to it are reduced, as are its chances to pursue a developed appellate agenda. For the CLP to achieve the kind of influence it hopes to have in court it must take steps to develop a multi-faceted approach to goal setting that includes improving its media exposure and developing a reputation among its core constituency. These are all necessary steps for improving the quality of cases that come its way. The CLP appears to be addressing these concerns.

Throughout the book, I have made two broad types of comparison—I compare New Christian Right litigators to each other, but I also make comparisons between New Christian Right litigators and the broader movement. I find that New Christian Right litigators exhibit characteristics very different from other movement organizations that engage in legislative lobbying and electioneering. Even litigators like the CLP maintain a distinctive approach to law and social conflict. Despite its close association with a parent organization espousing typical movement views on the role of religion in public life, the CLP's understanding of its role as litigator is deeply influenced by legal and social philosophy as well as religious ideology. It blends these influences in a way that adapts to secular and legal norms of respect for precedent and incremental development of law. Some New Christian Right law firms are better able to take advantage of the norms of courts than others. However, their assessment of American law and culture is tempered by the values transmitted through their legal education. To answer the question posed in the title of this chapter, they are not simply good Christians or good lawyers. They are truly good Christian lawyers.

Overall, this analysis has revealed some important recent developments in the litigating wing of the New Christian Right. These developments impact its ability to pursue its goals in court. Perhaps most importantly, various firms are acquiring competencies that allow them to lay claim to the title of movement leader. The changes in the organizational structure of the ACLJ and its adjusted focus on broad policy influence have provided other firms with the opportunity to take on new roles. Recently, both the Liberty Counsel and the CLP have assumed new and major responsibilities as movement standard bearers. As Brian Fahling has noted, "[t]he field is changing rapidly, and we would never have considered the kind of growth that would bring us into the place that the ACLJ once occupied."

> At one time the ACLJ was the premier firm and it got a lot of high-profile cases, had great resources. Now that has changed a bit and Mat Staver's Liberty Counsel is becoming more of the premier law firm.

In this respect, my analysis is both timely and important. A new era in conservative Christian litigation has begun at almost precisely the same time that a new set of issues has risen to prominence. The sexual orientation issue area in particular raises important challenges for New Christian Right litigators in terms of their ability to sustain the endorsement of liberal values such as tolerance so characteristic of their litigation efforts in the 1990s. In important respects, this book has developed initial answers to questions about how these new movement leaders will approach new issues and challenges, and what we can expect from New Christian Right litigators in the future.

Table 5.1. Categories of Litigation Behavior and Related Subcategories

Category	*Subcategory*
Case Sponsorship	
	– Full Test Case Strategy: trial court to court of last resort
	– Test Case Strategy from intermediate appellate to court of last resort
	– Test Case Strategy from trial to intermediate appellate court with denial of *certiorari*
	– Test Case Strategy from trial to intermediate appellate court with no petition for *certiorari*
	– One-Shot Appellate Case Sponsorship (appellate court level only)
	– One-Shot Trial Case Sponsorship (trial court level only)
Counsel on Brief	
Amicus curiae	

Table 5.2. Comparison by Type of Participation

Group	Case Sponsorship			On Brief	Amicus	Total
	Test Case (Trial and Appellate)	One Shot Appellate Only	One Shot Trial Only			
ACLJ	65	26	33	13	56	193[a]
	(34)	(14)	(17)	(6)	(29)	(100)[b]
LC	34	11	36	3	22	106
	(32)	(10)	(34)	(3)	(21)	(100)
CLP	13	18	18	0	19	68
	(19)	(26.5)	(26.5)	(0)	(28)	(100)

Source: Lexis/Nexis Legal Database

Note(s):

[a] = Instances of group participation

[b] = Percentage of overall litigation agenda

Table 5.3. Instances of Participation as Case Sponsor throughout Appellate Process

Group	Trial to CLR Full Test Case	Int. App. To CLR	Trial to Int. App. [a]	Trial to Int. App. [b]	N [c]
ACLJ	8 (29)	2 (6)	4 (10)	10 (20)	24 (65)
LC	1 (6)	0 (0)	3 (11)	8 (17)	12 (32)
CLP	0 (0)	0 (0)	1 (2)	5 (11)	6 (13)

Source: Lexis/Nexis Legal Database

Note(s):

[a] = First number equals number of actual cases. Number in parentheses equals number of instances of litigation by the group in those cases.

[b] = Cases did not include a petition for *certiorari* review after an appellate court ruling.

[c] = Cases included a petition for *certiorari* review after an appellate court ruling, which petition was denied.

CLR = Court of Last Resort (state or federal)

Int. App. = Intermediate Appellate Court

Table of Cases

ACLJ Participation

ACLU Neb. Found. v. City of Plattsmouth, 358 F. 3d 1020 (2004).

ACLU of Ohio Foundation v. Ashbrook, 211 F. Supp. 2d 873 (2002).

ACLU of Ohio v. Capitol Square Review Board, 20 F. Supp. 2d 1176 (1998).

ACLU of Ohio v. City of Stow, 29 F. Supp. 2d 845 (1998).

ACLU v. Capitol Square Review & Advisory Board, 243 F. 3d 289 (2001).

ACLU v. Mercer County, 240 F. Supp. 2d 623 (2003).

ACLU v. Reno, 929 F. Supp. 824 (1996).

Altman v. Minnesota Dept. of Corrections, 251 F. 3d 1199 (2001).

Amandola v. Town of Babylon, 251 F. 3d 339 (2001).

Arizona Civ. Lib. Union v. Dunham, 112 F. Supp. 2d 927 (2000).

Ashcroft v. ACLU, 124 S. Ct. 2783 (2003).

Baker v. Adams County, 310 F. 3d 927 (2002).

Berger v. Rensselaer Sch. Corp, 982 F. 2d 1160 (1993).

Black v. City of Atlanta, 35 F. 3d 516 (1994).

Blocker v. SBA, 916 F. Supp. 37 (1996).

Board v. Jews for Jesus, 482 U.S. 569 (1987).

Boerne v. Flores, 521 U.S. 507 (1997).

Books v. City of Elkhart, 235 F. 3d 292 (2000).

Books v. City of Elkhart, 239 F. 3d 826 (2001).

Boy Scouts of America v. Dale, 530 U.S. 640 (2000).

Branch Ministries, Inc. v. Rossotti, 211 F. 3d 137 (2000).

Bray v. Alexandria Women's Health Clinic, 506 U.S. 263 (1993).

Brooks v. North Carolina State Bar, 1996 U.S. Dist. LEXIS 16447 (1996).

Bush v. Gore, 531 U.S. 98 (2000).

Bynum v. Fort Worth ISD, 41 F. Supp. 2d 641 (1999).

Bynum v. United States Capitol Police Bd., 93 F. Supp. 2d 50 (2000).

Campbell v. St. Tammany Parish Sch. Bd., 533 U.S. 913 (2001).

Cannon v. Denver, 998 F. 2d 867 (1993).

Capitol Square Review Board v. Pinette, 515 U.S. 753 (1995).

Ceniceros v. Board, 106 F. 3d 878 (1995).

Chandler v. Siegelman, 530 U.S. 1256 (2000).

Children of the Rosary v. City of Phoenix, 154 F. 3d 972 (1998).

Christian Coalition Int'l v. United States, 2000 U.S. Dist. LEXIS 11861 (2000).

Church on the Rock v. City of Albuquerque, 84 F. 3d 1273 (1996).

Coalition of Clergy v. Bush, 310 F. 3d 1153 (2002).

Cruzan v. Director, 497 U.S. 261 (1990).

Cruzan v. Minneapolis Public Sch. Sys., 165 F. Supp. 2d 964 (2001).

Daily v. N.Y. City Housing Authority, 221 F. Supp. 2d 390 (2002).

Denver Area ETC, Inc. v. FCC, 518 U.S. 727 (1996).

Doe v. Sundquist, 106 F. 3d 702 (1997).

Dong v. Slattery, 84 F. 3d 82 (1996).

Edwards v. City of Santa Barbara, 150 F. 3d 1213 (1998).

Elk Grove U.S.D. v. Newdow, 124 S. Ct. 2301 (2003).

Ellis v. City of La Mesa, 990 F. 2d 1518 (1993).

Eulitt v. Maine Dept. of Education, 2003 U.S. Dist. LEXIS 13892 (2003).

Ex parte State ex rel James v. ACLU of Alabama, 711 So. 2d 952 (1998).

Fleming v. Jefferson County School District, 298 F. 3d 918 (2002).

Freedom from Religion Found. v. City of Marshfield, 203 F. 3d 487 (1999).

Freethought Society v. Chester County, 334 F. 3d 247 (2003).

Friends of the Vietnam Mem. v. Kennedy, 984 F. Supp. 18 (1997).

Frye v. Police Department of Kansas City, 260 F. Supp. 2d 796 (2003).

Full Gospel Tabernacle v. Community Sch. Dist. 27, 164 F. 3d 829 (1999).

Gentala v. City of Tucson, 213 F. 3d 1055 (1999).

Gibson v. Lee County School Dist., 1998 U.S. Dist. LEXIS 2696 (1998).

Good News Club v. Milford Central School, 533 U.S. 98 (2000).

Grace Bible Fellowship Inc. v. Maine Sch. Admin., 941 F. 2d 45 (1991).

Hamdi v. Rumsfeld, 124 S. Ct. 2633 (2004).

Harris v. Joint School District No. 241, 62 F. 3d 1233 (1995).

Henderson v. Stanton, 1998 U.S. App. LEXIS 30884 (1998).

Hill v. Colorado, 530 U.S. 703 (2000).

Hills v. Scottsdale Unified School District, 329 F. 3d 1044 (2003).

Hoffman v. Hunt, 126 F. 3d 575 (1997).

Hsu v. Roslyn Union Free School Dist. No. 3, 85 F. 3d 839 (1996).

Hyman v. City of Louisville, 132 F. Supp. 2d 528 (2001).

In Re Hodge, 220 B.R. 386 (1998).

In re Inquiry Concerning a Judge, 345 N.C. 632 (1997).

Jackson v. Jarman, 1998 U.S. Dist. LEXIS 939 (1998).

Jews for Jesus v. Jewish Community Relations Council, 968 F. 2d 286 (1992).

Jews for Jesus v. Massachusetts Bay Transp. Auth., 984 F. 2d 1319 (1993).

Kandel v. White, 339 Md. 432 (1995).

Kaplan v. Prolife Action League of Greensboro, 347 N.C. 342 (1997).

Kimbley v. Lawrence County, 119 F. Supp. 2d 856 (2000).

Kirkeby v. Furness, 905 F. Supp. 727 (1995).

Kiryas Joel Village School District v. Grumet, 512 U.S. 687 (1994).

Knight v. Connecticut Dept. of Pub. Health, 275 F. 3d 156 (2001).

Lamb v. Newton-Livingston, Inc., 551 N.W. 2d 333 (1996).

Lamb's Chapel v. Center Moriches School District, 508 U.S. 384 (1993).

Lawrence v. Texas, 539 U.S. 558 (2003).

Lee v. Int'l. Society for Krishna Consciousness, 505 U.S. 830 (1992).

Lee v. Wiesman, 505 U.S. 577 (1992).

Leebaert v. Harrington, 332 F. 3d 134 (2003).

Liberty Christian Center v. Board of Education, 8 F. Supp. 2d 176 (1998).

Locke v. Davey, 124 S. Ct. 1307 (2004).

Lutheran Church–Missouri Synod v. FCC, 141 F. 3d 344 (1998).

Madsen v. Women's Health Clinic, 512 U.S. 753 (1994).

Mahoney v. Babbitt, 113 F. 3d 219 (1997).

Mahoney v. Lewis, 2001 U.S. App. LEXIS 4014 (2001).

McGuire v. Reilly, 260 F. 3d 36 (2001).

Milwaukee Women's Med Servs. V. Brock, 2 F. Supp. 1172 (1998).

Mitchell v. Helms, 530 U.S. 793 (1999).

Moore v. City of Van, 238 F. Supp. 2d 837 (2003).

National Endowment for the Arts v. Finley, 524 U.S. 569 (1998).

New York v. Operation Rescue, 273 F. 3d 184 (2001).

Newdow v. Bush, 89 Fed. Appx. 624 (2004).

Nichol v. Arin Intermediate Unit 28, 268 F. Supp. 2d 536 (2003).

North Carolina Civil Liberties Union v. Constangy, 947 F. 2d 1145 (1991).

NOW v. Operation Rescue, 47 F. 3d 667 (1995).

NOW v. Schiedler, 510 U.S. 249 (1994).

Operation Rescue v. Women's Health Ctr., Inc., 634 So. 2d 1156 (1999).

Pennsylvania v. Labron, 518 U.S. 938 (1996).

People by Abrams v. Terry, 45 F. 3d 17 (1995).

Phillips v. Collings, 256 F. 3d 843 (2001).

Planned Parenthood of Michigan v. Engler, 860 F. Supp. 406 (1994).

Planned Parenthood v. Casey, 505 U.S. 833 (1992).

Prince v. Jacoby, 303 F. 3d 1074 (2002).

Reno v. ACLU, 521 U.S. 844 (1997).

Republican Party of Minnesota v. Kelly, 534 U.S. 1054 (2002).

Riely v. Reno, 860 F. Supp. 693 (1994).

Romer v. Evans, 517 U.S. 620 (1996).

Rosenberger v. University of Virginia, 515 U.S. 819 (1995).

Rumsfeld v. Padilla, 124 S. Ct. 2711 (2004).

Rust v. Sullivan, 500 U.S. 173 (1990).

SD Myers, Inc. v. City and County of San Francisco, 253 F. 3d 461 (2001).

Sabelko v. City of Phoenix, 120 F. 3d 161 (1997).

Santa Fe I.S.D. v. Doe, 530 U.S. 290 (2000).

Scheidler v. NOW, 537 U.S. 393 (2003).

Schenck v. Pro-Choice Network of Western New York, 519 U.S. 357 (1997).

Schmidt v. Cline, 127 F. Supp. 2d 1169 (2000).

Society for Krishna Consciousness v. Lee, 505 U.S. 672 (1992).

Stanley v. Lawson Co., 993 F. Supp. 1084 (1997).

State ex rel Angela M.W. v. Kruzicki, 209 Wis. 2d 112 (1997).

State ex rel. Thompson v. Jackson, 199 Wis. 2d 714 (1996).

Stenberg v. Carhart, 530 U.S. 914 (2000).

Strout v Albanese, 178 F. 3d 57 (1999).

*Strout v. Commissioner,*13 F. Supp. 2d 112(1998).

Tarsney v. O'Keefe, 225 F. 3d 929 (2000).

Trinity United Methodist Parrish v. Board, 907 F. Supp. 707 (1995).

Turner Broadcasting v. FCC, 910 F. Supp. 734 (1995).

United States v. Alaw, 327 F. 3d 1217 (2003).

United States v. American Library Association, 539 U.S. 194 (2003).

United States v. Arena, 180 F. 3d 380 (1999).

United States v. Kokinda, 497 U.S. 720 (1990).

United States v. Mohoney, 247 F. 3d 279 (2001).

United States v. Recio, 537 U.S. 270 (2002).

United States v. Schenck, 1994 U.S. Dist. LEXIS 1632 (1994).

United States v. Terry, 17 F. 3d 575 (1994).

United States v. Winstar Corp., 518 U.S. 839 (1996).

University of Wisconsin v. Southworth, 529 U.S. 217 (1999).

Vacoo v. Quill, 521 U.S. 793 (1996).

Virts v. Consol. Freightways Corp., 285 F. 3d 508 (2002).

Waguespack v. Rodriguez, 1998 U.S. Dist. LEXIS 10147 (1998).

Westside Community Schools v. Mergens, 496 U.S. 226 (1990).

Women's Health Ctr. of Duluth v. Operation Rescue, 1994 Minn. App. LEXIS 303 (1994).

Women's Health Servs., P.A. v. Operation Rescue, 24 F. 3d 107 (1994).

Zelman v. Simmons-Harris, 536 U.S. 639 (2001).

Zobrest v. Catalina Foothills School District, 509 U.S. 1(1992).

Liberty Counsel Participation

ACLU of Tenn., Inc. v. Rutherford Couty, 209 F. Supp. 2d 799 (2002).

ACLU v. McCreary County, 354 F. 3d 438 (2004).

ACLU v. Mercer County, 240 F. Supp. 2d 623 (2003).

Adler v. Duval County School District, 250 F. 3d 1330 (2001).

American Bible College v. State Board of Ind. Colleges, 653 So. 2d 1034 (1995).

Beach v. Leon County School Board, Unpublished opinion (1993).

Board of Regents v. Southworth, 529 U.S. 217 (2000).

Boerne v. Flores, 521 U.S. 507 (1997).

Brock v. Boozman, 2002 U.S. Dist. LEXIS 15479 (2002).

Brown v. City of Bainbridge Island, Unpublished opinion (1996).

Campbell v. St. Tammany Parish Sch. Bd., 300 F. 3d 526 (2002).

Capitol Square Review Bd. V. Pinette, 515 U.S. 753 (1998).

Cheffer v. McGregor, 6 F. 3d 705 (1994).

Cheffer v. Reno, 55 F. 3d 1517 (1995).

Cheffer v. Reno, No. 94-611-CIV-ORL-18 (1994).

Christ's Bride Ministries v. SEPTA, 148 F. 3d 242 (1998).

Connor v. Palm Beach County, Unpublished opinion (1995).

Daytona Rescue Mission v. City of Daytona Beach, 885 F. Supp. 1554 (1995).

Deida v. City of Milwaukee, 192 F. Supp. 2d 899 (2002).

Elk Grove U.S.D. v. Newdow, 124 S. Ct. 2301 (2003).

Falwell v. City of Lynchburg, 198 F. Supp. 2d 765 (2002).

Falwell v. Miller, 203 F. Supp. 2d 624 (2002).

First Baptist Church v. Miami-Dade County, 768 So. 2d 1114 (2000).

Freedom from Religion Foundation v. City of Marshfield, 203 F. 3d 487 (1999).

Friedman v. Clarkstown Cent. Sch. District, 75 Fed. Appx. 815 (2003).

Gernetzke v. Kenosha Unified Sch. Dist. No. 1, 274 F. 3d 464 (2002).

Good News Club v. Milford Central School, 533 U.S. 98 (2000).

Grant v. Fairview Hosp. & Healthcare Servs., 2004. U.S. Dist. LEXIS 2653 (2004).

Hill v. Colorado, 530 U.S. 703 (2000).

Hoover v. Wagner, 47 F. 3d 845 (1995).

Hsu v. Rosyln Union, 85 F. 3d 1530 (1996).

Jackson v. Benson, 218 Wis. 2d 835 (1998).

Jews for Jesus v. Broward County Aviation Dept., Unpublished opinion (1995).

Jews for Jesus v. Hillsborough Cnty. Aviation Auth., 162 F. 3d 627 (1998).

Johnston-Loehner v. O'Brien, 7 F. 3d 241 (1993).

Juzwick v. Borough of Dormont, 2001 U.S. Dist. LEXIS 25536 (2001).

Knutson v. Milwaukee Public Schools, Unpublished opinion (1997).

Largess v. Supreme Judicial Court for Massachusetts, 317 F. Supp. 2d 77 (2004).

Lawrence v. Texas, 539 U.S. 558 (2003).

Lee v. Weisman, 112 S. Ct. 2649 (1992).

Libertad v. Welch, 53 F. 3d 428 (1995).

Locke v. Davey, 124 S. Ct. 1307 (2004).

Madsen v. Women's Health Center, 512 U.S. 753 (1994).

Martin v. City of Gainesville, 800 So. 2d 687 (2001).

Mendelsohn v. City of St. Cloud, 719 F. Supp. 1065 (1989).

Midwest Pregnancy Care Center v. Independence, MS, Unpublished opinion (1995).

Moore v. City of Asheville, 290 F. Supp. 2d 664 (2003).

Morris v. City of West Palm Beach, 194 F. 3d 1203 (1999).

Muller v. Jefferson Lighthouse School, 98 F. 3d 1530 (1996).

National Endowment for the Arts v. Finley, 524 U.S. 569 (1997).

North Florida Women's Health & Counseling Services v. State, 866 So. 2d 612 (2003).

Operation Rescue v. Women's Health Center, 626 So. 2d 664 (1993).

Peachlum v. City of York, 333 F. 3d 429 (2003).

Peck v. Baldwinsville Sch. Bd. of Educ., 7 Fed. Appx. 74 (2001).

Santa Fe v. Jane Doe, 530 U.S. 290 (2000).

Scheidler v. NOW, 537 U.S. 393 (2003).

Schenck v. Pro-Choice Network of Western New York, 519 U.S. 357 (1997).

Sherman v. City of West Palm Beach, 89 F. 3d 855 (1996).

Simmons-Harris v. Goff, 86 Ohio St. 3d 1 (1999).

Smith v. Treshman, Unpublished opinion (1995).

Snyder v. Greater Orlando Aviation Authority, Unpublished opinion (1993).

State v. Limon, 83 P. 3d 229 (2004).

Suncoast Educational v. City of North Port, Unpublished opinion (1995).

Teens For Life v. Flagler County School Board, Unpublished opinion (1995).

Touchstone v. McDermott, 120 F. Supp. 2d 1055 (2000).

True Life Choice v. Dept. of H.R.S., 74 F. 3d 1251 (1995).

True Life Choice v. Dept. of H.R.S., 914 F. Supp. 507 (1994).

Turner v. Habersham County, 290 F. Supp. 2d 1362 (2003).

Van Orden v. Perry, 351 F. 3d 173 (2004).

Victory Outreach Ministries v. Tallahasee Housing Auth., Unpublished opinion (1994).

Westfield High Sch. L.I.F.E. Club v. City of Westfield, 249 F. Supp. 2d 98 (2003).

Wigg v. Sioux Falls Sch. Dist. 49-5, 274 F. Supp. 2d 1084 (2003).

Wishnatsky v. Fargodome Authority, Unpublished opinion (1995).

Wixtrom v. Dept. of Children & Families (In re J. D. S.), 864 So. 2d 534 (2004).

Women's Emergency Network v. Bush, 214 F. Supp. 2d 1316 (2002).

Women's Emergency Network v. Bush, 323 F. 3d 937 (2003).

Women's Emergency Network v. Dickinson, 214 F. Supp. 2d 1308 (2002).

Wright v. Okaloosa County Sch. Dist., Unpublished opinion (1997).

American Family Association's
Center for Law and Policy Participation

Action for Children's TV v. FCC, 932 F. 2d 1504 (1991).

American Family Association v. San Francisco, 277 F. 3d 1114 (2002).

American Library Assn. v. Barr, 794 F. Supp. 412 (1992).

Asquith v. City of Beaufort, 911 F. Supp. 974 (1995).

Baker v. Adams County S.D., 2002 U.S. Dist. LEXIS 26226 (2002).

Barnes v. Glen Theatre, Inc., 501 U.S. 560 (1991).

Berger v. Port Authority, 150 F. Supp. 2d 504 (2001).

Berger v. Rensselaer Cent. Sch. Corp., 982 F. 2d 1160 (1993).

Bischoff v. Osceola County, 222 F. 3d 874 (2000).

Brown v. Polk County, 61 F. 3d 650 (1995).

Brown v. Woodland Joint Unified Sch. Dist.,27 F. 3d 1373(1993).

Cafe 207, Inc. v. St. Johns City, 989 F. 2d 1136 (1993).

Channel Four Television Co. Lmt. v. Wildmon & AFA, 1992 U.S. Dist. LEXIS 6598 (1992).

Crampton v. Ervin, 2000 U.S. Dist. LEXIS 3148 (2000).

Doe v. Heck, 327 F. 3d 492 (2003).

Equality Foundation v. City of Cincinnati, 54 F. 3d 261 (1995).

Ex parte State ex rel James v. ACLU of Alabama, 1998 Ala. LEXIS 19 (1998).

Faustin v. City and County of Denver, 268 F. 3d 942 (2001).

FW/PBS, Inc. v. City of Dallas, 493 U.S. 215 (1990).

Gabriel v. City of Plano, 202 F. 3d 741 (2000).

Henderson v. Stadler, 265 F. Supp. 2d 699 (2003).

Hodgson v. Minnesota, 497 U.S. 417 (1990).

Howe v. City of Yuma, 1997 U.S. App. LEXIS 18422 (1997).

In re Advisory Opinion to the AG, 632 So. 2d 1018 (1994).

Ingebretsen v. Jackson Pub. Sch. Dist., 864 F. Supp. 1473 (1994).

Ingebretsen v. Jackson Pub. Sch. Dist., 88 F. 3d 274 (1996).

Kaplan v. Pro-Life Action League, 123 N.C. App. 720 (1996).

Largess v. Supreme Judicial Court, 317 F. Supp. 2d 77 (2004).

Lindsey v. City of Beaufort, 911 F. Supp. 962 (1995).

Lytle v. Brewer, 77 F. Supp. 2d 730 (1999).

Lytle v. Doyle, 326 F. 3d 463 (2003).

Lytle v. Griffith, 240 F. 3d 404 (2000).

Madsen v. Women's Health Center, 512 U.S. 753 (1994).

McKusick v. City of Melbourne, 96 F. 3d 478 (1996).

Mississippians v. Mabus, 793 F. Supp. 699 (1992).

Ohio v. Akron Center for Reproductive Health, 497 U.S. 502 (1990).

Okwedy v. Molinari, 150 F. Supp. 2d 508 (2001).

Operation Rescue v. Women's Health Ctr., Inc., 644 So. 2d 86 (1994).

Osborne v. Ohio, 495 U.S. 103 (1990).

Reyes v. City of Lynchburg, 1998 U.S. Dist. LEXIS 16745 (1998).

Reyes v. City of Lynchburg, 300 F. 3d 449 (1999).

Riley v. Jackson, 99 F. 3d 757 (1996).

Sable Communs. of California, Inc. v. FCC, 492 U.S. 115 (1989).

Saxe v. State College Area School District, 240 F. 3d 200 (2000).

Sechler v. State College Area School District, 121 F. Supp. 2d 439 (2000).

Stenberg v. Carhart, 530 U.S. 914 (2000).

Steverson v. City of Vicksburg, 900 F. Supp. 1 (1994).

Tennison v. Paulus, 144 F. 3d 1285 (1998).

Trewhella v. City of Lake Geneva, 249 F. Supp. 2d 1057 (2003).

United States v. McMillan, 946 F. Supp. 1254 (1995).

United States v. Thomas, 1996 U.S. App. LEXIS 4529 (1996).

United States v. Thomas, 74 F. 3d 701 (1996).

United States v. Vasquez, 145 F. 3d 74 (1998).

United States v. Wilson, 73 F. 3d 675 (1995).

Webster v. Reproductive Health Services, 492 U.S. 490 (1989).

Wildmon v. Berwick Universal Pictures, 983 F. 2d 21 (1992).

Wojnarowicz v. American Family Assn., 745 F. Supp. 130 (1991).

Notes

Preface

1. Steven P. Brown, *Trumping Religion* (Tuscaloosa, AL: University of Alabama Press, 2002).

2. Fritz Detwiler, *Standing on the Premises of God: The Christian Right's Fight to Redefine Public Schools* (New York: New York University Press, 1999).

3. Hans J. Hacker, "Defending the Faithful: Conservative Christian Litigation in American Politics." In *The Interest Group Connection*, eds. Paul S. Herrnson, Ronald G. Shaiko, and Clyde Wilcox, 2nd ed (Washington, DC: CQ Press, 2005).

4. Gregg Ivers, "Please, God, Save this Honorable Court: The Emergence of the Conservative Religious Bar." In *The Interest Group Connection*, eds. Paul S. Herrnson, Ronald G. Shaiko, and Clyde Wilcox (Chatham, NJ: Chatham House, 1998).

5. David E. Guinn, *Faith on Trial: Communities of Faith, the First Amendment, and the Theory of Deep Diversity* (Lanham, MD: Lexington Books, 2002), 3.

6. Stephen L. Carter, *The Culture of Disbelief: How American Law and Politics Trivializes Religious Belief* (New York: Basic Books, 1993), 57.

Chapter One

1. *Largess v. Supreme Judicial Court for Massachusetts*, 317 F. Supp. 2d 77 (2004).

2. *Goodridge v. Department of Public Health,* 798 N.E. 2d 941 (2003).

3. U.S. Constitution, Article IV, § iv.

4. *Largess v. Supreme Judicial Court for Massachusetts*, 3.

5. Liberty Counsel, "Supreme Court Declines to Issue Emergency Order Stopping Same Sex Marriage in Massachusetts," 14 May 2004, http://www.lc.org/libertyalert /2004/la051404b.htm.

6. Allen Pusey, "Falwell Has High Hopes as Law School Opens," *Dallas Morning News*, 25 August 2004, sec. A, 11.

7. The others include Regent University Law School and Ave Maria Law School.

8. For example, *Harris v. McRae* (448 U.S. 297, 1980) involved a challenge to the so-called Hyde Amendment, a federal regulation severely limiting federally funded abortions. Pro-life groups including Americans United for Life, Catholics for Life and Feminists for Life filed *amicus curiae* briefs supporting state regulations in *Akron v. Akron Center for Reproductive Health* (462 U.S. 416, 1983), *Planned Parenthood v. Ashcroft* (462 U.S. 476, 1983) and *Simopoulos v. Virginia* (462 U.S. 506, 1986). In many other cases the Christian Right supported state efforts to pass "model legislation" imposing comprehensive limitations on abortion rights and services. These took the form of consent provision, parental or spousal notification, doctor limitations, funding provisions, and record-keeping requirements.

However, pro-life efforts at coordinating litigation were often chaotic. This was particularly true in *Akron v. Akron Reproductive Health Services*. See Barbara H. Craig and David M. O'Brien, *Abortion and American Politics* (Chatham, NJ: Chatham House

Publishers, 1991). In *Akron* the Court considered a model city ordinance that included all of the provisions noted above, plus an expansive definition of the state's interest in preserving human life. Pro-life leaders urged the Reagan administration to argue for directly overturning *Roe*. The administration was reluctant to do so, drawing public criticism from pro-life groups. Thus, while the federal government argued that courts should end judicial supervision of states' abortion regulations on grounds of federalism, pro-life groups submitted *amicus curiae* briefs urging the Court to overturn *Roe*. The lack of a clear and coordinated argument hampered the pro-life position in court.

9. See *Board of Education of Westside Community Schools v. Mergens*, 496 U.S. 226 (1990); *Lamb's Chapel v. Center Moriches School District*, 508 U.S. 384 (1993); *Rosenberger v. University of Virginia*, 515 U.S. 819 (1995); and *U.S. v. Kokinda*, 497 U.S. 720 (1990). The core logic of this strategy has transferred over to abortion protestation cases. See *Madsen v. Women's Health Clinic*, 512 U.S. 753 (1994); and *Schenck v. Pro-Choice Women's Network*, 519 U.S. 357 (1997).

10. *Board of Westside Community Schools v. Mergens*, 496 U.S. 226 (1990).

11. *Boy Scouts v. Dale,* 530 U.S. 640 (2000).

12. *Board of Regents v. Southworth*, 529 U.S. 217 (2000).

13. *Santa Fe I.S.D. v. Doe,* 530 U.S. 290 (2000).

14. See *Hill v. Colorado*, 530 U.S. 703 (2000); *Good News Bible Club v. Milford Central School District*, 533 U.S. 98 (2001); and *Locke v. Davey*, 124 S. Ct. 1307 (2004). While not always successful in convincing courts, New Christian Right litigators presented the basic free expression argument in each of these cases.

15. Pusey, "Falwell Has High Hopes."

16. Alan Wolfe, "The Opening of the Evangelical Mind," *Atlantic Monthly* 286, no. 4 (2000): 55–76.

17. Harvey Cox, "The Warring Visions of the Religious Right," *Atlantic Monthly* 281, no. 4 (1995).

18. For an overview of attributes of Protestant Fundamentalist and Evangelical populations, see Steven P. Brown, *Trumping Religion* (Tuscaloosa: University of Alabama Press, 2002), 1–3. See also Nina J. Easton, *Gang of Five* (New York: Simon and Schuster, 2000), 217. She notes that the targeted constituency of the Christian Coalition does not reside in the "homogenous Bible Belt towns" of the South. They are primarily "college-educated with comfortable incomes" residing in suburbs whose motivations were not based on socioeconomic status, but on moral issues related to family. Easton, summarizing Ralph Reed's strategy of mobilization notes, "The prototypical member would be the thirtyish, college-educated, stay-at-home mother of three . . . not the pin-curl lady watching *The 700 Club* from her trailer park home." See also Mark J. Rozell and Clyde Wilcox, *Second Coming: The New Christian Right in Virginia Politics* (Baltimore, MD: Johns Hopkins University Press, 1996); and Clyde Wilcox, *Onward Christian Soldiers? The Religious Right in American Politics*, 2nd ed. (Boulder, CO: Westview Press, 1996). Wilcox reports that those identifying themselves as Protestant Evangelicals and with the New Christian Right have more than the average level of social-connectedness and are deeply involved in an identifiable network of professional, social, and civic organizations. Further, there is some evidence that grassroots Evangelicals exhibit less racial bias and more acceptance of Jews than the average American.

19. Wilcox, *Onward Christian Soldiers?*, 217.

20. Easton, *Gang of Five*, 16.

21. Examples abound. Wilcox notes an instance in which core constituencies of the

New Christian Right have been advised that "A vote for Bill Clinton is a vote against God." Wilcox, *Onward Christian Soldiers?*, 109.

22. Wilcox, *Onward Christian Soldiers?*, 110.

23. Multiple sources cite the "goal" of the New Christian Right as "reclaiming America" or "redefining America." See Fritz Detwiler, *Standing on the Premises of God: The Christian Right's Fight to Redefine Public Schools* (New York: New York University Press, 1999); Brown, *Trumping Religion*; and Wilcox, *Onward Christian Soldiers?*. Regardless, it is not difficult to argue that the goal of the conservative Christian social and political movement (as with any other movement) is to transform American culture and values.

24. Much of the early rhetoric of the movement can be attributed in part to theologians and conservative thinkers like Francis Schaeffer who interpret the history of religion and the current American cultural clash as a battle between forces that adhere to a biblical worldview and those of secular humanism. In fact, Detwiler attributes much of the language used to describe the social and political missions of leading New Christian Right organizations (e.g., Focus on the Family, Christian Defense League, and the Moral Majority) to the casting of cultural conflict in these dualistic terms. As he notes, "That language is now the lingua franca of the movement." Detwiler, *Standing on the Premises of God*, 16.

25. Craig and O'Brien, *Abortion and American Politics*, 52.

26. The Moral Majority in particular fell victim to its own issue cycle. When issues are placed on the congressional agenda they quickly lose saliency with lawmakers and the public, especially when Congress takes action on a particular issue within a congressional term. Furthermore, New Christian Right leaders lacked the political savvy to avoid political and organizational burnout. For an extended treatment of the Moral Majority and its influence on congressional policy making see Matthew C. Moen, *The Transformation of the Christian Right* (Tuscaloosa: University of Alabama Press, 1992); and Peter L. Benson and Dorothy L. Williams, *Religion on Capitol Hill: Myths and Realities* (San Francisco: Harper and Row, 1982), 168–84.

27. *Planned Parenthood v. Casey,* 505 U.S. 833 (1992).

28. Craig and O'Brien, *Abortion and American Politics*.

29. Brown, *Trumping Religion*.

30. Paul Weyrich, "The Moral Minority," *Christianity Today* 43 (6 September 1999): 44, as quoted in Brown, *Trumping Religion*, 4.

31. In fact, some among liberal pressure groups saw these statements as political ploys to whip up a frenzy of support among conservative Christian constituencies.

32. See Rousas Rushdoony's *The Messianic Character of American Education* (1963), *The Independent Republic: Studies in the Nature and Meaning of American History* (1964), and Francis Schaeffer's *Escape from Reason* (1968) and *The God Who is There* (1968) for the theological/philosophical foundations of this dominant and dualistic interpretation of the Christian church in Western history. The call to arms issued by New Christian Right leaders in the 1970s had its roots in the writings of these two men. As Detwiler notes, this manner of framing cultural conflict had provided the foundation for New Christian Right political action—"[c]ontemporary Christian Right leaders frame their understanding of the present condition of American society and their proposed solutions within the structure of Schaeffer's and Rushdooney's thought." Detwiler, *Standing on the Premises*, 16. Furthermore, Brown notes the significance to New Christian Right public interest law firms of Schaeffer's condemnation of Christian attorneys who "should have seen the changes taking place [within American law and

culture] and stood on the wall and blown the trumpets loud and clear." Brown, *Trumping Religion*, 6.

33. Moen, *The Transformation of the Christian Right*, 29.

34. New Christian Right lawyers participated in a great number of cases immediately after *Roe v. Wade*, 410 U.S. 113 (1973). The overwhelming majority involved abortion rights litigation, in keeping with the goals of the legislative lobbyists. Largely, conservative Christian attorneys worked in tandem with states and the federal government to pass and then defend abortion legislation. The Christian Right supported state efforts to pass "model legislation" imposing comprehensive limitations on abortion rights and services. These took the form of consent provision, parental or spousal notification, doctor limitations, funding provisions, and record-keeping requirements. See *Belloti v. Baird*, 443 U.S. 622 (1976); *Planned Parenthood v. Danforth*, 505 U.S. 833 (1975); *Beal v. Doe*, 432 U.S. 438 (1977); *Maher v. Roe*, 432 U.S. 464 (1977); and *Poelker v. Doe* 432 U.S. 519 (1977). *Harris v. McRae*, 448 U.S. 297 (1980), involved a challenge to the so-called Hyde Amendment, a federal regulation severely limiting federally funded abortions. The movement lobbied the Carter administration to actively defend the legislation. Furthermore, pro-life groups including Americans United for Life, Catholics for Life, and Feminists for Life filed *amicus curiae* briefs supporting state regulations in *Akron v. Akron Center for Reproductive Health,* 462 U.S. 416 (1983); *Planned Parenthood v. Ashcroft*, 462 U.S. 476 (1983); and *Simopoulos v. Virginia*, 462 U.S. 506 (1986). However, it was not until the late 1980s that the movement began to spin off independent public interest law firms dedicated solely to pursuing sophisticated litigation strategies.

35. John Moore, "The Lord's Litigators." *National Journal*, 2 July 1994.

36. Aaron Wildavsky, "Choosing Preferences by Constructing Institutions: A Cultural Theory of Preference Formation," *American Political Science Review* 81, no. 1 (March 1987): 3–22.

37. Ibid., 6.

38. Ibid., 3.

39. Options which, as Wildasvsky's critics rightly point out, involve conflict and lack of consensus. As Laitin notes, "there is rarely a value consensus within a culture," and he criticizes Wildavsky for not recognizing the importance of "diverse strands of opinion and conflicting values." See David D. Laitin; and Aaron Wildavsky, "Political Culture and Political Preferences," *American Political Science Review* 82, no. 2 (June 1988): 589. Within the larger milieu, "shared values" often means simply what range of options are socially viable, even if conflicting. However, this is not such a great difficulty for the present study. On the level of cultural and social movements, can one really wonder whether the Religious Right is indistinguishable from other segments of American society that oppose the Right politically and socially? Certainly, readily identifiable conflict exists within the conservative Christian movement (consider the turmoil caused within conservative Christian interest groups over abortion clinic violence and the killing of abortion doctors in the late 1980s and early 1990s). But, the issues that spark debate do not necessarily undermine the shared values that characterize the broad movement.

40. Wildavsky, "Choosing Preferences," 4.

41. For example, Wildavsky cites Michael and Becker (1976) as defining the traditional view of preferences within the rational choice discipline. They state that "all human behavior can be viewed as involving participants who maximize their utility from a stable set of preferences." Wildavsky goes on to note that within the rational choice model of inquiry, "[I]f preferences are fixed and outside the process of choice, then we

cannot inquire into how preferences are formed. The least interesting behavior, instrumental actions, may be explained by preferences; but about the most interesting, preferences themselves, nothing can be said." Wildavsky, "Choosing Preferences," 5.

42. David D. Laitin, *Hegemony and Culture: Politics and Religious Change among the Yoruba* (Chicago: University of Chicago Press, 1986), x.

43. Detwiler, *Standing on the Premise of God*, 4.

44. Ibid., 135–45.

45. See Doug McAdam and David A. Snow, "Introduction–Social Movements: Conceptual and Theoretical Issues," in *Social Movements: Readings on Their Emergence, Mobilization, and Dynamics*, ed. Doug McAdam and David A. Snow (Los Angeles: Roxbury Press, 1997).

46. Brown, *Trumping Religion*, 2.

47. For the extensive literature on the political apparatus of the New Christian Right, its efforts to influence electoral politics, and its broader policy influence in issues areas including education, abortion policy, church and state, and so on., and its network of institutions including churches, media, education, think-tanks, and institutes, see Detwiler, *Standing on the Premises of God,*135; Wilcox, *Onward Christian Soldiers?*; Robert B. Fowler and Alan D. Hertzke, *Religion and Politics in America: Faith, Culture, and Strategic Choices* (Boulder, CO: Westview Press, 1995); Moen, *The Transformation of the Religious Right;* and Mark Rozell and Clyde Wilcox, eds., *God at the Grassroots, 1996: The Christian Right in the 1996 Elections* (Lanham, MD: Rowman and Littlefield,1997).

48. In point of fact, scholars have been insisting for years that the New Christian Right is not a monolithic institution and that considerable variation in attitudes and beliefs exists across the spectrum of core and ancillary constituencies, elite leaders, and activists. However, whenever such variation is discovered by the media, considerable surprise is always expressed. For an example, see Cox, "The Warring Visions of the Religious Right." The abstract of his work reads: "Regent University is the intellectual and theological center of the Christian Coalition. What is it like there? Does an inverse political correctness rule? What theology is taught, and what are its political implications? On a recent visit the author, a noted Harvard theologian, found some surprising answers—among them, that the 'Christian right' is no monolith."

49. When a person or group that is not a named party in a lawsuit requests permission to file a brief in that case, we refer to this as *amicus curiae* participation. The term *amicus curiae* is Latin for "friend of the court." *Amicus curiae* generally have a strong interest in a case or a material interest in its outcome. They submit in support of one party or another in the case.

50. See Karen O'Connor, *Women's Organizations' Use of the Courts* (Lexington, MA: D.C. Heath and Company, 1980); and Lee Epstein, *Conservatives in Court* (Knoxville: University of Tennessee Press, 1985).

51. Epstein, *Conservatives in Court*, 48.

52. See Gary King, Robert O. Keohane, and Sidney Verba, *Designing Social Inquiry: Scientific Inference in Qualitative Research* (Princeton, NJ: Princeton University Press, 1994); Allen H. Barton and Paul F. Lazarsfeld, "Some Functions of Qualitative Analysis in Social Research," *Frankfurter Beitrage Zur Soziologie*, Band 1, 1955.

Chapter Two

1. Messianic Judaism includes Jewish people who believe Jesus is the Messiah of both Jews and Gentiles.

2. Dahlia Lithwick, "Rock of Ages and a Hard Space: The Supreme Court Searches for Breathing Room in Its Religion Cases," *Slate Magazine*, 2 December 2003, http://slate.msn.com/id/2091850.

3. *Bray v. Alexandria Women's Health Clinic*, 506 U.S. 263 (1993).

4. Justice Ruth Bader Ginsburg and Jay Sekulow's mother, Natalie Sekulow, graduated from James Madison High School in Brooklyn, New York, which is still in existence today.

5. *Board of Education of Westside Community Schools v. Mergens*, 496 U.S. 248 (1990).

6. From this point forward (except where noted) all quotations are from Jay Sekulow and Joel Thornton, interview by author, tape recording, Atlanta, Georgia, 20 August 1998; and Jay Sekulow, telephone interview, tape recording, 17 September 2004.

7. Frank J. Murray, "Activist Lawyer to Represent Florida Abortion Doctor's Killer," *Washington Times*, 6 October 1995, sec. A, 10.

8. Ibid.

9. *Branch Ministries, Inc. v. Rossoti*, 341 U.S. App. D.C. 166 (2000).

10. Marc Fisher, "Unlikely Crusaders; Jay Sekulow, 'Messianic Jew' of the Christian Right," *Washington Post*, 21 October 1997, sec. D, 01.

11. *Board of Education of Westside Community Schools v. Mergens* (1990); *Campbell v. St. Tammany Parish Sch. Bd.*, 206 F. 3d 482 (2000); *Chandler v. Siegelman*, 530 U.S. 1256 (2000). In *Chandler* the ACLJ challenged a school policy that "assumed that virtually any religious speech in schools is attributable to the State." (230 F. 3d 1313, 2000 at 10). This case was decided immediately after the Supreme Court's ruling in *Santa Fe v. Doe*, a case that Sekulow argued and in which the Court struck down a school district policy allowing student-led religious messages. Thus, even while losing, Sekulow was able to distinguish *Santa Fe* from *Chandler* and gain a victory in court.

12. Gene Kapp, *Roanoke Times & World News*, 8 September 1995.

13. ACLJ, http://www.aclj.org.

14. In *Board of Airport Commissioners of Los Angeles v. Jews for Jesus, Inc.*, 482 U.S. 569 (1987), Sekulow's client was Jews for Jesus, Inc. However, the policy he challenged affected a large number of evangelists from various religions and sects including the two listed above.

15. Sekulow's official title is Member of the Faculty, United States Department of Justice Office of Legal Education. From this position he has acted as adviser to the attorney general.

16. When interviewed in September 2004 for this project, Sekulow noted that he worked on the USA Patriot Act from "concept to completion."

17. Fisher, "Unlikely Crusaders," 1997.

18. Ibid.

19. Ibid.

20. Cable News Network, *Crossfire*, 7 June 1993. Transcript #849. As quoted in Roman, "Center Uses Free Speech to Defend Religious Rights," *Washington Times*, 18 July 1993, sec. A, 4.

21. Furthermore, a brief, general search of the Lexis/Nexis news database reveals that Sekulow's name appears in 115 major newspaper articles between 1989 and 2004

(twenty-seven since the 2000 election). During that time period, he appeared or was interviewed on 192 television and cable news segments (100 since the 2000 election).

22. See FDCH Political Transcripts, 13 May 2004, Committee Hearing, Constitution Subcommittee.

23. Jay Sekulow, *From Intimidation to Victory: Regaining the Christian Right to Speak* (Lake Mary, FL: Creation House Publishers, 1990).

24. The *American Lawyer* later called Sekulow's performance that day "rude, aggressive and obnoxious." See Lyle Deniston, "Airport Speech Ban: Foiled by the Facts?" *American Lawyer* 9, no. 4 (May 1987): 119.

25. Elizabeth Gleick, "Onward Christian Lawyers," *Time Magazine*, 13 March 1995.

26. Gustav Niebuhr, "Conservatives' New Frontier: Religious Liberty Law Firms," *New York Times*, 8 July 1995, sec. 1, 1.

27. It was not even his second move. Robertson hired Keith Fournier as executive director.

28. That book was Jay Sekulow, *From Intimidation to Victory: Regaining the Christian Right to Speak* (1990).

29. See the section, below, entitled "Organizational Structure."

30. This kind of negative rhetoric has come at times from the ACLJ's founder, Rev. Pat Robertson. It is difficult at times to distinguish whether the goal of attacks on the Court is to focus the attention and interest of New Christian Right grassroots membership or an effort to strike out at the legitimacy of the institution (or, perhaps, both at once). However, although Sekulow preaches tolerance for legal incrementalism, it appears that few listen within the movement. For example, Robertson lashed out at the Court after its decision in *Lawrence v. Texas* striking down an anti-sodomy law. In a campaign launched just after the decision (called "Operation Supreme Court Freedom"), Robertson appealed to his constituencies to pray for three retirements from the Court, stating, "In short, by its distorted reading of the religion clause of the First Amendment to the United States Constitution and its 'discovery' of emanations from the Fourteenth Amendment called 'penumbras,' the Supreme Court is bringing upon this nation the wrath of God when the precious liberties that we love so much may be taken away from all of us. . . . One justice is 83 years old, another has cancer, and another has a heart condition. Would it not be possible for God to put it in the minds of these three judges that the time has come to retire? With their retirement and the appointment of conservative judges, a massive change in federal jurisprudence can take place." See http://www.cbn.com/special/ supremecourt/pledgetopray.asp (accessed 12 July 2004).

31. *Board of Westside Community School District v Mergens*, 496 U.S. 248 (1990).

32. The ACLJ web site on student rights and an ACLJ affiliate sponsored site on student rights was begun in 2002. See http://www.aclj.org/resources/studrts /bibleclubs/index.asp; http://www.juntosociety.com/legal/aclj/aclj_sr.htm (accessed 12 July 2004).

33. Jay Sekulow and Keith Fournier, *And Nothing But the Truth: Real Life Stories of American Defending their Faith and Protecting their Families* (Nashville, TN: Thomas Nelson, 1996).

34. Nancy Roman, "Center Uses Free Speech to Defend Religious Rights," *Washington Times*, 18 July 1993, sec. A, 4.

35. Niebuhr, "Conservatives' New Frontier: Religious Liberty Law Firms."

36. Roman, "Center Uses Free Speech."

37. Ibid.

38. For example, while the ACLJ remains very active defending the religious expressive rights of public school students, Sekulow believes the organization is simply

mopping up pockets of resistance to settled doctrines. During 2004, the ACLJ filed seven high-profile lawsuits around the country addressing public school policies discriminating against student-led Bible clubs. But, these were not cases with the potential to change or adapt policy on equal access or free expression. The ACLJ's program is described in detail at http://www.aclj.org/resources/studrts/bibleclubs/index.asp.

39. *Zelman v. Simmons-Harris*, 536 U.S. 639 (2002).

40. Gleick, "Onward Christian Lawyers."

41. *Schenck v. Pro-Choice Women's Network*, 519 U.S. 357 (1997)

42. The effort among New Christian Right litigators to coordinate across firms during the late 1990s was a dismal failure. The Alliance Defense Fund (ADF), originally established as a clearinghouse for monetary grants and national coordination, has devolved into just another New Christian Right litigating firm as founding members became disillusioned with Alan Sears' attempts to corral power within the movement.

43. Keith Fournier left the ACLJ in 1997 to lead a Catholic litigating interest group. Benjamin Bull left after 2000 for the Alliance Defense Fund.

44. As noted in following chapters, the Liberty Counsel and American Family Association's Center for Law and Policy have entered into such an informal agreement to litigate gay rights issues.

45. *United States. v. Kokinda*, 497 U.S. 720 (1990).

46. *Lamb's Chapel v. Center Moriches Union School*, 508 U.S. 384 (1993).

47. *NOW v. Scheidler*, 510 U.S. 249 (1994).

48. Sekulow sent Benjamin Bull to oversee the operations of the European Center for Law and Justice.

49. Steven P. Brown, *Trumping Religion* (Tuscaloosa: University of Alabama Press, 2002), 47.

50. *Locke v. Davey*, 124 S. Ct. 1307 (2004).

51. John Moore, "The Lord's Litigators." *National Journal*, 2 July 1994.

52. Gregg Ivers, "Please, God, Save this Honorable Court: The Emergence of the Conservative Religious Bar." In *The Interest Group Connection*, ed. Paul S. Herrnson, Ronald G. Shaiko, and Clyde Wilcox (Chatham, NJ: Chatham House, 1998).

53. Roman, "Center Uses Free Speech."

54. Sinha Sonejuhi, "ACLU Discusses Civil Liberties," *Flat Hat: Student Newspaper of the College of William and Mary,* 12 November 2001, 1. This author was present at the event when Kent Willis voiced support for the New Christian Right's position on expressive freedom in public schools, and asked him to repeat his statement of support for the record.

55. *Hill v. Colorado*, 530 U.S. 703 (2000).

56. *Locke v. Davey*, 124 S. Ct. 1307 (2004).

57. *Santa Fe Independent School District v. Doe*, 530 U.S. 290 (2000).

58. Sekulow refused to participate at the trial and intermediate appellate levels when invited by the school district. According to other New Christian Right attorneys, he did not believe that the case should have been appealed and would have preferred that the Court accept a case Mat Staver and the Liberty Counsel were litigating in Florida. See the extensive discussion of *Adler v. Duval County Sch. Bd.*, 206 F. 3d 1070 (2000), in chapter 3 of this book.

59. *Board of Regents v. Southworth*, 529 U.S. 217 (2000).

60. *Boy Scouts of America v. Dale*, 530 U.S. 640 (2000).

61. Since 1999, it has participated in a large number of cases and brought two important cases along through appellate review: *SD Myers, Inc. v. City and County of*

San Francisco, 253 F. 3d 461 (2001); *Altman v. Minnesota Dept. of Corrections*, 251 F. 3d 1199 (2001).

62. *Bowers v. Hardwick*, 478 U.S. 186 (1986).

63. *Goodridge v. Department of Public Health*, 440 Mass. 309 (2003), at 312.

64. Figures for 2004 represent only the first half of the judicial term for that year.

65 Karen O'Connor, *Women's Organizations' Use of the Courts* (Lexington, MA: D. C. Heath and Company, 1980).

66. Ibid., 3.

Chapter 3

1. Mathew D. Staver, "Injunctive Relief and the *Madsen* Test," *St. Louis University Law Review* 14 (1995): 465–478.

2. Staver founded of a successful workers' compensation practice in Florida, Staver and Associates, before selling it to move into full-time public interest litigiation.

3. He is president of Staver Air.

4. See the Liberty Counsel web site, http://www.lc.org.

5. Mark I. Pinsky, "Fight for Religious Liberty Brings Lawyer Few 'Amens,'" *Orlando Sentinel*, 9 September 1995, sec. D, 5.

6. Margaret A. Jacobs, "Employers' Religious Bias Not Tolerated, Case Shows." *Pittsburgh Post-Gazette*, 27 August 1995, sec. D, 1.

7. Oliver Thomas, Testimony before the United States Senate Judiciary Committee, *Federal Document Clearinghouse–Congressional Testimony*, 20 October 1995.

8. Staver is currently a member of First Baptist Church of Orlando, Florida. He left the Seventh-Day Adventist Church over doctrinal concerns related to Evangelicalism, primarily his perception that the denomination has purposefully isolated itself from society.

9. The film was most probably *Silent Scream*, which was widely disseminated among churches during the early 1980s.

10. From this point forward (except where noted) all quotations are from Mathew D. Staver and Nicole Arfaras-Kerr, interview by author, tape recording, Orlando, Florida., 17 December 1998; and Mathew D. Staver, telephone interview, tape recording, 3 March 2004.

11. Mark Curriden, "Defenders of the Faith: The Growth of Public-Service Christian Law Firms," *American Bar Association Journal* 80 (December 1994): 93.

12. Ibid.

13. Pinsky, "Fight for Religious Liberty."

14. Monaghan eventually became senior counsel with the ACLJ.

15. All quotations from Liberty Counsel staff attorney, Nicole Arfaras-Kerr are from an interview conducted in December 1998 at the office of the Liberty Counsel, Orlando, Florida.

16. Staver notes that the LC's primary focus was "refined" and did not change conceptually, except that the LC has placed litigation rather than education at the forefront of its mission. Staver has come to the conclusion that, while education remains a central component of its mission, the LC must be quicker to resort to litigation as a tool for resolving conflict.

17. Pinsky, "Fight for Religious Liberty."

18. Brown notes both the disapproval of movement critics to using the free speech clause to make "an end run around the Supreme Court's decisions mandating a separation of church and state" and resistance among some in the New Christian Right to the free expression argument. According to some within the movement "in seeking refuge in the free speech clause, New Christian Right lawyers may well have cheapened religion by linking it with pornography, commercial advertising, racial invectives, flag burning and other forms of 'protected speech.'" Steven P. Brown, *Trumping Religion* (Tuscaloosa: University of Alabama Press, 2002), 10.

19. Lyle Denniston, "Judges May Keep Protests from Blocking Abortion Clinics, Supreme Court Rules," *Baltimore Sun*, 1 July 1994, sec. A, 3.

20. John W. Kennedy, "Buffer–zone Case Tests Free Speech," *Christianity Today* 38 (20 June 1994): 48.

21. Brown, *Trumping Religion*, 30. Brown notes that the LC's average budget was around $500,000 per year.

22. See http://www.lc.org.

23. *Freedom from Religion Foundation v. City of Marshfield*, no. 98 C 270 (1998). Unpublished opinion of the U.S. District Court for the Western District of Wisconsin.

24. *Freedom from Religion Foundation v. City of Marshfield*, 203 F. 3d 487 (1999).

25. While the majority adopted the general position endorsed by the state and the LC on brief, the dissent in this case offered a scathing review of the LC's *amicus* brief and quoted directly from it.

26. *Operation Rescue v. Women's Health Center*, 626 So. 2d 664 (1993).

27. *First Baptist Church v. Miami–Dade County*, 768 So. 2d 1114 (2000); *Martin v. City of Gainesville*, 800 So. 2d 687 (2001).

28. *Jackson v. Benson*, 213 Wis. 2d 1 (1997).

29. *Deida v. City of Milwaukee*, 206 F. Supp. 2d 967 (2002).

30. *Wigg v. Sioux Falls School District 49–5*, 274 F. Supp. 2d 1084 (2003).

31. *ACLU v. Mercer County*, 240 F. Supp. 2d 623 (2003).

32. *Moore v. City of Asheville*, 290 F. Supp. 2d 664 (2003).

33. *Hebel, Robert v. West, Jason*, Case #04–0642, Supreme Court, Ulster County (2004); *Thomasso, Randy v. Newsom, Gavin and Alfaro, Nancy*, Case # CGC04–428794, Coordination Proceeding No 4365, Superior Court of California, County of San Francisco (2004). As this book went to press, the California Supreme Court barred Newsom from issuing marriage licenses to gays and invalidated those licenses Newsom had issued. See Dean Murphy, "California Supreme Court Rules Gay Unions Have No Standing," *New York Times*, 13 August 2004, http://www.nytimes.com/2004/08/13/national/13gays.html?th.

34. Liberty Counsel, *Liberator* 10, no. 1 (1999).

35. On the initial appeal, a three judge panel of the Eleventh Circuit overturned the trial court's decision, declaring the policy unconstitutional on grounds that students participating in the graduation ceremony and delivering the disputed message acted as agents of the state. Any religious content to the message would violate the First Amendment's prohibition against state sponsorship of religion. Shortly thereafter, the Eleventh Circuit vacated this decision and agreed to a rehearing *en banc* where Staver again prevailed and the policy was declared constitutional. The ACLU requested review by the Supreme Court. However, the case was never heard by the Supreme Court, which vacated the *en banc* decision and ordered a rehearing consistent with its decision in *Santa Fe*. Upon review (the third time the case was heard on appeal) the Eleventh Circuit reinstated its previous decision upholding the policy verbatim, declaring that the Court's ruling in *Santa Fe* did not require any change to its rationale. The ACLU appealed to the

Supreme Court again. The Court denied review, allowing the Eleventh Circuit's decision to stand.

36. *Adler v. Duval County Sch. Bd.*, 206 F. 3d 1070, 1075 (11th Cir. 2000) (en banc), vacated by 531 U.S. 801 (2000) (Mem.), and reinstated, 250 F. 3d 1330 (11th Cir. 2001) (en banc), cert. denied, no. 01–287, 2001 WL 984867 (U.S. Dec. 10, 2001).

37. Julie Hauserman, "School Singled Out Christian Group, Girl's Lawsuit Says," *St. Petersburg Times*, 16 January 1999.

38. Liberty Counsel, "High School Backs away from Attempts to Censor Graduation Speech about Faith in God," 7 June 2004, http://www/lc.org/libertyalert /2004/1a060704.htm#Mass.

39. *Hall v. Teague Middle School & Seminole County School Board, FL*, unpublished opinion of the United States District Court for the Middle District of Florida, Orlando Division (1998). This case was brought by the LC on behalf of a student-led Christian group excluded from school-wide diversity celebrations.

40. A case filed by the LC under the Protection of Pupil Rights Act. It challenges the use of student questionnaires on hot-button issues from sexuality to racism without parental consent or consultation.

41. Bruce Vielmetti, "Religious Group Sues Pamphlet-Free TIA." *St. Petersburg Times,* 15 August 1995.

42. *Christ's Bride Ministries, Inc. v. Southeastern Pennsylvania Transit Authority*, 148 F. 3d 242 (1998).

43. The city appealed to the Supreme Court, but its petition for *certiorari* review was denied. In mediation, the transit authority agreed to reimburse Christ's Bride Ministries for all legal costs and place the ads back on city buses.

44. *Madsen v. Women's Health Clinic*, 512 U.S. 753 (1994).

45. *Operation Rescue v. Women's Health Center*, 626 So. 2d 664 (1993).

46. *Cheffer v. McGregor*, 6 F. 3d 705 (1993).

47. These interests were defined as stopping violent protest, protecting access of clients to clinics, and the health of those persons using abortion facilities.

48. *True Life Choice v. HRS*, 914 F. Supp. 507 (1996).

49. Phil Long, "HRS Pays Legal Fees for Abortion Foes," *Miami Herald*, 29 March 1996.

50. *Burns v. Burns*, 253 Ga. App. 600 (2002). The case involved a challenge to the Georgia and federal defense of marriage acts after a parent asserted that Georgia must recognize (give full faith and credit to) a certificate of civil union obtained under the Vermont civil union law (2000). The Georgia court ruled that the Vermont civil union did not constitute a marriage, and that the State of Georgia was not bound to recognize the union under its own or the federal statutes. This case was the first such of its kind in the United States.

51. *Lofton, Steven et al. v. Kearney, Kathleen et al.*, 157 F. Supp. 2d 1372 (2001).

52. *Diaz, Ruben Sr., et al. v. New York City Dep't of Educ, et al.* (ongoing)

53. *Ash, William et al., v. Forman, Howard*, Case # 04–003279, 17th Judicial Circuit, Broward County, Florida (2004).

54. Jacobs, "Employers' Religious Bias Not Tolerated, Case Shows."

55. No instances of participation by the LC during the first two years of its existence were reported to and recorded by Lexis/Nexis Academic Universe.

56. Examination of IRS Form 990 for tax years 1994–1998 provided by the LC reveals an enormous leap from a budget of $44,800 in 1993 (the year that the LC filed suit in *Cheffer v. McGregor*) to almost $200,000 in 1994.

57. *Christ's Bride Ministries, Inc. v. Southeastern Pennsylvania Transit Authority*, 148 F. 3d 242 (1998).

58. They were both consolidated into the same case, *Madsen v. Women's Health Clinic*. See discussion of LC participation in that case, above.

Chapter 4

1. Benjamin Bull left the CLP to join Jay Sekulow and the American Center for Law and Justice as senior associate counsel. Bull eventually became the director of the European Center for Law and Justice, and then joined the Alliance Defense Fund.

2. Bruce Green left the CLP shortly after I interviewed him in 1998. He joined the Alliance Defense Fund to develop attorney-training programs, then left in 2000 to become the first dean of the Liberty University Law School.

3. From this point forward (except where noted) all quotations are from Steve Crampton, Bruce Green, Brian Fahling, Michael DiPrimo, or Tim Wildmon, interview by author, tape recording, Tupelo, Mississippi, 18 August 1998 and 16 December 2004.

4. Fredrick Clarkson, "Correcting Dangerous Myths about the Christian Right," *Institute for First Amendment Studies, Inc.* June/July 1993, http://www.apocalypse .bershire.net/~ifas/fw/9306/myths.html (accessed 12 December 1997).

5. Mike Harden, "Pornography Lurks Almost Everywhere in Watchdog's Eyes," *Columbus Dispatch*, 14 January 1998, Sec. E, 1.

6. Hubert Morken, "The Evangelical Legal Response to the ACLU: Religion, Politics, and the First Amendment," Paper prepared for the Annual Meeting of the American Political Science Association, Chicago, 3–6 September 1992.

7. Donald Wildmon as quoted in Harden, "Pornography Lurks Almost Everywhere in Watchdog's Eyes," 1.

8. Morken, "The Evangelical Legal Response to the ACLU," 8–9.

9. Karen Rouse, "Group has Lobbied for Disney Divestiture," *Fort Worth Star-Telegram*, 10 July 1998, sec. Metro, 2.

10. Daniel Jeffreys, "When a Wildmon Wreaks Havoc," *Independent* (London), 27 July 1995, sec. Life, 6.

11. Ibid.

12. Nat Hentoff, "RICO: Hazardous to Users and Targets," *Washington Post*, 9 December 1989, sec. A, 19.

13. Playboy's suit was dismissed without prejudice, providing the AFA protection from RICO actions in the future. Bull successfully argued for a summary judgment in the Penthouse suit.

14. Hentoff, "RICO: Hazardous to Users and Targets."

15. See *Cheffer v. Reno*, 55 F. 3d 1517 (1995), a challenge to the constitutionality of the Freedom of Access to Clinic Entrances (FACE) Act.

16. The CLP has never had to defend a ruling from review by the high court.

17. In point of fact, when interviewed in 1998 (long before the explosion of cases involving gay marriage during the early 2000s), Brian Fahling predicted that the gay rights issue would be come much more salient in the coming years, both for the public and for New Christian Right litigators. He also noted that the CLP was addressing legal

conflicts over gay rights at a time when most other New Christian Right litigators did not list the issue area among their top concerns.

18. The CLP is so highly mobile that even the ACLJ's "SWAT team" approach to litigation pales in comparison. While the ACLJ can appear in court within a matter of days, the CLP has been known to move within hours to obtain an injunction and court hearing. The parent organization's business fleet of aircraft assists the center when it becomes necessary to make an appearance in court quickly.

19. Morken, "The Evangelical Legal Response to the ACLU," 8–9.

20. Julia McCord, "Defending Religious Rights Non-profit Christian Law Organizations Gain Ground," *Omaha World Herald*, 29 April 1995, sec. SF, 57.

21. The AFA maintains a toll-free number for contacting core projects. The pre-recorded message includes an option for contacting law center personnel directly if callers believe their constitutional rights have been violated.

22. Cathy Franklin, "Pastor Sues City for Telling Church to Move from Storefront," *City News Service*, 15 July 1999.

23. Michael Luo, "Ousted Church Persuades City to Reverse Ban," *Los Angeles Times*, 22 July 1999, sec. B, 1.

24. Cathy Franklin, "Pastor Sues City."

25. See Family Research Council policy statements on state-level challenges to partial birth abortion bans, 1999 to present. In particular, see the press release entitled "Partial-Birth Abortion Ban Victories in Virginia and Missouri," http://www.frc.org/press/091799b.html, 17 September 1999. Also see release entitled "FRC Lauds 'Impartial' Appeals Court Decision on Partial-Birth Abortion Laws," http://www.frc.org/press/102799.html, 27 October 1999 (accessed 13 May 2004).

26. The other is the American Center for Law and Justice.

27. The other cases were *U.S. v. Riley* and *U.S. v. Scott*. The CLP participated in this case on appeal. See 145 F. 3d 74 (1998).

28. *Bischoff v. Osceola County* 222 F. 3d 874 (2000).

29. *Lytle v. Doyle* 326 F. 3d 463 (2003).

30. *Faustin v. City and County of Denver* 268 F. 3d 942 (2001).

31. *Brown v. Polk County* 61 F. 3d 650 (1995).

32. *Saxe v. State College Area School District* 240 F. 3d 200 (2001).

33. Brian Fahling, "Tampering with Our Cultural DNA," *American Family Association*, 19 November 2003, http://www.afa.net/clp/GetArticle.asp?id=15.

34. *Boy Scouts of America v. Dale*, 530 U.S. 640 (2000).

35. *Goodridge v. Department of Public Health,* 440 Mass. 309 (2003), at 312.

36. See John Curran, "N.J. Couples Seek Marriage Licenses," *Associated Press*, 9 March 2004; Gene Johnson, "Seattle Mayor Recognizes Employees' Gay Marriages," *Washington Post*, 9 March 2004, sec. A, 03.

37. *Kansas v. Limon* 83 P. 3d 229 (2004). See the comments *inter alia* on the LC's involvement in this case.

38. David Von Drehle, "Legal Confusion Over Gay Marriage," *Washington Post*, 27 February 2004, sec. A, 08.

39. Steven Crampton, "Letters to California Officials," 13 February 2004, http://www.afa.net/clp/ArticlesNew.asp.

40. Brian Fahling, "The Federal Marriage Amendment: A Necessary Response to an Imminent Threat," 16 February 2004, http://www.afa.net/clp/ArticlesNew.asp.

41. Cheryl Wetzstein, "Court's Authority over Marriage Law Challenged," *Washington Times*, 7 June 2004, http://www.washtimes.com/national/20040607-124837-6491r.htm.

42. American Family Association Center for Law and Policy, "Little Known Legal Theory Deployed in Effort to Restore Government to the People of Massachusetts," 11 May 2004, http://www.afa.net/clp/ReleaseDetail.asp?id=52.

43. Ibid.

44. In 2000, the CLP filed an *amicus* brief in *Steinberg v. Carhart,* 530 U.S. 914 (2000). In this case, the U.S. Supreme Court declared unconstitutional a Nebraska statute that criminalized the performance of partial birth abortion procedures.

45. See table 4.5. The table records twenty instances of CLP participation as sponsor on appeal (all occur in U.S. courts of appeal), and thirty-six instances of total federal appellate court participation.

46. These two (*Faustin v. City and County of Denver* and *Lytle v. Doyle*) are discussed above in detail.

Chapter 5

1. In particular, recent studies of legislative lobbying have enlarged the scope of influences scholars consider. See John Mark Hansen, *Gaining Access: Congress and the Farm Lobby, 1919–1981* (Chicago: University of Chicago Press, 1991); Richard L. Hall and Frank W. Wayman, "Buying Time: Moneyed Interests and the Mobilization of Bias in Congressional Committees," *American Political Science Review* 84, no. 3 (September 1990): 797–820; David Austen-Smith and John R. Wright, "Counteractive Lobbying," *American Journal of Political Science* 38, no. 1 (February 1994): 25–44; John P. Heinz, et al., *The Hollow Core: Private Interests in National Policy Making* (Cambridge: Harvard University Press, 1993). Hansen began to direct the efforts of scholars toward concepts related to achieving policy goals including access to policy makers and political uncertainty. This theme is also at the center of analyses that consider environmental limitations on policy influence and refine the concept of influence to include specific legislative favors, access to policy makers, information and resource provision, and the effect of "political intelligence" on constituency preferences. Scholars conclude that the structure of the political environment places significant limitations on interest group capacities for influence. Heinz, et al. note the effects of a politically uncertain environment on legislative lobbying activities. Thus, scholars have analyzed the ways that groups attempt to achieve their goals given external systemic limitations.

2. See Lee Epstein, *Conservatives in Court* (Knoxville: University of Tennessee Press, 1985); Karen O'Connor, *Women's Organizations' Use of the Courts* (Lexington, MA: D. C. Heath and Company, 1980); Karen O'Connor and Lee Epstein, "The Rise of Conservative Interest Group Litigation," *Journal of Politics* 45, no. 2 (May 1983): 479–89; Lee Epstein and Joseph Kobylka, *The Supreme Court and Legal Change: Abortion and the Death Penalty* (Chapel Hill: University of North Carolina Press, 1992); and Joseph F. Kobylka, "A Court-Created Context for Group Litigation: Libertarian Groups and Obscenity," *Journal of Politics* 49, no. 4 (November 1987): 1061–78. However, other traditionally qualitative works have combined a concern for internal group dynamics, expectations, and motivations with description of the social and legal environment as well as legal strategies employed to achieve policy aims. See Shaun Peters, *Judging Jehovah's Witnesses: Religious Persecution and the Dawn of the Rights Revolution* (Lawrence: University Press of Kansas, 1999). Peters links the environment of persecution against Jehovah's Witnesses to internal ideological positions on rights

within the ACLU, prompting it to seek policy change in the area of religious expression. Furthermore, those who study the Religious Right in court have been particularly (although not always systematically) concerned about motivations and internal characteristics of litigators. Also, see Steven P. Brown, *Trumping Religion* (Tuscaloosa: University of Alabama Press, 2002); and Fritz Detwiler, *Standing on the Premises of God: The Christian Right's Fight to Redefine Public Schools* (New York: New York University Press, 1999). Broad description of the ideological underpinnings of conservatism has been left to those who study grassroots mobilization and electioneering within the New Christian Right. For example, see Clyde Wilcox, *Onward Christian Soldiers?: The Religious Right in American Politics*, 2nd ed. (Boulder, CO: Westview Press, 2000); Clyde Wilcox and Ted G. Jelen, "Rethinking the Reasonableness of the Religious Right," *Review of Religious Research* 36 (1995): 263–76; and Kenneth Wald, *Religion and Politics in the United States* (New York: St. Martin's Press, 1997).

3. Lee Epstein, "Courts and Interest Groups," in *The American Courts: A Critical Assessment*, ed. John B. Gates and Charles A. Johnson, (Washington, DC: Congressional Quarterly Press, 1991), 335–71.

4. The previous chapter on the ACLJ provides an example in *Santa Fe v. Doe*, 530 U.S. 290 (2000). The ACLJ did not participate at trial or on appeal until the case was accepted for review by the Supreme Court. Sekulow exerted no influence on the lower court record. In effect, he lost control of this case and argued it before the Supreme Court in an effort to limit the damage that such a precedent might cause in the future.

5. The category "Test Case" in table 5.2 combines the following categories from table 5.1: Full Test Case Strategy, Test Case Strategy—intermediate appellate to court of last resort, Test Case Strategy—trial to intermediate appellate level with cert. denial, and Test Case Strategy—trial to intermediate appellate level with no cert petition. I treat these categories separately in table 5.3 below.

6. A group could, of course, make numerous appearances before courts while litigating the same case. Including the number of actual cases litigated (the first number in each cell) provides a slightly different picture of litigation than simply providing the number of instances (the second number in each cell) in which the group made an appearance as I have done up to this point.

7. In addition, the ACLJ sponsored three cases heard by state supreme courts, including one that was reviewed by the U.S. Supreme Court (*Hill v. Thomas*, 973 P. 2d 1246, 1999). Further, the ACLJ participated as Counsel on Brief in four more cases before the U.S. Supreme Court, bringing the total of cases in which it participated heavily before a court of last resort to nineteen.

8. The three cases Sekulow argued before the Supreme Court in which he did not participate at trial or at the intermediate appellate level were *Santa Fe I.S.D. v. Jane Doe*, 530 U.S. 290 (2000); *Bray v. Alexandria Women's Health Clinic*, 506 U.S. 263 (1993); and *Board v. Jews for Jesus*, 482 U.S. 569 (1987).

9. They are *Locke v. Davey*, 124 S. Ct. 1307 (2004); *Scheidler v. NOW*, 537 U.S. 393 (2003); *Campbell v. St. Tammany Parish*, 533 U.S. 913 (2001); *Chandler v. Siegelman*, 530 U.S. 1256 (2000); *Lamb's Chapel v. Center Moriches*, 508 U.S. 384 (1993); and *Westside Community Schools v. Mergens* 496 U.S. 226 (1990).

10. *Schenck v. Pro-Choice Network*, 519 U.S. 357 (1997); *U.S. v. Koklinda*, 497 U.S. 720 (1990).

11. *Hill v. Colorado*, 530 U.S. 703 (2000). In the third state supreme court case, the ACLJ only participated in the final stage. See *In re Inquiry Concerning a Judge*, 345 N.C. 632 (1997).

12. *Kaplan v. Prolife Action League of Greensboro*, 347 N.C. 342 (1997).

13. They are *Full Gospel Tabernacle v. Community School District 27*, 164 F. 3d 829 (1999); *Edwards v. City of Santa Barbara,* 150 F. 3d 1213 (1998); *Hoffman v. Hunt,* 126 F. 3d 575 (1997); and *U.S. v. Terry*, 17 F. 3d 575 (1994).

14. *Adler v. Duvall County School District II*, 250 F. 3d 1330 (2001). In this case, the Supreme Court granted *certiorari* review, but immediately remanded it to the intermediate appellate court for reconsideration in light of *Santa Fe v. Doe.* After reconsideration, the opposing party applied for Supreme Court review again, but that petition was denied. Since the Supreme Court never issued an opinion in this case, I have coded it as a case that moved from trial to intermediate appellate court with a denial of *certiorari* review.

15. Of course, in some of these cases the CLP prevailed and the burden to apply for higher review fell on its opponent. The CLP can hardly be blamed in these cases for not pursuing higher appellate review of a case in which it prevailed. However, even in cases in which the opposition prevailed at the intermediate appellate level, the CLP did not pursue further review.

16. As noted in chapter 4, the CLP's most profound appellate victory (in *Brown v. Woodland Joint ISD*, 27 F. 3d 1373 [1993], a religious establishment case) did not provide it with the opportunity to control or contribute to the court record at trial.

17. Kevin R. den Dulk, "Prophets in Caesar's Courts: The Legal Mobilization of Religious Groups" (Ph.D. diss., University of Wisconsin, 2000).

18. A reference to the French national policy limiting public displays of religious clothing and symbols in public schools.

19. Clement E. Vose, *Caucasians Only: The Supreme Court, the NAACP, and the Restrictive Housing Covenant Cases* (Los Angeles: University of California Press, 1959); Frank J. Sorauf, *The Wall of Separation: The Constitutional Politics of Church and State* (New Jersey: Princeton University Press, 1976); Karen O'Connor, *Women's Organizations' Use of the Courts* (Lexington, MA: D. C. Heath and Company, 1980).

20. *Schenck v. Pro-Choice Network Of Western New York*, 1996 U.S. TRANS LEXIS 64 (1996), at 50.

21. Clearly, playing by the rules of the Court does not mean that Sekulow, a tenacious and bulldogged fighter who takes every opportunity to win a case, pulls his punches. What follows is an excerpt from Petitioner's Reply Brief in Schenck:

> Respondents make passing reference to an alleged health risk of delaying abortion in response to protest activities. Resp. Br. at 16. It is certainly true that abortion, as the forcible interruption of the natural state of pregnancy, poses dangers to the woman, as even respondents' amici admit, ACOG Br. at 7 & nn. 6–7. But respondent Paul Davis, MD, testified that, at least through fourteen weeks of gestation, "I'm not dealing in the area where a delay would make any difference." Tr. 847–48. Furthermore, respondents themselves have no qualms about delaying their patients' abortions, not only to accommodate their own business schedule (abortions are not done every day of the week), but also whenever they conclude the pregnant woman should wait and reconsider. . . .

22. Brown, *Trumping Religion*, 10.

23. Fahling refers a trial court ruling in the case *Jaffree v. James*, 554 F. Supp. 1130 (S.D. Ala. 1983). In this case, Judge Brevard Hand argued that the doctrine of incorporation, or applying portions of the Bill of Rights to state governments as part of

the definition of due process found in the Fourteenth Amendment, is an illegitimate construction of the Constitution and the intent of that amendment's framers. See Gregg Ivers, *Redefining the First Freedom* (New Brunswick, PA: Transaction Publishers, 1993), 11.

24. The CLP does not dispute this conclusion. It views the legal environment as particularly hostile to its worldview. One CLP attorney noted that he feels real and personal intolerance from the legal system, and works out the application of principles "in a political and legal culture that despises my faith."

25. David R. Manwaring, *Render Unto Caesar: The Flag-Salute Controversy* (Chicago: University of Chicago Press, 1962); Richard C. Cortner, *A Mob Intent on Death: The NAACP and Arkansas Riot Cases* (Boston: University Press of New England, 1988).

26. For example, Epstein notes that the number of case studies of the ACLU after Vose's *Caucasians Only* was approximately fifty-one (see Epstein, *Conservatives in Court*, 7).

27. Frank J. Sorauf, *Wall of Separation;* Epstein, *Conservatives in Court.*

28. Marc Galanter, "Why the 'Haves' Come Out Ahead: Speculations on the Limits of Legal Change." *Law and Society Review* 9, no. 1 (fall 1974): 95–160; Joseph F. Kobylka, *The Politics of Obscenity: Group Litigation in a Time of Change* (New York: Greenwood Press, 1991); O'Connor, *Women's Organizations Use of the Courts.*

29. Sorauf, *Wall of Separation.*

30. Kim Lane Scheppele and Jack L. Walker Jr., "The Litigation Strategies of Interest Groups," in *Mobilizing Interest Groups in America*, ed. Jack Walker Jr. (Ann Arbor: University of Michigan Press, 1991).

31. See Susan Olson, *Clients and Lawyers: Securing the Rights of Disabled Persons* (Westport, CT: Greenwood Press, 1984).

32. See page 21 of this text, and page 186 n21 for a brief survey of Sekulow's media appearances.

Bibliography

Alvord, Valerie. "Group's Lawsuit Targets City, NFL; Seeks OK to Leaflet Fans at Super Bowl." *San Diego Union-Tribune*, 24 January 1998.

American Center for Law and Justice. http://www.aclj.org.

American Family Association Center for Law and Policy. "Abortion Clinics Agree to Pay Protester $3,000 to Settle Claims of Abuse of Legal Process." Press Release, 14 December 1998.

———. "AFA Center for Law and Policy Wins Trio of Pro-Life Cases." *AFA Journal*, March 1999. http://www.afa.net/law/9903.html.

———, "Little Known Legal Theory Deployed in Effort to Restore Government to the People of Massachusetts," 11 May 2004, http://www.afa.net/clp/ReleaseDetail.asp?id=52.

———. "Moral Lynching in Lynchburg." *AFA Action Letter*, April 1998.

———. "Partial-Birth Abortion and the Inevitable Delivery Theory." 14 May 1999. http://www.afa.net/law/990514.htm.

———. "A Victory for Free Speech in Idaho County Court." Press Release, 15 March 1999.

———. http://www.afa.net/clp/.

Andrews, James H. "Religious Right Fights for Rights." *Christian Science Monitor*, 7 February 1994, 14.

Austen-Smith, David, and John R. Wright. "Counteractive Lobbying," *American Journal of Political Science* 38, no. 1 (February 1994): 25–44.

Barker, Lucius J., and Twiley W. Barker Jr. *Freedom, Courts, Politics: Studies in Civil Liberties*. Trenton, NJ: Prentice Hall, 1965.

Baum, Lawrence. *The Puzzle of Judicial Behavior*. Ann Arbor: University of Michigan Press, 1997.

Benson, Peter L., and Dorothy L. Williams, *Religion on Capitol Hill: Myths and Realities*. San Francisco: Harper and Row, 1982.

Berry, Jeffrey M. *The Interest Group Society*. 2nd ed. Glenview, IL: Scott, Foresman Press, , 1989.

———. *Lobbying for the People*. Princeton, NJ: Princeton University Press, 1977.

Blanchard, D. A. *The Anti-Abortion Movement and the Rise of the Religious Right: From Polite to Fiery Protest*. New York: Twayne Publishers, 1994.

Booth, Wayne C., Gregory G. Colomb, and Joseph M. Williams. *The Craft of Research*. Chicago: University of Chicago Press, 1995.

Brisbin, R. A. J. *Justin Anton Scalia and the Conservative Revival*. Baltimore, MD: Johns Hopkins University Press, 1997.

Brown, Steven P. *Trumping Religion: The New Christian Right, the Free Speech Clause, and the Courts*. Tuscaloosa: University of Alabama Press, 2002.

Browne, William P. "Organized Interests and Their Issue Niches: A Search for Pluralism an a Policy Domain." *Journal of Politics* 52, no. 2 (May 1990): 477–509.

Buckley, William F., Jr. "The NEA and Censorship." *National Review*, 9 July 1990, 62.

Byrnes, Timothy A., and Mary C. Segers. *The Catholic Church and the Politics of Abortion*. Boulder: Westview Press, 1992.

Cable News Network. "Groups Fail to Block Same-Sex Marriage Licenses." Original broadcast date, 13 February 2004. http://www.cnn.com/2004/US/West/02/13/samesex.marriage.

———. "Massachusetts Court Rules Ban on Gay Marriage Unconstitutional." Original broadcast date, 4 February 2004. http://www.cnn.com/2003/LAW/11/18/samesex.marriage.ruling.

———. "State's Constitution Was Basis for Ruling." Original broadcast date, 18 November 2003. http://www.cnn.com/2003/LAW/11/18/samesex.ruling.

Caldeira, Gregory A., and John R. Wright. "Amicus Curiae before the Court: Who Participates, When and How Much?" *Journal of Politics* 52, no. 3 (August 1990): 782–806.

———. "Lobbying for Justice: Organized Interests, Supreme Court Nominations and the United States Senate." *American Journal of Political Science* 42, no. 2 (April 1998): 499–523.

———. "Organized Interests and Agenda Setting in the U.S. Supreme Court." *American Political Science Review* 82, no. 4 (December 1988): 1109–27.

Carelli, Richard. "Challenge to Oregon School System Rejected." *Associated Press Washington Dateline*, 11 January 1999.

Carter, Stephen L. *The Culture of Disbelief: How American Law and Politics Trivializes Religious Belief.* New York: Basic Books, 1993.

Cigler, Allan J., and Burdett A. Loomis, eds. *Interest Group Politics.* 4th ed. Washington, DC: Congressional Quarterly Press, 1994.

———. *Interest Group Politics.* 3rd ed. Washington DC: Congressional Quarterly Press, 1991.

Clark, Peter B., and James Q. Wilson. "Incentive Systems: A Theory of Organizations." *Administrative Science Quarterly* 6 (1961):129.

Clarkson, Fredrick. "Correcting Dangerous Myths about the Christian Right," *Institute for First Amendment Studies, Inc.*, June/July 1993. http://www.apocalypse.bershire.net/~ifas/fw/9306/myths.html.

Clayton, Cornell W. "The Supreme Court and Political Jurisprudence: New and Old Institutionalisms." In *Supreme Court Decision-Making: New Institutional Approaches*, edited by Cornell Clayton and Howard Gillman. Chicago: University of Chicago Press, 1999.

Cole, Jeff. "Board Keeps Good Friday Holiday; County's Designation Can Stand Up to Legal Challenges, Florida-Based Liberty Counsel Tell Supervisors." *Milwaukee Journal Sentinel*, 9 January 1997.

Cox, Harvey. "The Warring Visions of the Religious Right." *Atlantic Monthly* 276, no. 5 (1995): 59–69.

Craig, Barbara H., and David M. O'Brien. *Abortion and American Politics.* Chatham, NJ: Chatham House Publishers, 1991.

Crampton, Steven, "Letters to California Officials," 13 February 2004. http://www.afa.net/clp/ArticlesNew.asp.

———. "The Tyranny of T.V." *American Family Association Center for Law and Policy*, 5 May 1999. http://www.afa.net/law/990505.htm.

Curran, John. "N.J. Couples Seek Marriage Licenses." *Associated Press*, 9 March 2004.

Curriden, Mark. "Defenders of the Faith: The Growth of Public-Service Christian Law Firms." *American Bar Association Journal* 80 (December 1994): 86.

Cusac, Ann Marie. "Suing for Jesus." *Progressive* 61, no. 4 (April 1997): 30.

den Dulk, Kevin R. "The Legal Mobilization of the New Christian Right: Resources, Strategies, and Impact." Paper prepared for the Annual Meeting of the Midwest Political Science Association, Chicago, 23–26 April 1998.

———— "Prophets in Caesar's Courts: The Legal Mobilization of Religious Groups." Ph.D. diss., University of Wisconsin, 2000.

Denniston, Lyle. "Airport Speech Ban: Foiled by the Facts?" *American Lawyer* 9, no. 4 (May 1987): 119.

———— "Judges May Keep Protests from Blocking Abortion Clinics, Supreme Court Rules." *Baltimore Sun*, 1 July 1994, sec. A, 3.

Detwiler, Fritz. *Standing on the Premises of God: The Christian Right's Fight to Redefine Public Schools*. New York: New York University Press, 1999.

Douglas, Mary, and Aaron Wildavsky. *Risk and Culture: An Essay on the Selection of Technical and Environmental Dangers*. Los Angeles: University of California Press, 1982.

Doughney, Mike, and Lauren S. Kneisly. "AFA Severs Ties with Operation Rescue National." *Biblical America Resistance Front*, 5 June 1998. http://www.barf.org/archive/operation_rescue_national/pr-980605a.txt.

Easton, Nina J. *Gang of Five*. New York: Simon and Schuster, 2000.

Epstein, Lee. *Conservatives in Court*. Knoxville: University of Tennessee Press, 1985.

Epstein, Lee, and Jack Knight. *The Choices Justices Make*. Washington, DC: Congressional Quarterly Press, 1998.

————. "Mapping Out the Strategic Terrain: The Informational Role of *Amici curiae*." In *Supreme Court Decision-Making: New Institutional Approaches*, edited by Cornell Clayton and Howard Gillman. Chicago: University of Chicago Press, 1999.

Epstein, Lee, and Joseph Kobylka. "Courts and Interest Groups." In *The American Courts: A Critical Assessment*, ed. John B. Gates and Charles A. Johnson, 335–71. Washington, DC: Congressional Quarterly Press, 1991.

————. *The Supreme Court and Legal Change: Abortion and the Death Penalty*. Chapel Hill: University of North Carolina Press, 1992.

Fahling, Brian. "The Federal Marriage Amendment: A Necessary Response to an Imminent Threat," 16 February 2004. http://www.afa.net/clp/ArticlesNew.asp.

————. "How History Became Unconstitutional in Kentucky." *American Family Association*, 17 May 2000. http://www.afa.net/clp/clp51700.asp.

————"The Possibilities of Cooperation in Our Divided Culture." *American Family Association*, 9 February 2004. http://www.afa.net/clp/GetArticle.asp?id=21.

————. "Supreme Court Restores Constitutional Balance." *Family Research Counsel, Reagan Information Interchange*, 30 June 1997. http://www.reagan.com.

————. "Tampering with Our Cultural DNA." *American Family Association*, 19 November 2003. http://www.afa.net/clp/GetArticle.asp?id=15.

Falik, M. *Ideology and Abortion Politics*. New York: Praeger Publishers, 1983.

Farley, Christopher J. "Without a Prayer: The Debate over Religion in Public Schools Is Born Again in Mississippi." *Time Magazine*, 20 December 1993, 41.

Fetterman, D. M. *Ethnography Step by Step*. Newbury Park, NJ: Sage Publications, 1989.

Fikac, Peggy. "Judge Chastises IRS over Treatment of Christian Employee Group." *Associated Press*, 22 November 1997.

Fisher, Marc. "Unlikely Crusaders; Jay Sekulow, 'Messianic Jew' of the Christian Right." *Washington Post*, 21 October 1997, sec. D, 01.

Fowler, Robert B., and Alan D. Hertzke. *Religion and Politics in America: Faith, Culture, and Strategic Choices*. Boulder, CO: Westview Press, 1995.

Franklin, Cathy. "Pastor Sues City for Telling Church to Move from Storefront." *City News Service*, 15 July 1999.

Gage, Beverly. "Anti-Abortion on Trial." *New Haven Advocate*, 1997.

Galanter, Marc. "Why the 'Haves' Come out Ahead: Speculations on the Limits of Legal Change." *Law and Society Review* 9, no. 1 (fall 1974): 95–160.

Gillman, Howard. "The Court as an Idea, Not a Building (or a Game): Interpretive Institutionalism and the Analysis of Supreme Court Decision-Making." In *Supreme Court Decision-Making: New Institutional Approaches*, edited by Cornell Clayton and Howard Gillman. Chicago: University of Chicago Press, 1999.

Gillman, Howard, and Cornell Clayton. "Beyond Judicial Attitudes: Institutional Approaches to Supreme Court Decision Making." In *Supreme Court Decision-Making: New Institutional Approaches*, edited by Cornell Clayton and Howard Gillman. Chicago: University of Chicago Press,1999.

Gleick, Elizabeth. "Onward Christian Lawyers." *Time Magazine*, 13 March 1995.

Greenberg, J. *Litigation for Social Change: Methods, Limits, and Role in Democracy*. New York: Association of the Bar of the City of New York, 1974.

Guinn, David E. *Faith on Trial: Communities of Faith, the First Amendment, and the Theory of Deep Diversity*. Lanham, MD: Lexington Books, 2002.

Hacker, Hans J. "Defending the Faithful." In *The Interest Group Connection*, edited by Paul S. Herrnson, Ronald G. Shaiko, and Clyde Wilcox. 2nd ed. Washington, DC: Congressional Quarterly Press, 2005.

Hall, Richard L., and Frank W. Wayman. "Buying Time: Moneyed Interests and the Mobilization of Bias in Congressional Committees." *American Political Science Review* 84, no. 3 (September 1990): 797–820.

Hansen, John Mark. *Gaining Access: Congress and the Farm Lobby, 1919–1981*. Chicago: University of Chicago Press, 1991.

Hansen, Kristin. "Partial-birth Abortion Ban Victories in Virginia and Missouri." *Family Research Counsel*. 17 September 1999. http://www.frc.org/press/091799b.html.

Harden, Mike. "Pornography Lurks Almost Everywhere in Watchdog's Eyes." *Columbus Dispatch*, 14 January 1998, sec. E, 1.

Hauserman, Julie. "School Singled Out Christian Group, Girl's Lawsuit Says." *St. Petersburg Times*, 16 January 1999.

Hentoff, Nat. "RICO: Hazardous to Users and Targets." *Washington Post*, 9 December 1989, sec. A, 19.

Heinz, John P., Edward O. Laumann, Robert L. Nelson, and Robert H. Salisbury. *The Hollow Core: Private Interests in National Policy Making*. Cambridge, MA: Harvard University Press, 1993.

Hertz, Susanne. *Caught in the Craossfire: A Year on Abortion's Front Line*. New York: Prentice Hall Press, 1991.

Hertzke, Alan D. *Representing God in Washington*. Knoxville: University of Tennessee Press, 1988.

Hladky, Mary. "Hailed. But How Hardy: New Anti-Bias Law May Be More a Symbol." *Miami Daily Business Review*, 4 December 1998, sec. B, 1.

Hofrenning, D. *In Washington but Not of It: Prophetic Politics of Religious Lobbyists*. Philadelphia, PA: Temple University Press, 1995.

Hojnacki, Marie. "Interest Groups' Decisions to Join Alliances or Work Alone." *American Journal of Political Science* 41, no. 1 (January 1997): 61–87.

Hula, Kevin. "Rounding up the Usual Suspects: Forging Interest Group Coalitions." In *Interest Group Politics*, edited by Allan J. Cigler and Burdett A. Loomis. Washington, DC: Congressional Quarterly Press, 1995.

Ivers, Gregg. "Please, God, Save This Honorable Court: The Emergence of the Conservative Religious Bar." In *The Interest Group Connection*, edited by Paul S. Herrnson, Ronald G. Shaiko, and Clyde Wilcox. Chatham, NJ: Chatham House, 1998.

———. *Redefining the First Freedom: The Supreme Court and the Consolidation of State Power.* New Brunswick, PA: Transaction Publishers, 1993.

———. *To Build a Wall: American Jews and Separation of Church and State.* Charlottesville: University of Virginia Press, 1995.

Jacobs, Margaret A. "Employers' Religious Bias not Tolerated, Case Shows." *Pittsburgh Post-Gazette* , 27 August 1995, sec. D, 1.

Jeffreys, Daniel. "When a Wildmon Wreaks Havoc." *Independent* (London), 27 July 1995, sec. Life, 6.

Jelen, Ted G. *To Serve God and Mammon.* Boulder, CO: Westview Press, 2000.

Johnson, Gene. "Seattle Mayor Recognizes Employees' Gay Marriages." *Washington Post*, 9 March 2004, sec. A, 03.

Kennedy, John W. "Buffer–zone Case Tests Free Speech." *Christianity Today* 38, no. 7 (20 June 1994): 48.

Kobylka, Joseph F. "A Court-Created Context for Group Litigation: Libertarian Groups and Obscenity. *Journal of Politics* 49, no. 4 (November 1987): 1061–78.

———.*The Politics of Obscenity: Group Litigation in a Time of Change.* New York: Greenwood Press, 1991.

Koshner, Andrew Jay. *Solving the Puzzle of Interest Group Litigation.* Westport, CT: Greenwood Press, 1998.

Laitin, David D. *Hegemony and Culture: Politics and Religious Change among the Yoruba.* Chicago: University of Chicago Press, 1986.

Laitin, David D., and Aaron Wildavsky. "Political Culture and Political Preferences." *American Political Science Review* 82, no. 2 (June 1988): 589–597.

Laumann, Edward O., and David Knoke. *The Organizational State: Social Choice in National Policy Domains.* Madison: University of Wisconsin Press, 1987.

Liberty Counsel. http://www.lc.org.

Liberty Counsel. "High School Backs away from Attempts to Censor Graduation Speech About Faith in God," 7 June 2004. http://www/lc.org/libertyalert/2004/1a060704.htm#Mass.

Liberty Counsel. "Liberty Counsel Files Two Suits against New Paltz Mayor," 3 March 2004. http://www.lc.org/pressrelease/2004/nr030304.htm.

Liberty Counsel. "Supreme Court Declines to Issue Emergency Order Stopping Same Sex Marriage in Massachusetts," 14 May 2004. http://www.lc.org/libertyalert /2004/la051404b.htm (accessed 11 June 2004)

Lithwick, Dahlia. "Rock of Ages and a Hard Space: The Supreme Court Searches for Breathing Room in Its Religion Cases." *Slate Magazine*, 2 December 2003. http://slate.msn.com/id/2091850.

Long, Phil. "HRS Pays Legal Fees for Abortion Foes." *Miami Herald*, 29 March 1996.

Luo, Michael. "Ousted Church Persuades City to Reverse Ban." *Los Angeles Times*, 22 July 1999, sec. B, 1.

———. "They Call It Church; City Calls It Illegal." *Los Angeles Times*, 16 July 1999, sec. B, 1.

Maltzman, Forrest, James E. Spriggs II, and Paul J. Wahlbeck. *Crafting Law on the Supreme Court: The Collegial Game.* New York: Cambridge University Press, 2000.

————. "Strategy and Judicial Choice: New Institutionalist Approaches to Supreme Court Decision Making." In *Supreme Court Decision-Making: New Institutional Approaches*, edited by Cornell Clayton and Howard Gillman. Chicago: University of Chicago Press, 1999.

Manwaring, David R. *Render unto Caesar: The Flag-Salute Controversy*. Chicago: University of Chicago Press, 1962.

McAdam, Doug, and David A. Snow, eds. *Social Movements: Readings on Their Emergence, Mobilization, and Dynamics*. Los Angeles: Roxbury Press, 1997.

McCord, Julia. "Defending Religious Rights: Non-profit Christian Law Organizations Gain Ground." *Omaha World Herald*, 29 April 1995, sec. SF, 57.

McFarland, A. S. *Common Cause: Lobbying in the Public Interest*. Chatham, NJ: Chatham House Publishers, 1984.

McGuire, Kevin T. "Amici Curiae and Strategies for Gaining Access to the Supreme Court." *Political Research Quarterly* 47 (1994): 821–838.

McKeegan, M. *Abortion Politics: Mutiny on the Rights*. Toronto, CA: Maxwell Macmillan Press, 1992.

Moe, Terry M. "A Calculus of Group Membership." *American Journal of Political Science* 24, no. 4 (November 1980): 593–632.

Moen, Matthew C. *The Transformation of the Christian Right*. Tuscaloosa: University of Alabama Press, 1992.

Moen, Matthew C., and Lynn Gustafson. *The Religious Challenge to the State*. Philadelphia: Temple University Press, 1992.

Moore, John. "The Lord's Litigators." *National Journal*, 2 July 1994.

Morken, Hubert. "The Evangelical Legal Response to the ACLU: Religion, Politics, and the First Amendment." Paper prepared for the Annual Meeting of the American Political Science Association, Chicago, 3–6 September 1992.

Murray Frank J. "Activist Lawyer to Represent Florida Abortion Doctor's Killer." *Washington Times*, 6 October 1995, sec. A, 10.

Niebuhr, Gustav. "Conservatives' New Frontier: Religious Liberty Law Firms." *New York Times*, 8 July 1995, sec. 1, 1.

————. "Victory on Religion Rulings was Limited, Groups Say." *New York Times*, 5 July 1995, sec. 1, 1.

O'Connor, Karen. *No Neutral Ground?: Abortion Politics in an Age of Absolutes*. Boulder, CO: Westview Press, 1996.

————. *Women's Organizations' Use of the Courts*. Lexington, MA: D. C. Heath and Company, 1980.

O'Connor, Karen, and Lee Epstein. "The Rise of Conservative Interest Group Litigation." *Journal of Politics* 45, no. 2 (May 1983): 479–489.

Olsen, Ken. "Federal Suit Filed over Parade Bust: Protester Seeks Damages, Court Order Allowing Right to Picket Next Aryan March." *Spokane Spokesman-Review*, 2 April 1999.

Olson, Mancur, Jr. *The Logic of Collective Action: Public Goods and the Theory of Groups*. Cambridge: Harvard University Press, 1971.

Olson, Susan. *Clients and Lawyers: Securing the Rights of Disabled Persons*. Westport, CT: Greenwood Press, 1984.

Oritz, Vikki, and Lori Holly. "County Sued over Parks' Literature Policy." *Milwaukee Journal Sentinel*, 22 January 1999.

Peshkin, A. "Understanding Complexity: A Gift of Qualitative Research." *Anthropology and Education Quarterly* 19 (1988): 416–424.

Peters, Shawn F. *Judging Jehovah's Witnesses: Religious Persecution and the Dawn of the Rights Revolution*. Lawrence: University Press of Kansas, 1999.

Petracca, Mark P. "The Rediscovery of Interest Group Politics." In *The Politics of Interests: Interest Groups Transformed*, edited by Mark P. Petracca. Boulder, CO: Westview Press, 1992.

Pinsky, Mark I. "Fight for Religious Liberty Brings Lawyer Few 'Amens.'" *Orlando Sentinel*, 9 September 1995, sec. D, 5.

———. "Legal Weapon: Jay Sekulow is the Christian Right's Leading Lion in the Judicial Arena." *Los Angeles Times*, 2 September 1993, sec. E, 1.

Puoliot, Janine S. "Rising Complaints of Religious Bias." *U.S. Chamber of Commerce–Nation's Business*, February 1996.

Pusey, Allen."Falwell Has High Hopes as Law School Opens." *Dallas Morning News*, 25 August 2004, sec. A, 11.

Roman, Nancy. "Center Uses Free Speech to Defend Religious Rights." *Washington Times*, 18 July 1993, sec. A, 4.

Rosenberg, Gerald N. *The Hollow Hope: Can Courts Bring About Social Change?* Chicago: University of Chicago Press, 1991.

Rouse, Karen. "Group Has Lobbied for Disney Divestiture." *Fort Worth Star-Telegram*, 10 July 1998, sec. Metro, 2.

Rozell, Mark J., and Clyde Wilcox. *God at the Grassroots, 1996: The Christian Right in the 1996 Elections*. Lanham, MD: Rowman and Littlefield, 1997.

———. *Second Coming: The New Christian Right in Virginia Politics*. Baltimore, MD: Johns Hopkins University Press, 1996.

Salisbury, Robert H., John P. Heinz, Edward O. Laumann, and Robert Nelson. "Who Works with Whom? Interest Group Alliances and Opposition." *American Political Science Review* 81, no. 4 (December 1987): 1217–1234.

Salisbury, Robert H. "An Exchange Theory of Interest Groups." *Midwest Journal of Political Science* 13, no. 1 (February 1969): 1–32.

Scheppele, Kim Lane, and Jack L. Walker Jr. "The Litigation Strategies of Interest Groups." In *Mobilizing Interest Groups in America*, edited by Jack Walker Jr., 157–183. Ann Arbor: University of Michigan Press, 1991.

Schwartz, Bernard. *The New Right and the Constitution: Turning Back the Legal Clock*. Boston: Northeastern University Press, 1990.

Sekulow, Jay. *From Intimidation to Victory: Regaining the Christian Right to Speak*. Lake Mary, FL: Creation House, 1990.

———. As quoted by NBC Nightly News, 22 October 1997.

Sekulow, Jay, and Keith Fournier. *And Nothing But the Truth: Real Life Stories of American Defending their Faith and Protecting their Families*. Nashville, TN: Thomas Nelson, 1996.

Sheeran, Patrick J. *Women, Society, the State, and Abortion: A Structuralist Analysis*. New York: Praeger Publishers, 1987.

Songer, Donald R., and Reginald Sheehan. "Interest Group Success in the Courts: Amicus Participation in the Supreme Court," *Political Research Quarterly* 46 (June 1993): 339–354.

Songer, Donald R., and Ashlyn Kuersten. "The Success of Amici in State Supreme Courts." *Political Research Quarterly* 48 (March 1995): 31–42.

Sorauf, Frank J. *The Wall of Separation: The Constitutional Politics of Church and State*. Princeton, NJ: Princeton University Press, 1976.

Spriggs, James F., II, and Paul J. Wahlbeck. "Amicus Curiae and the Role of Information at the Supreme Court." *Political Research Quarterly* 50 (June 1997): 365–386.

Stafford, Tim. "Move over ACLU." *Christianity Today* 37 (25 October 1993): 20.

Staggenborg, Suzanne. *The Pro-Choice Movement: Organization and Activism in the Abortion Conflict.* New York: Oxford University Press, 1991.

Staver, Mathew D. "ACLU Files Suit to Evict Churches From School Buildings." *The Liberator* 10, no. 4 (April 1999).

———. "Another Victory for Student-Initiated Graduation Messages." *Liberator* 9, no. 6 (June 1998).

———"The Battle over Bible Clubs." *Liberator* 10, no. 2 (February 1999).

———. "FCA Meets for the First Time in Manatee High School's History." *The Liberator* 10, no. 5 (May 1999).

———. "Graduation Prayer Victory." *Liberator* 10, no. 7 (May 1999).

———. "Injunctive Relief and the *Madsen* Test," *St. Louis University Law Review* 14 (1995): 465–478.

———. "They're Baaack!" *Liberator* 9, no. 11 (November 1998).

Thomas, Oliver. Testimony before the United States Senate Judiciary Committee. *Federal Document Clearinghouse - Congressional Testimony.* 20 October 1995.

Tribe, Laurence H. *Abortion: The Clash of Absolutes.* New York: W. W. Norton and Company, 1990.

Truman, David B. *The Governmental Process: Political Interests and Public Opinion.* New York: Alfred A. Knopf, Inc., 1971.

Utter, G. H., and J. W. Storey. *The Religious Right: A Reference Manual.* Santa Barbara, CA: ABC-CLIO, 1995.

Vielmetti, Bruce. "Religious Group Sues Pamphlet-Free TIA." *St. Petersburg Times,* 15 August 1995.

Von Drehle, David. "Legal Confusion over Gay Marriage." *Washington Post,* 27 February 2004, sec. A, 08.

Vose, Clement E. *Caucasians Only: The Supreme Court, the NAACP, and the Restrictive Covenant Cases.* Berkeley: University of California Press, 1959.

Wald, Kenneth. *Religion and Politics in the United States.* New York: St. Martin's Press, 1997.

Westfall, Bruce. "Lawsuit Opposes Benefits Policy." *Columbian* (Vancouver, WA.) sec. B, 1.

Wetzstein, Cheryl. "Court's Authority over Marriage Law Challenged," *Washington Times,* 7 June 2004.
http://www.washtimes.com/national/20040607-124837-6491r.htm.

Wilcox, Clyde. *Onward Christian Soldiers? The Religious Right in American Politics.* 2nd ed. Boulder, CO: Westview Press, 2000.

Wilcox, Clyde, and Ted G. Jelen. "Rethinking the Reasonableness of the Religious Right." *Review of Religious Research* 36 (1995): 263–276.

Wildavsky, Aaron. "Choosing Preferences by Constructing Institutions: A Cultural Theory of Preference Formation." *American Political Science Review* 81, no. 1 (March 1987): 3–22.

Wilson, James Q. *Political Organizations.* New York: Basic Books, Inc., 1973.

Wilson, Janet. "Suit Targets Volunteer Training Program." *Los Angeles Times,* 5 March 1998, sec. B, 4.

Wolfe, Alan. "The Opening of the Evangelical Mind." *Atlantic Monthly* 286, no. 4 (2000): 55–76.

Index

About the Author

Hans J. Hacker received his Ph.D. in 2000 from the Ohio State University where he was a University Fellowship recipient. From 1998 to 2002, he taught public law at the University of Maryland, the College of William and Mary, and the Johns Hopkins University, D.C. Center for Graduate Programs. In 2003, he joined the faculty at Stephen F. Austin State University as assistant professor of political science and pre-law program adviser. He has served as a consultant to NASA Center for Educational Technology on the *Foundations of Freedom: The History of the United States Constitution* project. His research and teaching interests lie in the areas of interest group litigation, law and society, civic and political engagement, and the historical connections between economic, political, and civil rights doctrines in the United States. He is the author of "Defending the Faithful: Conservative Christian Litigation in American Politics," in Herrnson, Shaiko, and Wilcox's *The Interest Group Connection*.